AMERICA THROUGH THE LOOKING GLASS

AMERICA THROUGH THE LOOKING GLASS

a historical reader in
popular culture
volume II

Edited by
DAVID BURNER
State University of New York at Stony Brook

ROBERT D. MARCUS
State University of New York at Stony Brook

JORJ TILSON

Prentice-Hall, Inc., Englewood Cliffs, New Jersey

Library of Congress Cataloging in Publication Data

BURNER, DAVID comp.
America through the looking glass.

1. United States—Popular culture—History—Sources.
I. Marcus, Robert D. joint comp.
II. Tilson, Jorj, joint comp. III. Title.
E169.1.B939   917.3'03   73-21852
ISBN   0-13-024000-1 (v. 2)

© 1974 by Prentice-Hall, Inc., Englewood Cliffs, New Jersey.

PRINTED IN THE UNITED STATES OF AMERICA

10   9   8   7   6   5   4   3   2   1

Cover *Illustration:* Mirror, c. 1865. Cast-iron frame, American flag, and monument
with eagle. Two female figures once painted red, white, and blue. Two weeping
willows and trophy of laurel, shield, ramrod, and arrow.—From *Index of American Design*

PRENTICE-HALL INTERNATIONAL, INC., LONDON
PRENTICE-HALL OF AUSTRALIA, PTY. LTD., SYDNEY
PRENTICE-HALL OF CANADA, LTD., TORONTO
PRENTICE-HALL OF INDIA PRIVATE LIMITED, NEW DELHI
PRENTICE-HALL OF JAPAN, INC., TOKYO

N 1 0 6

to
Arthur Marcus
the memory of Arthur Burner (1925–1973)
Robert Burner
Tim Tilson
brothers and friends

contents

part 2   the electronic age: since 1910   143

AMERICA THROUGH THE LOOKING GLASS

introduction

American popular culture is the mirror of American life; it is, in fact, the way most people see themselves. Like other mirrors, this one can give a true picture, a distorted one, or even a grotesque image. But we examine this reflection of American life, because it gives the only view that would be fully recognizable to the common men and women of the nation's past whose experience constitutes our history.

Culture is, quite simply, the subjective resources that members of a group possess: the body of beliefs, practices, rituals, goals, patterns of behavior that people have available to cope with life. It is the "inside" of which society or social structure is the "outside." No analysis of the activities of a people would be complete without examining both the objective structure of society—the institutions and actual relationships among people—and the culture, the way experience is subjectively organized.

In American history the backbone of every textbook is its account of the nation's institutions. Students come away with a shadowy vision of the people of the past "responding" to the frontier, to industrialism, to the rise of a welfare state, and to the country's role in world politics.

The past becomes what happened to people, not what people did or who they were. An introduction to their culture, to their sense of the world, to their amusements, customs, and passions is an obvious first step toward righting this balance.

The study of popular culture is a relatively recent intellectual discipline that has only begun to affect historical studies. It grew up since the 1930s, principally as a branch of literary criticism. Some custodians of high culture, convinced that they could no longer simply avoid the subject, embraced the distinction between serious and popular culture —in short to prevent the infection from spreading. Others applied the canons of serious criticism to popular culture to discover that popular entertainers like Charlie Chaplin were in fact artists or that tragedy, a traditional theme of high culture, could be found in popular media. Still, so long as esthetic standards dominated inquiry, the second-class character of popular culture could only be confirmed. And the emphasis on contemporary materials left historians with little of value to use when they sought to describe popular culture in the past.

The historical study of ideas often reinforced the tendency to ignore or isolate popular culture. Much intellectual history studied culture in the old nineteenth-century sense—the best that has been thought and felt. This, however, does little toward recapturing the way most people in the past encountered the world. The theory of virtual representation—that the elites of society can speak for the lowly—has long since vanished from political thought and ought to quit the cultural scene as well. The culture of the great and powerful is not the culture of the masses. Even the greatest works of art—Dante's poetry or Shakespeare's plays—do not speak for an age; they speak for less than that—a class or a group or a tendency, and they speak for more, transcending their age and touching the concerns of humanity in some way general and timeless. As humanists, we study them without worrying about what they tell us of the past. As historians, we study them as we would any other cultural artifact, for what they say about the man or woman who created them and the audience they reached. They provide a valuable entrée to one part of the past, not some royal road to broad insight.

Another discipline that has restricted inquiry into popular culture is the study of folklore. Like the literary critic, the folklorist saw popular culture as an alien force, undermining folk expression. He defined folklore as culture passed directly by word of mouth without the intermediaries of print or electronic media. Only such culture could be genuinely of the people. Popular culture using folk themes became known as "fakelore"—a pejorative term if there ever was one. Popular culture, then, became whatever was neither high culture nor folk culture, something both inferior and inauthentic; and most scholars gave it a rather wide berth. Only in the last few years have folklorists realized the artificial limits of their definition, recognizing that much vital folk culture moves in and out of print and electronic media without ceasing to be authentically of the common imagination.

Most of these problems of definition disappear when one focuses on historical rather than esthetic questions. Viewed historically, popular culture means any form of expression or custom that achieves popularity among a large group of people. It can include the high culture created by a single self-conscious artist (e.g., Shakespeare, whose plays were a staple of touring companies a century ago) and the folk artifacts that enter media such as print or phonograph records. Once into the consciousness of a substantial group both become indistinguishable parts of the community's cultural endowment. Transformed into popular culture, they function no differently from the products composed commercially for popular audiences.

In short, popular culture and all culture is a process, not a specific kind of product. Students of high culture call this process "tradition"; folklorists speak of "the folk process." Both mean something living and evolving out of the imaginations of specific groups of people. Still, popular culture, because of its low academic pedigree and its concentration on the present, achieved a far more limiting definition than is implied in the image of a free-flowing process. Most people, their gazes narrowed to the electronic media, the professional entertainer, and the mass-produced popular book, magazine, or comic, envision popular culture as a consumer item created by professionals for a passive audience.

This static definition does not at all conform to most historical experience and even eliminates a good deal of contemporary culture from consideration. Much popular culture was created wholly or in part by the people who enjoyed it. Transmission by the folk process meant a continuous modification of what was inherited. Even the transmission of commercially produced popular entertainment was once a more active process. Sheet music, for example, was printed for playing on the piano and singing at home. Similarly, in transmitting the culture of home economics, the cooking, and housekeeping, and childrearing books, and even the sex manuals that dot the American past and clot the American present assume a more active role on the part of the ultimate consumer than, say, the motion picture. Rituals such as quilting bees, barn raisings,

Fourth of July fireworks, cookouts, coffee klatches, garage sales, dormitory bull sessions, bar hopping, and neighborhood cancer fund drives reflect as much popular culture as listening to *Amos 'n' Andy* or watching *All in the Family*. The whole world of how-to-do-it books is a continuing index to the popular mind. Popular culture, then, is not simply mankind as a vast audience: it is whatever provides materials for people to use in their daily lives—to use to give meaning to their experience.

Popular culture so defined encompasses the whole cycle of human life from midwifery and childrearing practices through marriage rituals and success images to the art of tombstone inscriptions. Most beliefs about hygiene and health come through the conduit of popular culture augmented by, perhaps, less science than we like to think. Humor becomes a part of the culture as do religious practices and beliefs. Instruction comes in schoolbooks, etiquette manuals (extremely influential in the nineteenth century), and how-to-do-it books of every description (perhaps even more prevalent a hundred years ago than now). Even political life once had much the form of popular entertainment and then as now helped to mold people's perception of the world. Domestic architecture and fashions in clothing fixed some of the most basic parts of people's imaginations, teaching particular standards of beauty, of order, of seemliness. A wide range of materials addressed to both children and adults affected the meanings people found in work, the views they took of the environment, their visions of people they had never seen, or their stereotypes of people they encountered daily.

This broad and indefinite expanse of the American mind is the subject of the book before you. Its organization reflects no limiting theoretical definition of popular culture. Some of the selections—e.g., the various songs—appear for their obvious popularity. Other selections—occasionally rather obscure ones—represent customs and attitudes that had wide currency. The diary—written in French—of a budding scientist, Lester Frank Ward, was not a best seller: we include it because it recounts the feelings of a mid-nineteenth century young man in love. Some other items report on widespread practices: Mrs. Trollope would be highly insulted to find her writings included in a book on popular culture, but her rather clinical description of a revival is an invaluable portrait of Americans expressing themselves.

Historians have recently become aware of the degree to which they have concentrated on elites and neglected the "underside" of American history. This book aims at moving yet another step: to examine the "inside" of American history, of the way Americans experienced their world. Such an emphasis has the advantage of exposing many of the most interesting and readable documents that a culture produces as well as introducing new nonwritten sources, such as the everyday objects—toys, decorations, gadgets—displays in the illustrations taken from the Index of American Design. Since motion pictures, an important part of popular culture, can be readily available for classroom use in a way that radio or video tapes cannot, we have included an illustrated guide to movies and information on how to locate them. The authors have always found their students enthusiastic about having motion pictures as part of a course; the major problem in using films is relating them to other sources of information and preventing movies from dominating all discussion. Tying such media to other forms of popular culture and organizing them in a way that will supplement American history text-books hopefully will help solve that problem and integrate popular culture sources into the broader consideration of the American past.

part 1 the industrial age, 1870-1910

Industrialization beginning in the 1840s in the United States, brought major transformations in American life by the Civil War. In the years after the war, industry pushed its way into the lives and the thinking of almost every American. This force, national in scope, had a dual result: on the one hand, it sucked new groups into its vortex and spread their manners and folkways to a national audience, gradually increasing the complexity and heterogeneity of American mores. People everywhere, not just in cities, saw the fruits of urban culture—the products, the magazines and newspapers, the fashions. Men and women of every class viewed the styles and doings of the rich. A national audience studied the vices of the urban netherworld and heard the grievances of farmers and laborers.

On the other hand, this same process exerted pressure toward standardization. Boys and girls everywhere could read the same adventure stories. Teachers knew what other teachers did in the classroom. Technology smoothed out regional variations in work practices and even in household chores while creating cheap goods which enabled the mass of people to emulate the style of the rich: cast-iron sculpture, imitation plate, inexpensive books, machine-made lace.

Popular culture helped Americans retain their optimism and sense of direction amid the bewildering and sometimes threatening changes wrought by industry. The covert themes bubbling their way to the top of this often opaque melting pot differ little from the more formal ideas of high culture. An emphasis on what Theodore Roosevelt called "The Strenuous Life" as a masculine ideal appears again and again in children's literature, in adventure stories like Tarzan and Fu Manchu, in sports, and in the cult of the Civil War—virtually a national religion of the age. A taste for adventure—witness the admiration for the dashing Richard Harding Davis—was considered particularly good equipment for the rapidly changing world of industrial America.

This popular culture also emphasized morality. The belief that moral categories described reality, that the good would triumph and the evil suffer, was a rarely challenged assumption. Popular art expressed a simple version of the moralism that also informs the speeches of Woodrow Wilson or the complex novels of William Dean Howells and Henry James. Owen Wister's *The Virginian* cast the western romance in its classic form of a morality play—the white hats and horses against the black hair and painted faces of the Indians. Russell Conwell and Anthony Comstock both assumed that virtue would be rewarded and vice punished. Carry Nation acted secure in the belief that God was on her side (in fact, she claimed that he had told her so). Yet here and there one detects in popular culture glimmerings of a more desperate view of the world similar to the vision of a few iconoclasts of high culture like the pessimistic novelist Theodore Dreiser. Huckleberry Finn is one long account of what people considered the opposite of virtue being rewarded; Edward Crapsey viewed prostitutes to some extent as victims of society rather than of their own vices; Edwin Markham's "The Man With the Hoe" astonished Americans precisely because its antihero was a victim of society rather than a moral agent. Markham's imagery, however, suggests a European peasant rather than an American farmer and implies that people not responsible for their plight are by definition un-American.

This popular culture also shares with all of American life a pervasive materialism that seems to comport oddly with moral idealism. Yet, as George Santayana had remarked, the American had typically been an idealist working on matter. The forthcoming materialism of Russell Conwell, Ward McAllister, or Thomas Edison seems to mesh with a concern for morality with scarcely a whirl of clashing gears. Americans accepted the hardships and uncertainties of industrialization precisely because of the great material rewards promised in the future. If these rewards went to moral and venturesome men and virtuous women there was no apparent conflict between the constraints of morality and the hunger after wealth. Only when Americans began to suspect that the race was not always to the swift, wealth to the virtuous, or the fair to the brave would the potential friction between materialism and idealism become a problem.

Finally, popular culture was shot through with racism. In this period even scientists offered racial explanations for social and political trends. Sax Rohmer trades artfully on the "Yellow Peril" that worried Americans early in the century. The Coon songs reflect racist stereotypes of sensual and lackadaisical blacks. It requires little psychological sophistication to realize that white Americans were projecting their own fears onto black scapegoats. During the time that these overtly sexual songs became popular, Americans engaged in a national debate over divorce, showed panic over the "White Slave Trade," and conducted drives against prostitution. Such projections relieve anxiety about problems without facing them. They too are part of the classical function of popular culture: to enable people to cope with the changes that take place in their lives or to escape in their imaginations from what they cannot handle.

education and children's literature

Twain's portrait of schoolhouse learning, with its stress on oratory and genteel culture, is faithful to the experience of most nineteenth-century Americans who received an education. The famous McGuffey Readers, used throughout the century, were merely selections of oratory prefaced by instructions on how to declaim the contents aloud. (From *The Adventures of Tom Sawyer,* 1876.)

MARK TWAIN: TOM SAWYER'S BOUT
WITH SCHOOLBOOKS

Eloquence—and the Master's Gilded Dome

Vacation was approaching. The schoolmaster, always severe, grew severer and more exacting than ever, for he wanted the school to make a good showing on "Examination" day. His rod and his ferule were seldom idle now—at least among the smaller pupils. Only the biggest boys, and young ladies of eighteen and twenty, escaped lashing. Mr. Dobbins's lashings were very vigorous ones, too; for although he carried, under his wig, a perfectly bald and shiny head, he had only reached middle age and there was no sign of feebleness in his muscle. As the great day approached, all the tyranny that was in him came to the surface; he seemed to take a vindictive pleasure in punishing the least shortcomings. The consequence was, that the smaller boys spent their days in terror and suffering and their nights in plotting revenge. They threw away no opportunity to do the master a mischief. But he kept ahead all the time. The retribution that followed every vengeful success was so sweeping and majestic that the boys always retired from the field badly worsted. At last they conspired together and hit upon a plan that promised a dazzling victory. They swore in the sign-painter's boy, told him the scheme, and asked his help. He had his own reasons for being delighted, for the master boarded in his father's family and had given the boy ample cause to hate him. The master's wife would go on a visit to the country in a few days, and there would be nothing to interfere with the plan; the master always prepared himself for great occasions by getting pretty well fuddled, and the sign-painter's boy said that when the dominie had reached the proper condition on Examination Evening he would "manage the thing" while he napped in his chair; then he would have him awakened at the right time and hurried away to school.

In the fullness of time the interesting occasion arrived. At eight in the evening the school-house was brilliantly lighted, and adorned with wreaths and festoons of foliage and flowers. The master sat throned in his great chair upon a raised platform, with his blackboard behind him. He was looking tolerably mellow. Three rows of benches on each side and six rows in front of him were occupied by the dignitaries of the town and by the parents of the pupils. To his left, back of the rows of citizens, was a spacious temporary platform upon which were seated the scholars who were to take part in the exercises of the evening; rows of small boys, washed and dressed to an intolerable state of discomfort; rows of gawky big boys; snowbanks of girls and young ladies clad in lawn and muslin and conspicuously conscious of their bare arms, their grand-mothers' ancient trinkets, their bits of pink and blue ribbon and the flowers in their hair. All the rest of the house was filled with non-participating scholars.

The exercises began. A very little boy stood up and sheepishly recited, "You'd scarce expect one of my age to speak in public on the stage," etc.—accompanying himself with the painfully exact and spasmodic gestures which a machine might have used—supposing the machine to be a trifle out of order. But he got through safely, though cruelly scared, and got a fine round of applause when he made his manufactured bow and retired.

A little shamefaced girl lisped "Mary had a little lamb," etc., performed a compassion-inspiring curtsy, got her meed of applause, and sat down flushed and happy.

Tom Sawyer stepped forward with conceited confidence and soared into the unquenchable and indestructible "Give me liberty or give me death" speech, with fine fury and frantic gesticulation, and broke down in the middle of it. A ghastly stage-fright seized him, his legs quaked under him and he was like to choke. True, he had the manifest sympathy of the house—but he had the house's silence, too, which was even worse than its sympathy. The master frowned, and this completed the disaster. Tom struggled awhile and then retired, utterly defeated. There was a weak attempt at applause, but it died early.

"The Boy Stood on the Burning Deck" followed; also "The Assyrian Came Down," and other declamatory gems. Then there were reading exercises and a spelling-fight. The meager Latin class recited with honor. The prime feature of the evening was in order now—original "compositions" by the young ladies. Each in her turn stepped forward to the edge of the platform, cleared her throat, held up her manuscript (tied with dainty ribbon), and proceeded to read, with labored attention to "expression" and punctuation. The themes were the same that had been illuminated upon similar occasions by their mothers before them, their grandmothers, and doubtless all their ancestors in the female line clear back to the Crusades, "Friendship" was one; "Memories of Other Days"; "Religion in History"; "Dream Land"; "The Advantages of Culture"; "Forms of Political Government Compared and Contrasted"; "Melancholy"; "Filial Love"; "Heart Longings," etc., etc.

A prevalent feature in these compositions was a nursed and petted melancholy; another was a wasteful and opulent gush of "fine language"; another was a tendency to lug in by the ears particularly prized words and phrases until they were worn entirely out; and a peculiarity that conspicuously marked and marred them was the inveterate and intolerable sermon that wagged its crippled tail at the end of each and every one of them. No matter what the subject might be, a brain-racking effort was made to squirm it into some aspect or other that the moral and religious mind could contemplate with edification. The glaring insincerity of these sermons was not sufficient to compass the banishment of the fashion from the schools, and it is not sufficient to-day; it never will be sufficient while the world stands, perhaps. There is no school in all our land where the young ladies do not feel obliged to close their compositions with a sermon; and you will find that the sermon of the most frivolous and the least religious girl in the school is always the longest and the most relentlessly pious. But enough of this. Homely truth is unpalatable.

Let us return to the "Examination." The first composition that was read was one entitled "Is this, then, Life?" Perhaps the reader can endure an extract from it:

In the common walks of life, with what delightful emotions does the youthful mind look forward to some anticipated scene of festivity! Imagination is busy sketching rose-tinted pictures of joy. In fancy, the voluptuous votary of fashion sees herself amid the festive throng, "the observed of all observers." Her graceful form, arrayed in snowy robes, is whirling through the mazes of the joyous dance; her eye is brightest, her step is lightest in the gay assembly.

In such delicious fancies time quickly glides by, and the welcome hour arrives for her entrance into the elysian world, of which she has had such bright dreams. How fairylike does everything appear to her enchanted vision! Each new scene is more charming than the last. But after a while she finds that beneath this goodly exterior, all is vanity: the flattery which once charmed her soul now grates harshly upon her ear; the ballroom has lost its charms; and with wasted health and embittered heart she turns away with the conviction that earthly pleasures cannot satisfy the longings of the soul!

And so forth and so on. There was a buzz of gratification from time to time during the reading, accompanied by whispered ejaculations of "How sweet!" "How eloquent!" "So true!" etc., and after the thing had closed with a peculiarly afflicting sermon the applause was enthusiastic.

Then arose a slim, melancholy girl, whose face had the "interesting" paleness that comes of pills and indigestion, and read a "poem." Two stanzas of it will do:

A Missouri Maiden's Farewell to Alabama

Alabama, good-by! I love thee well!!
But yet for a while do I leave thee now!
Sad, yes, sad thoughts of thee my heart doth swell,
And burning recollections throng my brow!
For I have wandered through thy flowery woods;
Have roamed and read near Tallapoosa's stream;
Have listened to Tallassee's warring floods,
And wooed on Coosa's side Aurora's beam.

Yet shame I not to bear on o'er-full heart,
Nor blush to turn behind my tearful eyes;
'Tis from no stranger land I now must part,
'Tis to no strangers left I yield these sighs.
Welcome and home were mine within this State,
Whose vales I leave—whose spires fade fast from me;
And cold must be mine eyes, and heart, and tête,
When, dear Alabama! they turn cold on thee!

There were very few there who knew what "*tête*" meant, but the poem was very satisfactory, nevertheless.

Next appeared a dark-complexioned, black-eyed, black-haired young lady, who paused an impressive moment, assumed a tragic expression, and began to read in a measured, solemn tone.

A Vision

Dark and tempestuous was night. Around the throne on high not a single star quivered; but the deep intonations of the heavy thunder constantly vibrated upon the ear; whilst the terrific lightning reveled in angry mood through the cloudy chambers of heaven, seeming to scorn the

power exerted over its terror by the illustrious Franklin! Even the boisterous winds unanimously came forth from their mystic homes, and
blustered about as if to enhance by their aid the wildness of the scene.

At such a time, so dark, so dreary, for human sympathy my very
spirit sighed; but instead thereof,

"My dearest friend, my counselor, my comforter and guide—
My joy in grief, my second bliss in joy," came to my side.

She moved like one of those bright beings pictured in the sunny walks of
fancy's Eden by the romantic and young, a queen of beauty unadorned
save by her own transcendent loveliness. So soft was her step, it failed
to make even a sound, and but for the magical thrill imparted by her
genial touch, as other unobtrusive beauties, she would have glided away
unperceived—unsought. A strange sadness rested upon her features, like
icy tears upon the robe of December, as she pointed to the contending
elements without, and bade me contemplate the two beings presented.

This nightmare occupied some ten pages of manuscript and wound
up with a sermon so destructive of all hope to non-Presbyterians that it
took the first prize. This composition was considered to be the very
finest effort of the evening. The mayor of the village, in delivering the
prize to the author of it, made a warm speech in which he said that it
was far the most "eloquent" thing he had ever listened to, and that Daniel
Webster himself might well be proud of it.

It may be remarked, in passing, that the number of compositions in
which the word "beauteous" was over-fondled, and human experience
referred to as "life's page," was up to the usual average.

Now the master, mellow almost to the verge of geniality, put his
chair aside, turned his back to the audience, and began to draw a map of
America on the blackboard, to exercise the geography class upon. But
he made a sad business of it with his unsteady hand, and a smothered
titter rippled over the house. He knew what the matter was and set himself to right it. He sponged out lines and remade them; but he only
distorted them more than ever, and the tittering was more pronounced.
He threw his entire attention upon his work, now, as if determined not
to be put down by the mirth. He felt that all eyes were fastened upon
him; he imagined he was succeeding, and yet the tittering continued; it
even manifestly increased. And well it might. There was a garret above,
pierced with a scuttle over his head; and down through this scuttle
came a cat, suspended around the haunches by a string; she had a rag
tied about her head and jaws to keep her from mewing; as she slowly
descended she curved upward and clawed at the string, she swung
downward and clawed at the intangible air. The tittering rose higher
and higher—the cat was within six inches of the absorbed teacher's head

—down, down, a little lower, and she grabbed his wig with her desperate claws, clung to it, and was snatched up into the garret in an instant with her trophy still in her possession! And how the light did blaze abroad from the master's bald pate—for the sign-painter's boy had *gilded* it!

That broke up the meeting. The boys were avenged. Vacation had come.

(*Note.—The pretended "compositions" quoted in this chapter are taken without alteration from a volume entitled "Prose and Poetry, by a Western Lady"—but they are exactly and precisely after the school-girl pattern, and hence are much happier than any mere imitations could be.*)

Fiction for young people commanded huge sales early in the twentieth century, and many of the series that survived for generations—the Hardy Boys, the Rover Boys, Frank Merriwell, and the Bobbsey Twins, came from that period. They taught their audience a little about the world, confirmed most of the prevailing stereotypes about other peoples, and are illuminating glimpses into the popular mind of the not-very distant past. (Selection from Edward Strate-Meyer, *Into the Heart of Africa*, 1906.)

THE ROVER BOYS: INTO THE HEART OF AFRICA

"Well, I sincerely trust we have no more such adventures."

The speaker was Randolph Rover. He was seated on an old bench in one of the rooms of the fort, binding up a finger which had been bruised in the fray.

It was two hours later, and the fight had come to an end some time previous. Nobody was seriously hurt, although Sam, Dick, and Aleck were suffering from several small wounds, Aleck had had his ear clipped by a bullet from Captain Villaire's pistol and was thankful that he had not been killed.

Baxter, the picture of misery, was a prisoner. The bully's face was much swollen and one eye was in deep mourning. He sat huddled up in a heap in a corner and wondering what punishment would be dealt out him. "I suppose they'll kill me," he groaned, and it may be added that he thought he almost deserved that fate.

"You came just in time," said Dick. "Captain Villaire was about to torture us into writing letters home asking for the money he wanted as a ransom. Baxter put it into his head that we were very rich."

"Oh, please don't say anything more about it!" groaned the unfortunate bully. "I—I—that Frenchman put up this job all on his own hook."

"I don't believe it," came promptly from Randolph Rover. "You met him at Boma; you cannot deny it."

"So I did; but he didn't say he was going to capture you, and I—"

"We don't care to listen to your falsehoods, Baxter," interrupted Dick sternly. "You are fully as guilty as anybody. You admitted it before."

Cujo had gone off to watch Captain Villaire and his party. He now came back, bringing word that the brigand had taken a fallen tree and put out on the Congo and was drifting down the stream along with several of his companions in crime. "Him won't come back," said the tall African. "Him had enough of um fight."

Nevertheless the whole party remained on guard until morning, their weapons ready for instant use. But no alarm came, and when day dawned they soon made sure that they had the entire locality around the old fort to themselves, the Frenchman with a broken arm having managed to crawl off and reach his friends. What to do with Dan Baxter was a conundrum.

"We can't take him with us, and if we leave him behind he will only be up to more evil," said Dick. "We ought to turn him over to the British authorities."

"No, no, don't do that," pleaded the tall youth. "Let me go and I'll promise never to interfere with you again."

"Your promises are not worth the breath used in uttering them," replied Tom. "Baxter, a worse rascal than you could not be imagined. Why don't you try to turn over a new leaf?"

"I will—if you'll only give me one more chance," pleaded the former bully of Putnam Hall.

The matter was discussed in private, and it was at last decided to let Baxter go, providing he would promise to return straight to the coast.

"And remember," said Dick, "if we catch you following us again we will shoot you on sight."

"I won't follow—don't be alarmed," was the low answer, and then Baxter was release and conducted to the road running down to Boma. He was given the knife he had carried, but the Rovers kept his pistol, that he might not be able to take a long-range shot at them. Soon he was out of their sight, not to turn up again for a long while to come.

It was not until the heat of the day had been spent that the expedition resumed its journey, after an excellent meal made from the supplies Captain Villaire's party had left behind in their hurried flight.

Some of the remaining supplies were done up into bundles by Cujo, to replace those which had been lost when the natives hired by Randolph Rover had deserted.

"It's queer we didn't see anything of that man and woman from the inn," remarked Dick, as they set off. "I reckon they got scared at the very start."

They journeyed until long after nightfall, "to make up for lost time," as Mr. Rover expressed it, and so steadily did Cujo push on that when a halt was called the boys were glad enough to rest. They had reached a native village called Rowimu. Here Cujo was well known and he readily procured good accommodations for all hands.

The next week passed without special incident, excepting that one afternoon the whole party went hunting, bringing down a large quantity of birds and several small animals, including an antelope, which to the boys looked like a Maine deer excepting for the peculiar formation of its horns.

"I wonder how Mr. Blaze is making out?" said Tom, when they were returning to camp from the hunt.

"Oh, I reckon he is blazing away at game," laughed Sam, and Tom at once groaned over the attempted joke.

"Perhaps we will meet him some day—if he's in this territory," put in Dick. "But just now I am looking for nobody but father."

"And so are all of us," said Tom and Sam promptly.

They were getting deeper and deeper into the jungle and had to take good care that they did not become separated. Yet Cujo said he understood the way perfectly and often proved his words by mentioning something which they would soon reach, a stream, a little lake, or a series of rocks with a tiny waterfall. "Been ober dis ground many times," said the guide.

"I suppose this is the ground Stanley covered in his famous expedition along the Congo," remarked Dick, as they journeyed along. "But who really discovered the country, Uncle Randolph?"

"That is a difficult question to answer, Dick. The Portuguese, the Spanish, and the French all claim that honor, along with the English. I fancy different sections were discovered by different nationalities. This Free State, you know, is controlled by half a dozen nations."

"I wonder if the country will ever be thoroughly civilized?"

"It will take a long while, I am afraid. Christianity will have to come first. Many of the tribes in Africa are, you must remember, without any form of religion whatever, being even worse than what we call heathens, who worship some sort of a God."

"Don't they believe in anything?" asked Sam.

"Nothing, Sam. And their morality is of the lowest grade in consequence. They murder and steal whenever the chance offers, and when they think the little children too much care for them they pitch them into the rivers for the crocodiles to feed upon."

"The beasts!" murmured Tom. "Well, I reckon at that rate, civilization can't come too quick, even if it has to advance behind bayonets and cannon."

Andrew Carnegie's famous public libraries were not given without strings attached. Towns had to agree to their maintenance. Mr. Dooley, Thomas Finley Dunne's sagacious Irish barkeeper, explains the effect of this on taxes and looks America's greatest gift horse squarely in the mouth. (Selection from Finley Peter Dunne, *Dissertations by Mister Dooley*, 1906.)

FINLEY PETER DUNNE: THE CARNEGIE LIBRARIES

"Has Andhrew Carnaygie given ye a libry yet?" asked Mr. Dooley. "Not that I know iv," said Mr. Hennessy.

"He will," said Mr. Dooley. "Ye'll not escape him. Befure he dies he hopes to crowd a libry on ivry man, woman, an' child in the' counthry. He's given thim to cities, towns, villages, an' whistlin' stations. They're tearin' down gas-houses an' poor-houses to put up libries. Befure another year, ivry house in Pittsburg that ain't a blast-furnace will be a Carnaygie libry. In some places all th' buildin's is libries. If ye write him f'r an autygraft he sinds ye a libry. No beggar is iver turned impty-handed fr'm th' dure. Th' pan-handler knocks an' asts f'r a glass iv milk an' a roll. 'No, sir,' says Andhrew Carnaygie, 'I will not pauperize this onworthy man.' Nawthin is worst f'r a beggar-man thin to make a pauper iv him. Yet it shall not be said iv me that I give nawthin' to th' poor. Saunders, give him a libry, an' if he still insists on a roll tell him to roll th' libry. F'r I'm humorous as well as wise,' he says."

"Does he give th' books that go with it?" asked Mr. Hennessy.

"Books?" said Mr. Dooley. "What ar-re ye talkin' about? D'ye know what a libry is? I suppose ye think it's a place where a man can go, haul down wan iv his fav'rite authors fr'm th' shelf, an' take a nap in it. That's not a Carnaygie libry. A Carnaygie libry is a large, brown-stone, impenethrible buildin' with th' name iv th' maker blown on th' dure. Libry, fr'm th' Greek wurruds, libus, a book, an' ary, sildom,—sildom a book. A Carnaygie libry is archytechoor, not lithrachoor. Lithrachoor will be riprisinted. Th' most cillybrated dead authors will be honored be havin' their names painted on th' wall in distinguished comp'ny, as thus: Andhrew Carnaygie, Shakespeare; Andhrew Carnaygie, Byron; Andhrew Carnaygie, Bobby Burns; Andhrew Carnaygie, an' so on. Ivry author is guaranteed a place next to pure readin' matther like a bakin' powdher advertisemint, so that whin a man comes along that niver heerd iv Shakespeare he'll know he was somebody, because there he is on th' wall. That's th' dead authors. Th' live authors will stand outside an' wish they were dead.

"He's havin' gr-reat spoort with it. I r-read his speech th' other day, whin he laid th' corner-stone iv th' libry at Pianola, Ioway. Th' entire popylation iv this lithry cinter gathered to see an' hear him. There was th' postmaster an' his wife, th' blacksmith an' his fam'ly, the station agent, mine host iv th' Farmers' Exchange, an' some sthray live stock. 'Ladies an' gintlemen,' says he. 'Modesty compels me to say nawthin' on this occasion, but I am not be be bulldozed,' he says. 'I can't tell ye how much pleasure I take in disthributin' monymints to th' humble name around which has gathered so manny hon'rable associations with mesilf. I have been a very busy little man all me life, but I like hard wurruk, an' givin' away me money is th' hardest wurruk I iver did. It fairly makes me teeth ache to part with it. But there's wan consolation. I cheer mesilf with th' thought that no matther how much money I give it don't do any particular person anny good. Th' worst thing ye can do f'r anny man is to do him good. I pass by th' organ-grinder on th' corner with a savage glare. I bate th' monkey on th' head whin he comes up smilin' to me window, an' hurl him down on his impecyoonyous owner. None iv me money goes into th' little tin cup. I cud kick a hospital, an' I lave Wall Sthreet to look afther th' widow an' th' orphan. Th' submerged tenth, thim that can't get hold iv a good chunk iv th' goods, I wud cut off fr'm th' rest iv th' wurruld an' prevint fr'm bearin' th' haughty name iv papa or th' still lovelier name iv ma. So far I've got on'y half me wish in this matther.

" 'I don't want poverty an' crime to go on. I intind to stop it. But how? It's been holdin' its own f'r cinchries. Some iv th' gr-reatest iv former minds has undertook to prevint it an' has failed. They didn't know how. Modesty wud prevint me agin fr'm sayin' that I know how, but that's nayether here nor there. I do. Th' way to abolish poverty an' bust crime is to put up a brown-stone buildin' in ivry town in th' counthry with me name over it. That's th' way. I suppose th' raison it wasn't thried befure was that no man iver had such a name. 'Tis thrue me efforts is not appreciated ivrywhere. I offer a city a libry, an' oftentimes it replies an' asks me f'r something to pay off th' school debt. I rayceive degraded pettyshuns fr'm so-called proud methropolises f'r a gas-house in place iv a libry. I pass thim by with scorn. All I ask iv a city in rayturn f'r a fifty-thousan'-dollar libry is that it shall raise wan millyon dollars to maintain th' buildin' an' keep me name shiny, an' if it won't do that much f'r lithrachoor, th' divvle take it, it's onworthy iv th' name iv an American city. What ivry community needs is taxes an' lithrachoor. I give thim both. Three cheers f'r a libry an' a bonded debt! Lithrachoor, taxation, an' Andhrew Carnaygie, wan an' insiprable, now an' foriver! They'se nawthin' so good as a good book. It's betther thin food; it's betther thin money. I have made money an' books, an' I like me books betther thin me money. Others don't, but I do. With these few wurruds I will conclude. Modesty wud prevint me fr'm sayin' more, but I have to catch a thrain, an' cannot go on. I stake ye to this libry, which ye will have as soon as ye raise th' money to keep it goin'. Stock it with useful readin', an' some day ye're otherwise pauper an' criminal childher will come to know me name whin I am gone an' there's no wan left to tell it thim.'

"Whin th' historyan comes to write th' histhry iv th' West he'll say: 'Pianola, Ioway, was a prosperous town till th' failure iv th' corn crop in nineteen hundherd an' wan, an' th' Carnaygie libry in nineteen hundherd an' two. Th' govermint ast f'r thirty dollars to pave Main Street with wooden blocks, but th' gr-reat philanthropist was firm, an' the libry was sawed off on th' town. Th' public schools, th' wurruk-house, th' wather wurruks, an' th' other penal instichoochions was at wanst closed, an' th' people begun to wurruk to support th' libry. In five years th' popylation had deserted th' town to escape taxation, an' now, as Mr. Carnaygie promised, poverty an' crime has been abolished in th' place, th' janitor iv th' buildin' bein' honest an' well paid.'

"Isn't it good f'r lithrachoor, says ye? Sure, I think not, Hinnissy. Libries niver encouraged lithrachoor anny more thin tombstones encourage livin'. No wan iver wrote annythin' because he was tol' that a hundherd years fr'm now his books might be taken down fr'm a shelf in a granite sepulcher an' some wan wud write 'Good' or 'This man is crazy' in th' margin. What lithrachoor needs is fillin' food. If Andhrew wud put a kitchen in th' libries an' build some bunks or even swing a few hammocks where livin' authors cud crawl in at night an' sleep while waitin' f'r this enlightened nation to wake up an' discover th' Shakespeares now on th' turf, he wud be givin' a rale boost to lithrachoor. With th' smoke curlin' fr'm th' chimbley, an' hundherds iv potes settin' aroun' a table loaded down with pancakes an' talkin' pothry an' prize-fightin', with hundherds iv other potes stacked up nately in th' sleepin'-rooms an' snorin' in wan gran' chorus, with their wives holdin' down good-payin' jobs as libraryans or cooks, an' their happy little childher playin' through th' marble corrydors, Andhrew Carneygie wud not have lived in vain. Maybe that's th' on'y way he knows how to live. I don't believe in libries.

They pauperize lithrachoor. I'm f'r helpin' th' boys that's now on th' job. I know a pote in Halsted Sthreet that wanst wrote a pome beginnin', 'All th' wealth iv Ind,' that he sold to a magazine f'r two dollars, payable on publycation. Lithrachoor don't need advancin'. What it needs is advances f'r lithrachoors. Ye can't shake down posterity f'r th' price.

"All th' same, I like Andhrew Carnaygie. Him an' me ar-re agreed on that point. I like him because he ain't shamed to give publicly. Ye don't find him puttin' on false whiskers an turnin' up his coat-collar whin he goes out to be benivolent. No, sir. Ivry time he dhrops a dollar it makes a noise like a waither fallin' down-stairs with a tray iv dishes. He's givin' th' way we'd all like to give. I niver put annything in th' poor-box, but I wud if Father Kelly wud rig up like wan iv thim slot-machines, so that whin I stuck in a nickel me name wud appear over th' altar in red letters. But whin I put a dollar in th' plate I get back about two yards an' hurl it so hard that th' good man turns around to see who done it. Do good be stealth, says I, but see that th' burglar-alarm is set. Anny benivolent money I hand out I want to talk about me. Him that giveth to th' poor, they say, lindeth to th' Lord; but in these days we look f'r quick returns on our invistmints. I like Andhrew Carnaygie, an', as he says, he puts his whole soul into th' wurruk."

"What's he mane be that?" asked Mr. Hennessy.

"He manes," said Mr. Dooley, "that he's gin'rous. Ivry time he gives a libry he gives himsilf away in a speech."

L. Frank Baum's *The Wizard of Oz* is not only an enduring children's tale but also a satire on American politics in the 1890s. With a little brains, a little courage, and a pair of silver slippers, the people of Kansas could easily overthrow their oppressors. Baum vigorously supported the populists and their Free Silver policy in the 1890s. The Emerald City was, after all, green, and Dorothy killed the wicked witch of the East. But Baum's story, later a famous and enduring film with Judy Garland, has charmed children long after its politics are forgotten by all save historians. (Selection from L. Frank Baum, *The Wizard of Oz*, 1900.)

L. FRANK BAUM: *THE WIZARD OF OZ*

Even with eyes protected by the green spectacles, Dorothy and her friends were at first dazzled by the brilliancy of the wonderful City. The streets were lined with beautiful houses, all built of green marble and studded everywhere with sparkling emeralds. They walked over a pavement of the same green marble, and where the blocks were joined together were rows of emeralds, set closely, and glittering in the brightness of the sun. The windowpanes were of green glass, even the sky above the City had a green tint, and the rays of the sun were green.

There were many people, men, women and children, walking about, and these were all dressed in green clothes and had greenish skins. They looked at Dorothy and her strangely assorted company with wondering eyes, and the children all ran away and hid behind their mothers when they saw the Lion; but no one spoke to them. Many shops stood in the street, and Dorothy saw that everything in them was green. Green candy and green popcorn were offered for sale, as well as green shoes, green hats and green clothes of all sorts. At one place a man was selling green lemonade, and when the children bought it Dorothy could see that they paid for it with green pennies.

There seemed to be no horses nor animals of any kind; the men carried things around in little green carts, which they pushed before them. Everyone seemed happy and contented and prosperous.

The Guardian of the Gates led them through the streets until they came to a big building, exactly in the middle of the City, which was the Palace of Oz, the Great Wizard. There was a soldier before the door, dressed in a green uniform and wearing a long green beard.

"Here are strangers," said the Guardian of the Gates to him, "and they demand to see the Great Oz."

"Step inside," answered the soldier, "and I will carry your message to him."

So they passed through the palace gates and were led into a big room with a green carpet and lovely green furniture set with emeralds. The soldier made them all wipe their feet upon a green mat before entering this room, and when they were seated he said politely,

"Please make yourselves comfortable while I go to the door of the Throne Room and tell Oz you are here."

They had to wait a long time before the soldier returned. When, at last, he came back, Dorothy asked,

"Have you seen Oz?"

"Oh, no," returned the soldier; "I have never seen him. But I spoke to him as he sat behind his screen and gave him your message. He says he will grant you an audience, if you so desire; but each one of you must enter his presence alone, and he will admit but one each day. Therefore, as you must remain in the Palace for several days, I will have you shown to rooms where you may rest in comfort after your journey."

"Thank you," replied the girl; "that is very kind of Oz."

The soldier now blew upon a green whistle, and at once a young girl, dressed in a pretty green silk gown, entered the room. She had lovely green hair and green eyes, and she bowed low before Dorothy as she said,

"Follow me and I will show you your room."

So Dorothy said good-bye to all her friends except Toto and taking the dog in her arms followed the green girl through seven passages and up three flights of stairs until they came to a room at the front of the Palace. It was the sweetest little room in the world, with a soft, comfortable bed that had sheets of green silk and a green velvet counterpane. There was a tiny fountain in the middle of the room, that shot a spray of green perfume into the air, to fall back into a beautifully carved green marble basin. Beautiful green flowers stood in the windows, and there was a shelf with a row of little green books. When Dorothy had time to open these books she found them full of queer green pictures that made her laugh, they were so funny.

In a wardrobe were many green dresses, made of silk and satin and velvet; and all of them fitted Dorothy exactly.

"Make yourself perfectly at home," said the green girl, "and if you wish for anything ring the bell. Oz will send for you tomorrow morning."

She left Dorothy alone and went back to the others. These she also led to rooms, and each one of them found himself lodged in a very pleasant part of the Palace. Of course this politeness was wasted on the Scarecrow; for when he found himself alone in his room he stood stupidly in one spot, just within the doorway, to wait till morning. It would not rest him to lie down, and he could not close his eyes; so he remained all night staring at a little spider which was weaving its web in a corner of the room, just as if it were not one of the most wonderful rooms in the world. The Tin Woodman lay down on his bed from force of habit, for he remembered when he was made of flesh; but not being able to sleep he passed the night moving his joints up and down to make sure they kept in good working order. The Lion would have preferred a bed of dried leaves in the forest, and did not like being shut up in a room; but he had too much sense to let this worry him, so he sprang upon the bed and rolled himself up like a cat and purred himself asleep in a minute.

The next morning, after breakfast, the green maiden came to fetch Dorothy, and she dressed her in one of the prettiest gowns made of green brocaded satin. Dorothy put on a green silk apron and tied a green ribbon around Toto's neck, and they started for the Throne Room of the Great Oz.

First they came to a great hall in which were many ladies and gentlemen of the court, all dressed in rich costumes. These people had nothing to do but talk to each other, but they always came to wait outside the Throne Room every morning, although they were never permitted to see Oz. As Dorothy entered they looked at her curiously, and one of them whispered,

"Are you really going to look upon the face of Oz the Terrible?"

"Of course," answered the girl, "if he will see me."

"Oh, he will see you," said the soldier who had taken her message to the Wizard, "although he does not like to have people ask to see him. Indeed, at first he was angry, and said I should send you back where you came from. Then he asked me what you looked like, and when I mentioned your silver shoes he was very much interested. At last I told him about the mark upon your forehead, and he decided he would admit you to his presence."

Just then a bell rang, and the green girl said to Dorothy,

"This is the signal. You must go into the Throne Room alone."

She opened a little door and Dorothy walked boldly through and found herself in a wonderful place. It was a big, round room with a high arched roof, and the walls and ceiling and floor were covered with large emeralds set closely together. In the center of the ceiling was a great light, as bright as the sun, which made the emeralds sparkle in a wonderful manner.

But what interested Dorothy most was the big throne of green marble that stood in the middle of the room. It was shaped like a chair and sparkled with gems, as did everything else. In the center of the chair was an enormous Head, without body to support it or any arms or legs whatever. There was no hair upon this head, but it had eyes and nose and mouth, and was bigger than the head of the biggest giant.

As Dorothy gazed upon this in wonder and fear the eyes turned slowly and looked at her sharply and steadily. Then the mouth moved, and Dorothy heard a voice say:

"I am Oz, the Great and Terrible. Who are you, and why do you seek me?"

It was not such an awful voice as she had expected to come from the big Head; so she took courage and answered,

"I am Dorothy, the Small and Meek. I have come to you for help."

The eyes looked at her thoughtfully for a full minute. Then said the voice:

"Where did you get the silver shoes?"

"I got them from the Wicked Witch of the East, when my house fell on her and killed her," she replied.

"Where did you get the mark upon your forehead?" continued the voice.

"That is where the good Witch of the North kissed me when she bade me good-bye and sent me to you," said the girl.

Again the eyes looked at her sharply, and they saw she was telling the truth. Then Oz asked,

"What do you wish me to do?"

"Send me back to Kansas, where my Aunt Em and Uncle Henry are," she answer earnestly. "I don't like your country, although it is so beautiful. And I am sure Aunt Em will be worried over my being away so long."

The eyes winked three times, and then they turned up to the ceiling and down to the floor and rolled around so queerly that they seemed to see every part of the room. And at last they looked at Dorothy again.

"Why should I do this for you?" asked Oz.

"Because you are strong and I am weak; because you are a Great Wizard and I am only a helpless little girl," she answered.

"But you were strong enough to kill the wicked Witch of the East," said Oz.

"That just happened," returned Dorothy simply; "I could not help it."

"Well," said the Head, "I will give you my answer. You have no right to expect me to send you back to Kansas unless you do something for me in return. In this country everyone must pay for everything he gets. If you wish me to use my magic power to send you home again you must do something for me first. Help me and I will help you."

"What must I do?" asked the girl.

"Kill the wicked Witch of the West," answered Oz.

"But I cannot!" exclaimed Dorothy, greatly surprised.

"You killed the Witch of the East and you wear the silver shoes, which bear a powerful charm. There is now but one Wicked Witch left in all this land, and when you can tell me she is dead I will send you back to Kansas—but not before."

The little girl began to weep, she was so disappointed; the eyes winked again and looked at her anxiously, as if the Great Oz felt that she could help him if she would.

"I never killed anything willingly," she sobbed, "and even if I wanted to, how could I kill the Wicked Witch? If you, who are Great and Terrible, cannot kill her yourself, how do you expect me to do it?"

"I do not know," said the Head; "but that is my answer, and until the Wicked Witch dies you will not see your Uncle and Aunt again. Remember that the Witch is Wicked—tremendously Wicked—and ought to be killed. Now go, and do not ask to see me again until you have done your task."

Sorrowfully Dorothy left the Throne Room and went back to where the Lion and the Scarecrow and the Tin Woodman were waiting to hear what Oz had said to her.

"There is no hope for me," she said sadly, "for Oz will not send me home until I have killed the Wicked Witch of the West; and that I can never do."

Her friends were sorry, but could do nothing to help her; so she went to her own room and lay down on the bed and cried herself to sleep.

The next morning the soldier with the green whiskers came to the Scarecrow and said,

"Come with me, for Oz has sent for you."

So the Scarecrow followed him and was admitted into the great Throne Room, where he saw, sitting in the emerald throne, a most lovely lady. She was dressed in green silk gauze and wore upon her flowing green locks a crown of jewels. Growing from her shoulders were wings, gorgeous in color and so light that they fluttered if the slightest breath of air reached them.

When the Scarecrow had bowed, as prettily as his straw stuffing would let him, before this beautiful creature, she looked upon him sweetly, and said,

"I am Oz, the Great and Terrible. Who are you, and why do you seek me?"

Now the Scarecrow, who had expected to see the great Head Dorothy had told him of, was much astonished; but he answered her bravely.

"I am only a Scarecrow, stuffed with straw. Therefore I have no brains, and I come to you praying that you will put brains in my head instead of straw, so that I may become as much a man as any other in your dominions."

"Why should I do this for you?" asked the lady.

"Because you are wise and powerful, and no one else can help me," answered the Scarecrow.

"I never grant favors without some return," said Oz; "but this much I will promise. If you will kill for me the Wicked Witch of the West I will bestow upon you a great many brains, and such good brains that you will be the wisest man in all the Land of Oz."

"I thought you asked Dorothy to kill the Witch," said the Scarecrow, in surprise.

"So I did. I don't care who kills her. But until she is dead I will not grant your wish. Now go, and do not seek me again until you have earned the brains you so greatly desire."

The Scarecrow went sorrowfully back to his friends and told them what Oz had said; and Dorothy was surprised to find the great Wizard was not a Head, as she had seen him, but a lovely lady.

"All the same," said the Scarecrow, "she needs a heart as much as the Tin Woodman."

On the next morning the soldier with the green whiskers came to the Tin Woodman and said,

"Oz has sent for you. Follow me."

So the Tin Woodman followed him and came to the great Throne Room. He did not know whether he would find Oz a lovely lady or a Head, but he hoped it would be the lovely lady. "For," he said to himself, "if it is the Head, I am sure I shall not be given a heart, since a head has no heart of its own and therefore cannot feel for me. But if it is the lovely lady I shall beg hard for a heart, for all ladies are themselves said to be kindly hearted."

But when the Woodman entered the great Throne Room he saw neither the Head nor the Lady, for Oz had taken the shape of a most terrible Beast. It was nearly as big as an elephant, and the green throne seemed hardly strong enough to hold its weight. The Beast had a head like that of a rhinoceros, only there were five eyes in its face. There were five long arms growing out of its body and it also had five long, slim legs. Thick, wooly hair covered every part of it, and a more dreadful-looking monster could not be imagined. It was fortunate the Tin Woodman had no heart at that moment, for it would have beat loud and fast from terror. But being only tin, the Woodman was not at all afraid, although he was much disappointed.

"I am Oz, the Great and Terrible," spake the Beast, in a voice that was one great roar. "Who are you, and why do you seek me?"

"I am a Woodman, and made of tin. Therefore I have no heart, and cannot love. I pray you to give me a heart that I may be as other men are."

"Why should I do this?" demanded the Beast.

"Because I ask it, and you alone can grant my request," answered the Woodman.

Oz gave a low growl at this, but said gruffly,

"If you indeed desire a heart, you must earn it."

"How?" asked the Woodman.

"Help Dorothy to kill the Wicked Witch of the West," replied the Beast. "When the Witch is dead, come to me, and I will then give you the biggest and kindest and most loving heart in all the Land of Oz."

So the Tin Woodman was forced to return sorrowfully to his friends and tell them of the terrible Beast he had seen. They all wondered greatly at the many forms the great Wizard could take upon himself, and the Lion said,

"If he is a beast when I go to see him, I shall roar my loudest, and so frighten him that he will grant all I ask. And if he is the lovely lady, I shall pretend to spring upon her, and so compel her to do my bidding. And if he is the great Head, he will be at my mercy; for I will roll this head all about the room until he promises to give us what we desire. So cheer up my friends, for all will yet be well."

The next morning the soldier with the green whiskers led the Lion to the great Throne Room and bade him enter the presence of Oz.

The Lion at once passed through the door, and glancing around saw, to his surprise, that before the throne was a Ball of Fire, so fierce and glowing he could scarcely bear to gaze upon it. His first thought was that Oz had by accident caught on fire and was burning up; but, when he tried to go nearer, the heat was so intense that it singed his whiskers, and he crept back tremblingly to a spot nearer the door.

Then a low, quiet voice came from the Ball of Fire, and these were the words it spoke:

"I am Oz the Great and Terrible. Who are you, and why do you seek me?" And the Lion answered,

"I am a Cowardly Lion, afraid of everything. I come to you to beg that you give me courage, so that in reality I may become the King of Beasts, as men call me."

"Why should I give you courage?" demanded Oz.

"Because of all Wizards you are the greatest, and alone have power to grant my request," answered the Lion.

The Ball of Fire burned fiercely for a time, and the voice said,

"Bring me proof that the Wicked Witch is dead, and that moment I will give you courage. But so long as the Witch lives you must remain a coward."

The Lion was angry at this speech, but could say nothing in reply, and while he stood silently gazing at the Ball of Fire it became so furiously hot that he turned tail and rushed from the room. He was glad to find his friends waiting for him, and told them of his terrible interview with the Wizard.

"What shall we do now?" asked Dorothy sadly.

"There is only one thing we can do," returned the Lion, "and that is to go to the land of the Winkies, seek out the Wicked Witch, and destroy her."

"But suppose we cannot?" said the girl.

"Then I shall never have courage," declared the Lion.

"And I shall never have brains," added the Scarecrow.

"And I shall never have a heart," spoke the Tin Woodman.

"And I shall never see Aunt Em and Uncle Henry," said Dorothy, beginning to cry.

"Be careful!" cried the green girl; "the tears will fall on your green silk gown, and spot it."

So Dorothy dried her eyes and said,

"I suppose we must try it; but I am sure I do not want to kill anybody, even to see Aunt Em again."

"I will go with you, but I'm too much of a coward to kill the Witch," said the Lion.

"I will go too," declared the Scarecrow, "but I shall not be of much help to you, I am such a fool."

"I haven't the heart to harm even a Witch," remarked the Tin Woodman; "but if you go I certainly shall go with you."

Therefore it was decided to start upon their journey the next morning, and the Woodman sharpened his axe on a green grindstone and had all his joints properly oiled. The scarecrow stuffed himself with fresh straw and Dorothy put new paint on his eyes that he might see better. The green girl, was very kind to them, filled Dorothy's basket with good things to eat, and fastened a little bell around Toto's neck with a green ribbon.

They went to bed quite early and slept soundly until daylight, when they were awakened by the crowing of a green cock that lived in the back yard of the palace, and the cackling of a hen that had laid a green egg.

sex and the family

In the course of the nineteenth century, the "spheres" of men and women became sharply differentiated: business, politics, saloons, sports, a whole rough-house world on one side; home, manners, church, gentility on the other. Here are some examples from the "man's world" tame enough to go into a household songbook. (Selections from *Heart Songs Dear to the American People*, 1909.)

HEART SONGS

My Moustache

1 My moustache is growing, Its genial warmth bestowing;
Its beauty charms the eye of all Broadway.
Come forth like a fairy so light and so airy,
And ramble o'er my upper lip so gay.

Refrain
Come! come! moustache come,
Come e'er the dye on thee fades;
Come forth like a fairy, so light and so airy,
And ramble o'er my upper lip so gay.

2 But when I am drinking, I oft times am thinking,
There's one thing you will hinder very much;
The rapturous blisses of sweet stolen kisses,
You'll scarcely let the girls our two lips touch.

My Last Cigar

1 'Twas off the blue Canary Isles, a glorious summer day,
I sat upon the quarterdeck, and whiffed my cares away;
And as the volumed smoke arose, like incense in the air,
I breath'd a sigh to think, in sooth, it was my last cigar.

Refrain
It was my last cigar, it was my last cigar;
I breath'd a sigh to think, in sooth, it was my last cigar.

2   I leaned upon the quarterrail, and looked down in the sea,
E'en there the purple wreath of smoke was curling gracefully.
O, what had I at such a time, to do with wasting care?
Alas! the trembling tear proclaimed it was my last cigar.

3   I watched the ashes as it came fast drawing to the end;
I watched it as a friend would watch beside a dying friend;
But still the flame crept slowly on, it vanished into air,
I threw it from me, spare the tale, it was my last cigar.

4   I've seen the land of all I love fade in the distance dim,
I've watched above the blighted heart, where once proud hope
   had been;
But I've never known a sorrow that could with that compare,
When off the blue Canary Isles, I smoked my last cigar.

Social mobility, opportunity, democracy, call it what you will—a society with enough fluidity to enable people to rise and fall is one that constantly requires its members to learn new manners to fit changing stations and styles. (From *The Manners that Win*, 1886.)

MANNERS THAT WIN

An introduction secured by you for the purpose of asking a favor does not entitle you to after recognition.

In giving introductions, always give the full name, as "Mrs. Jones, allow me to introduce my cousin, Frank Thornton;" not simply "my cousin Frank," which would leave poor Mrs. Jones in doubt as to what the name of the dear cousin might be.

Introductions should not be made in a public conveyance. Calling out a name makes the owner of it unpleasantly conspicuous.

To introduce a person, who is in any way objectionable, to a friend, is an insult.

Kissing in public, or in greetings, is confined to gushing school-girls and very intimate friends. Giving the hand is sufficiently cordial. Sensible people distinguish readily between real warm-heartedness and familiarity, and gushing demonstrativeness. Even between intimate friends, if in anywise public, it is a vulgar parade of affection. Only vulgar clowns salute friends by slapping them on the back, or an unceremonious poke.

If a gentleman talks with a lady on the street, he will hold his hat in his hand, unless she request him to replace it, which she will do if she is wellbred. . . .

First calls must be promptly returned, even if the second is never made.

Gentlemen, if making a formal call in the evening, retain hat and cane in hand until invited to lay them aside and spend the evening. This invitation should not be given, and if given, should not be accepted, on the occasion of a first call.

In receiving a gentleman caller, a gentleman meets him at the door, takes his hat and cane, and places a chair for him; a lady simply rises to bow, and resumes her place when the gentleman is seated.

A lady when calling keeps her parasol in her hand. Fidgeting in any way is ill-bred.

When a caller is ready to go, there is nothing to be done but to rise and go, expressing pleasure at finding friends at home. Apologies for long calls, looking at a watch, or remarking "Now I must go," are in bad taste. A straightforward, business-like getting out, without the nonsense of lingering or delay, is sensible and polite. Never resume a seat after rising to take leave. Double farewells are awkward.

Trivial subjects are in order for calls. Grave discussions and weighty subjects are out of place.

If strangers are in a room when a caller leaves, a slight bow in passing out is a sufficient recognition.

Married men need not make calls of ceremony. The wife leaves the husband's card.

Refreshments to callers are often offered in the country, but are not necessary in the city. . . .

Never draw near a fire in calling, unless invited.

In calling on an invalid, never go to the sick room until invited.

A gentleman who is a confirmed invalid may receive visits from a lady at his room, but in no other case.

Calls made by card or in person on the sick, must be returned as soon as sufficiently recovered.

Never remove gloves during a formal call.

It is an offense to call upon friends in reduced circumstances in the gorgeousness of an expensive wardrobe.

The mistress may not leave the room while visitors remain.

It is rude to open or finger the piano, or to examine furniture or pictures, or to change or displace any article, while waiting for the mistress.

It is rude to place one's chair so as to have the back to any one, to play with any article, or to seem to be aware of anything except the company present and its attractions.

In calling on friends, at a boarding-house or hotel, it is well to write the name of the friend on whom the call is made over your own, to guard against mistakes.

Gesticulations in conversation are always in bad taste. Declamation is one thing, and conversation another.

If flattered, seem not to hear or understand, or maintain a quiet dignity. Any expression of pleasure will incur the contempt of the flatterer.

Never notice or correct an error in the speech of another.

Whistling, lounging attitudes, fidgeting, fussing with the dress or any part of it, are all awkward and low-bred.

Whispering is atrocious, and interrupting or contradicting a speaker an insult.

Sitting or standing too close to one with whom you are conversing is rude, and to many exceedingly offensive.

Laughing in advance of the wit of what one is about to say is silly.

In dealing in scandal, as in robbery, the receiver is as bad as the thief.

Swearing, sneering, and private woes and affairs are banished from the talk of cultivated people.

Nick names are not recognized as well-bred in good society.

Boasting or parading wealth, possessions, or social position, or distinguished people who are relatives or friends, is a mark of a weak head and low breeding.

Never talk to a man about his business, unless he opens the subject. It seems to suggest that you fear that he cannot talk of anything else. Eschew all topics that may be painful or disagreeable. . .

The well-bred husband and wife, do not speak of each other as "Smith" or "Jones," nor as "my husband" or "my wife," except among relatives. "Mr. Smith" or "Mrs. Smith" is the proper phrase, in speaking of one's husband or wife, or in speaking to a friend of his or her husband or wife.

Punning is always to be avoided. An inveterate punster is an inveterate bore.

While business and professions are to be avoided as matters of conversation in society, it is always polite to show an interest in personal matters. A mother will always talk of her children, or a young lady of her last party.

A clear, distinct, but low, tone of voice is indicative of high breeding. . . . .

Never smack the lips, or make noises in the mouth or throat, or pick the teeth, or put the fingers in the mouth, wipe fingers on the table-cloth, or speak when the mouth is full, or slip back sleeves and cuffs as if about to take a round at fisticuffs.

Never eat all on your plate, never scrape it, or wipe it with bread, or stretch the feet or legs under the table to interfere with the opposite neighbor.

At a dinner for gentlemen guests only, the mistress presides, but retires after dinner.

To smoke or even ask to smoke in the presence of ladies is rude. Ladies may give permission, if out of doors, to keep gentlemen from running away after their cigars. To smoke in the streets in daylight is rude, or to smoke at all in rooms which ladies occupy, or in public places where ladies congregate.

It is not in accordance with etiquette to smoke a pipe in the street, or to smoke without permission in the presence of a clergyman, or to appear in the presence of ladies with clothes saturated with smoke; or to smoke a cigar without offering one to others present.

At a gentleman's party, the host only has a right to call for a toast or a song.

If a gentleman attends a ball without a lady, he should invite one of the ladies of the household to dance, and place himself at the disposal of the hostess for the benefit of "wall flowers."

A lady at a ball never gives her bouquet, fan, or gloves to a gentleman to hold during a dance, unless he is her husband, brother, or escort. . . .

In a ball-room a gentleman cannot be too careful not to injure the delicate fabrics worn by ladies.

Never make arrangements for the next dance while another is in progress.

Amateur musicians should always learn a few pieces to play or sing without notes. To carry music, without a special invitation to do so, is awkward, and to refuse to play or sing when invited, often appears selfish and ungracious.

It is dangerous to pay long visits, even to old friends, without a special invitation. If detained in a city where friends reside, don't drive at once to the house, as if your chief anxiety was to save your hotel bill, but let them know of your arrival from your hotel.

A special invitation should specify who is to go, and only those especially named should accept. It is always understood, however, that a wife may accompany her husband, and a husband may always join his wife.

The host should always meet a guest at the depot, or at least send some one.

The guest must conform to the habits of the family. The host and hostess will take pleasure in showing a guest all points of interest in the vicinity.

Visitors may be left to their own devices during the morning hours, but the hostess places music, books, etc., at their command. Attentions to guests should be kindly; fussiness is always annoying.

Neither hostess or guest may accept invitations which do not include the other.

The visitor uses a friend's servants as her own, while a guest in a house, so far as personal wants are concerned, but is careful not to be too exacting.

If any article of furniture in your own room suffers accident or injury, replace it quietly at your own expense.

A gentleman may bring a book, flowers, or confectionery, to the hostess, and a lady friend may bestow favors and kindness on the children. If a gift is made, it should be to the hostess, or if there are several children, to the youngest.

To eat confectionery or chew gum in the streets is a sign of low breeding.

In crossing a slippery walk, the gentleman may precede or follow the lady, as he can best render her assistance. He may offer his services to an entire stranger with perfect propriety.

To cross the street between the carriages of a funeral is disrespectful.

The gentleman nearest the door dismounts to assist a lady from an omnibus, when no attendant is employed to render necessary aid. He also passes up any lady's fare, and thus saves her from rising to her feet.

When a gentleman rises to offer his seat to a lady, she should thank him audibly, or at least with a polite bow for his courtesy. To turn his back, and force her to accept the courtesy in silence, is rude.

In walking with a lady, a gentleman should accommodate his steps to hers.

Loud talking or laughing in the street, or in any public place, is ill-bred. To look back at one who has passed, even if she has on a new dress which does not fit in the back, is not polite.

If a gentleman is about to leave a room, and meets a lady in the doorway, he raises his hat and steps aside for her to pass. If the door is closed, and both are entering or going out, he passes before her with a bow, opens the door and holds it open until she has passed.

Ladies should not enter places of business except on business. When in, ask for what is wanted as explicitly as possible, and do not consume the time of a salesman by examining things you know you do not want. Never try to cheapen goods; if the price is too high, go elsewhere. Don't stand at a counter when others are waiting, to make up your mind. Decide at once, or make way for others, and then take your time. Be careful not to injure goods by handling. Never give unnecessary trouble.

Never call a clerk who is waiting on some one else. Never lounge over a counter, or push aside or crowd up on another person, and never take hold of a piece of goods another is examining.

A gentleman walking with two ladies may give an arm to each, but no lady may take the arms of two gentlemen at the same time.

A gentleman carrying an umbrella, with a lady on each side of him, and the rain dripping from the umbrella over both, while he is dry, is too absurd a picture to name among the offenses against etiquette.

Don't try to shake hands with a friend across the street. Put out your hand only when quite near the friend.

Webster's *New International Dictionary* defines a "comstock" or "comstocker" as "a ludicrous prude especially in matters relating to morality in art." There is also "comstockery": "prudish concern in hunting down immorality especially in books, papers, and pictures." All these additions to the language come from the career of Anthony Comstock, whose "New York Society for the Suppression of Vice," armed with laws against using the mails to convey obscene materials, crusaded against every form of lewdness. (Selection from Anthony Comstock, *Traps for the Young*, 1883.)

ANTHONY COMSTOCK: *TRAPS FOR THE YOUNG*

And it came to pass that as Satan went to and fro upon the earth, watching his traps and rejoicing over his numerous victims, he found room for improvement in some of his schemes. The daily press did not meet all his requirements. The *weekly* illustrated papers of crime would do for young men and sports, for brothels, gin-mills, and thieves' resorts, but were found to be so gross, so libidinous, so monstrous, that every decent person spurned them. They were excluded from the home on sight. They were too high-priced for children, and too cumbersome to be conveniently hid from the parent's eye or carried in the boy's pocket. So he resolved to make another trap for boys and girls especially. . . .

One day while riding on the cars I purchased a copy of one of these papers. It is claimed to be "high-toned." The reader may judge of the *tone* when he learns that the copy now before me contains made-up stories with the following crimes woven into them. It must be premised that the following is taken from a single issue, and from parts of continued stories. To complete the grand total of infamies it would be necessary to commence at the beginning and go to the end of the fractional parts of the tales from which these extracts are taken.

The gist of these stories consists of—

A conspiracy against a school-girl.
One girl hired to personate a rich girl and marry a villain in her stead.
A man murdered by being blown up by explosives.
A beautiful girl, by lying and deceit, seeks to captivate one whom she
    loves.
Six assaults upon an officer while resisting arrests.
A conspiracy against an officer to prevent the arrest of a criminal.
A burglary.
An illegitimate child.
A woman murdered by masked burglars.
An attempt to force a beautiful girl to marry a scoundrel to save her
    benefactor.
Two attempts to coerce a girl to marry against her wishes.
One woman who died in New York comes to life in Italy.
Two attempted assassinations.
One confidence operator at work to swindle a stranger.
An assault on the highway.
A hired assassin.
A massacre by Indians.
One babe stolen to substitute for another.
An attempt to murder a child.
Two women concealing their secret-born babes.

A rich man is confronted in a castle by a woman he has ruined, who raises such an outcry that he becomes purple and rigid, while blood gushes from his mouth. The woman takes a vial from her pocket and instantly cures him.

One case of clandestine correspondence and meetings between a girl and her lover. This results in the girl running away at night and getting married to hide her shame. This is followed by a scene in their room, where the husband refuses to acknowledge his wife publicly; she being in a delicate condition pleads to have the marriage made public. The husband dares not do this for fear of arrest for other crimes. . . .

Again, these stories breed vulgarity, profanity, loose ideas of life, impurity of thought and deed. They render the imagination unclean, destroy domestic peace, desolate homes, cheapen woman's virtue, and make foul-mouthed bullies, cheats, vagabonds, thieves, desperadoes, and libertines. They disparage honest toil, and make real life a drudge and burden. What young man will serve an apprenticeship, working early and late, if his mind is filled with the idea that sudden wealth may be acquired by following the hero of the story? In real life, to begin at the foot of the ladder and work up, step by step, is the rule; but in these stories, inexperienced youth, with no moral character, take the foremost positions, and by trick and device, knife and revolver, bribery and corruption, carry everything before them, lifting themselves in a few short weeks to positions of ease and affluence. Moral courage with such is a thing to be sneered at and despised in many of these stories. If one is asked to drink and refuses, he is set up and twitted till he yields or is compelled to by force. The idea of doing anything from principle is ridiculous in the extreme. As well fill a kerosene-oil lamp with water and expect a brilliant light. And so, in addition to all else, there is early inculcated a distaste for the good, and the piercing blast of ridicule is turned upon the reader to destroy effectually all moral character. . . .

the world of work

The hard times encountered by farmers in the years after the Civil War brought forth some songs that are still sung. (*Anonymous.*)

DOWN ON PENNY'S FARM

1 Come you ladies and you gentlemen and listen to my song;
I'll sing it to you right but you might think it's wrong;
May make you mad, but I mean no harm:
It's all about the renters on Penny's farm.

Chorus:
It's hard times in the country,
Down on Penny's farm.

2 Now you move out on Penny's farm,
Plant a little crop of 'bacco and a little crop of corn.
He'll come around to plan and plot
Till he gets himself a mortgage on everything you got.

3 You go to the fields and you work all day,
Till way after dark, but you get no pay.
Promise you meat or a little lard,
It's hard to be a renter on Penny's farm.

4 Now here's George Penny come into town
With a wagon-load of peaches, not one of them sound.
He's got to have his money or somebody's check;
You pay him for a bushel and you don't get a peck.

5 Then George Penny's renters they come into town,
With their hands in their pockets and their heads hanging down.
Go in the store and the merchant will say:
"Your mortgage is due and I'm looking for my pay."

6 Goes down in his pocket with a trembling hand—
"Can't pay you all but I'll pay you what I can."

Then to the telephone the merchant makes a call:
"They'll put you on the chain gang if you don't pay it all."

THE FARMER IS THE MAN

1 Oh, the farmer comes to town
   With his wagon broken down,
   But, the farmer is the man who feeds them all.
   If you'll only look and see,
   I think you will agree
   That the farmer is the man who feeds them all.

   Chorus
   The farmer is the man,
   The farmer is the man,
   Lives on credit till the fall;
   Then they take him by the hand
   And they lead him from the land,
   And the merchant is the man who gets it all.

2 When the lawyer hangs around
   While the butcher cuts a pound,
   Oh, the farmer is the man who feeds them all,
   When the preacher and the cook
   Go a-strolling by the brook,
   Oh, the farmer is the man who feeds them all,

3 When the banker says he's broke
   And the merchant's up in smoke,
   They forget that it's the farmer feeds them all.
   It would put them to the test
   If the farmer took rest;
   Then they'd know that it's the farmer feeds them all.

   Last Chorus:
   The farmer is the man,
   The farmer is the man,
   Lives on credit till the fall—
   With the interest rate so high
   It's a wonder he don't die,
   For the mortgage man's the one who gets it all.

The labor movement continually took folk melodies or old hymns and turned them into union songs. Here is probably the most popular hymn of the nineteenth century—the melody of "John Brown's Body" and "The Battle Hymn of the Republic"—transformed into perhaps the most popular union song of the twentieth century. ("Solidarity Forever," words by Ralph Chaplin.)

"SOLIDARITY FOREVER"

1   When the union's inspiration through the workers' blood shall run,
There can be no power greater anywhere beneath the sun.
Yet what force on earth is weaker than the feeble strength of one?
But the union makes us strong.

Chorus:
Solidarity forever!
Solidarity forever!
Solidarity forever!
For the union makes us strong.

2   They have taken untold millions that they never toiled to earn,
But without our brain and muscle not a single wheel could turn.
We can break their haughty power, gain our freedom when we learn
That the union makes us strong

3   In our hands is placed a power greater than their hoarded gold,
Greater than the might of armies magnified a thousand fold.
We can bring to birth a new world from the ashes of the old,
For the union makes us strong.

Edwin Markham's "The Man with the Hoe" was a sensation in 1899: Americans thought of their farmers as sturdy, independent yeomen, not as peasants "stolid and stunned, a brother to the ox." A little later, Edgar Lee Masters etched the epitaphs of Spoon River, a rural town where lives were measured by words that conveyed the isolation of the times. (Selections from Edwin Markham, *The Man with the Hoe and Other Poems, 1899;* and Edgar Lee Masters, *Spoon River Anthology, 1906.*)

EDWIN MARKHAM: THE MAN WITH THE HOE

Written after seeing Millet's World-Famous Painting.

God made man in His own image,
in the image of God made He him.—*Genesis.*

Bowed by the weight of centuries he leans
Upon his hoe and gazes on the ground,
The emptiness of ages in his face,
And on his back the burden of the world.
Who made him dead to rapture and despair,
A thing that grieves not and that never hopes,
Stolid and stunned, a brother to the ox?
Who loosened and let down this brutal jaw?
Whose was the hand that slanted back this brow?
Whose breath blew out the light within this brain?
Is this the Thing the Lord God made and gave
To have dominion over sea and land;
To trace the stars and search the heavens for power;
To feel the passion of Eternity?
Is this the Dream He dreamed who shaped the suns
And pillared the blue firmament with light?
Down all the stretch of Hell to its last gulf
There is no shape more terrible than this—
More tongued with censure of the world's blind greed—
More filled with signs and portents for the soul—
More fraught with menace to the universe.

What gulfs between him and the seraphim!
Slave of the wheel of labor, what to him
Are Plato and the swing of Pleiades?
What the long reaches of the peaks of song,
The rift of dawn, the reddening of the rose?
Through this dread shape the suffering ages look;
Time's tragedy is in that aching stoop;
Through this dread shape humanity betrayed,
Plundered, profaned and disinherited,
Cries protest to the Judges of the World,
A protest that is also prophecy.
O masters, lords and rulers in all lands,
Is this the handiwork you give to God,

This monstrous thing distorted and soulquenched?
How will you ever straighten up this shape;
Touch it again with immortality;
Give back the upward looking and the light;
Rebuild in it the music and the dream;
Make right the immemorial infamies,
Perfidious wrongs, immedicable woes?
O masters, lords and rulers in all lands,
How will the Future reckon with this Man?
How answer his brute question in that hour
When whirlwinds of rebellion shake the world?
How will it be with kingdoms and with kings—
With those who shaped him to the thing he is—
When this dumb Terror shall reply to God,
After the silence of the centuries?

EDGAR LEE MASTERS, *SPOON RIVER ANTHOLOGY*

Frank Drummer

Out of a cell into this darkened space—
The end at twenty-five!
My tongue could not speak what stirred within me,
And the village thought me a fool
Yet at the start there was a clear vision,
A high and urgent purpose in my soul
Which drove me on trying to memorize
The Encyclopedia Britannica!

Deacon Taylor

I belonged to the church,
And to the party of prohibition;
And the villagers thought I died of eating watermelon.
In truth I had cirrhosis of the liver,
For every noon for thirty years,
I slipped behind the prescription partition
In Trainor's drug store
And poured a generous drink
From the bottle marked
"*Spiritus frumenti.*"

A. D. Blood

If you in the village think that my work was a good one,
Who closed the saloons and stopped all playing at cards,
And haled old Daisy Fraser before Justice Arnett,
In many a crusade to purge the people of sin;
Why do you let the milliner's daughter Dora,
And the worthless son of Benjamin Pantier
Nightly make my grave their unholy pillow?

Barney Hainsfeather

If the excursion train to Peoria
Had just been wrecked, I might have escaped with my life—
Certainly I should have escaped this place.
But as it was burned as well, they mistook me
For John Allen who was sent to the Hebrew Cemetery
At Chicago,
And John for me, so I lie here.
It was bad enough to run a clothing store in this town,
But to be buried here—*ach!*

Harry Wilmans

I was just turned twenty-one,
And Henry Phipps, the Sunday-school superintendent,
Made a speech in Bindle's Opera House.
"The honor of the flag must be upheld," he said,
"Whether it be assailed by a barbarous tribe of Tagalogs
Or the greatest power in Europe."
And we cheered and cheered the speech and the flag he waved
As he spoke.
And I went to the war in spite of my father,
And followed the flag till I saw it raised
By our camp in a rice field near Manila,
And all of us cheered and cheered it.
But there were flies and poisonous things;
And there was the deadly water,
And the cruel heat,
And the sickening, putrid food;

And the smell of the trench just back of the tents
Where the soldiers went to empty themselves;
And there were the whores who followed us, full of syphilis;
And beastly acts between ourselves or alone,
With bullying, hatred, degradation among us,
And days of loathing and nights of fear
To the hour of the charge through the steaming swamp,
Following the flag,
Till I fell with a scream, shot through the guts.
Now there's a flag over me in Spoon River!
A flag! A flag!

In the depression of the 1870s, middle-class Americans became more deeply aware of the insecure lives of the laboring class growing so rapidly in their midst. In 1883 the Senate held hearings on the relationship between capital and labor at which a Fall River, Massachusetts, mule-spinner testified. (From *Testimony, Senate Committee upon the Relations between Labor and Capital,* 1883.)

TESTIMONY OF THOMAS O'DONNELL

When he appeared before the committee, Thomas O'Donnell, a native of Ramsbotham, England, had been for eleven years a mule-spinner in the textile factories of Fall River, Massachusetts.

Sen. Blair: Are you a married man?—A. Yes, sir; I am a married man; have a wife and two children. I am not very well educated. I went to work when I was young, and have been working ever since in the cotton business; went to work when I was about eight or nine years old. I was going to state how I live. My children get along very well in summer time, on account of not having to buy fuel or shoes or one thing and another. I earn $1.50 a day and can't afford to pay a very big house rent. I pay $1.50 a week for rent, which comes to about $6.00 a month.

Q. That is, you pay this where you are at Fall River?—A. Yes, Sir.

Q. Do you have work right along?—A. No, sir; since that strike we had down in Fall River about three years ago I have not worked much more than half the time, and that has brought my circumstances down very much.

Q. Why have you not worked more than half the time since then?—A. Well, at Fall River if a man has not got a boy to act as "back-boy" it is very hard for him to get along. In a great many cases they discharge men in that work and put in men who have boys.

Q. Men who have boys of their own?—A. Men who have boys of their own capable enough to work in a mill, to earn $.30 or $.40 a day.

Q. Is the object of that to enable the boy to earn something for himself?—A. Well, no; the object is this: They are doing away with a great deal of mule-spinning there and putting in ring-spinning, and for that reason it takes a good deal of small help to run this ring work, and it throws the men out of work because they are doing away with the mules and putting these ring-frames in to take their places. For that reason they get all the small help they can to run these ring-frames. There are so many men in the city to work, and whoever has a boy can have work, and whoever has no boy stands no chance. Probably he may have a few months of work in the summer time, but will be discharged in the fall. That is what leaves me in poor circumstances. Our children, of course, are very often sickly from one cause or another, on account of not having sufficient clothes, or shoes, or food, or something. And also my woman; she never did work in a mill; she was a housekeeper, and for that reason she can't help me to anything at present, as many women do help their husbands down there, by working, like themselves. My wife never did work in a mill, and that leaves me to provide for the whole family. I have two children. . . .

Q. How much have you had within a year?—A. Since Thanksgiving I happened to get work in the Crescent Mill, and worked there exactly thirteen weeks. I got just $1.50 per day, with the exception of a few days that I lost—because in following up mule-spinning you are obliged to lose a day once in a while; you can't follow it up regularly.

Q. Thirteen weeks would be seventy-eight days, and, at $1.50 a day, that would make $117, less whatever time you lost?—A. Yes. I worked thirteen weeks there and ten days in another place, and then there was a dollar I got this week, Wednesday.

Q. Taking a full year back can you tell how much you have had?—A. That would be about fifteen week's work. . . .

Q. That would be somewhere about $133, if you had not lost any time?—A. Yes, sir.

Q. That is all you have had?—A. Yes, sir.

Q. To support yourself and wife and two children?—A. Yes, sir.

Q. Have you had any help from outside?—A. No, sir.

Q. Do you mean that yourself and wife and two children have had nothing but that for all this time?—A. That is all. I got a couple dollars' worth of coal last winter, and the wood I picked up myself. I goes around with a shovel and picks up clams and wood.

Q. What do you do with the clams—A. We eat them. I don't get them to sell, but just to eat, for the family. That is the way my brother lives, too, mostly. He lives close by us.

Q. How many live in that way down there?—A. I could not count them, they are so numerous. I suppose there are one thousand down there.

Q. A thousand that live on $150 a year?—A. They live on less.

Q. Less than that?—A. Yes; they live on less than I do.

Q. How long has that been so?—A. Mostly so since I have been married.

Q. How long is that?—A. Six years this month.

Q. Why do you not go West on a farm?—A. How could I go, walk it?

Q. Well, I want to know why you do not go out West on a $2,000 farm, or take up a homestead and break it and work it up, and then have it for yourself and family?—A. I can't see how I could get out West. I have got nothing to go with.

Q. It would not cost you over $1,500.—A. Well, I never saw over a $20 bill, and that is when I have been getting a month's pay at once. If someone would give me $1,500 I will go. . . .

Q. Are you a good workman?—A. Yes, sir.

Q. Were you ever turned off because of misconduct or incapacity or unfitness for work?—A. No, sir.

Q. Or because you did bad work?—A. No, sir.

Q. Or because you made trouble among the help?—A. No, sir.

Q. Did you ever have any personal trouble with an employer?—A. No, sir.

Q. You have not anything now you say?—A. No, sir.

Q. How old are you?—A. About thirty.

Q. Is your health good?—A. Yes, sir.

Q. What would you work for if you could get work right along; if you could be sure to have it for five years, staying right where you are?— A. Well, if I was where my family could be with me, and I could have work every day I would take $1.50, and be glad to. . . .

Q. You spoke of fuel—what do you have for fuel?—A. Wood and coal.

Q. Where does the wood come from?—A. I pick it up around the shore—any old pieces I see around that are not good for anything. There are many more that do the same thing.

Q. Do you get meat to live on much?—A. Very seldom.

Q. What kinds of meat do you get for your family?—A. Well, once in a while we get a piece of pork and some clams and make a clam chowder. That makes a very good meal. We sometimes get a piece of corn beef or something like that. . . .

Q. What have you eaten?—*A.* Well, bread mostly, when we could get it; we sometimes couldn't make out to get that, and have had to go without a meal.

Q. Has there been any day in the year that you have had to go with-anything to eat?—*A.* Yes, sir, several days.

Q. More than one day at a time?—*A.* No. . . .

Q. What have the children got on in the way of clothing?—*A.* They have got along very nicely all summer, but now they are beginning to feel quite sickly. One has one shoe on, a very poor one, and a slipper, that was picked up somewhere. The other has two odd shoes on, with the heel out. He has got cold and is sickly now.

Q. Have they any stockings?—*A.* He had got stockings, but his feet comes through them, for there is a hole in the bottom of the shoe.

Q. What have they got on the rest of their person?—*A.* Well, they have a little calico shirt—what should be a shirt; it is sewed up in some shape—and one little petticoat, and a kind of little dress.

Q. How many dresses has your wife got?—*A.* She has got one since she was married, and she hasn't worn that more than half a dozen times; she has worn it just going to church and coming back. She is very good in going to church, but when she comes back she takes it off, and it is pretty near as good now as when she bought it.

Q. She keeps that dress to go to church in?—*A.* Yes, sir.

Q. How many dresses aside from that has she?—*A.* Well, she got one here three months ago.

Q. What did it cost?—*A.* It cost $1.00 to make it and I guess about a dollar for the stuff, as near as I can tell.

Q. The dress cost $2.00?—*A.* Yes.

Q. What else has she?—*A.* Well, she has an undershirt that she got given to her, and she has an old wrapper, which is about a mile too big for her; somebody gave it to her.

Q. She did not buy it?—*A.* No. That is all that I know that she has. . . .

Q. Do you see any way out of your troubles—what are you going to do for a living—or do you expect to have to stay right there?—*A.* Yes. I can't run around with my family.

Q. You have nowhere to go to, and no way of getting there if there was any place to go to?—*A.* No, sir; I have no means nor anything, so I am obliged to remain there and try to pick up something as I can.

Q. Do the children go to school?—*A.* No, sir; they are not old enough; the oldest child is only three and a half; the youngest one is one and a half years old.

Q. Is there anything else you wanted to say?—*A.* Nothing further, except that I would like some remedy to be got to help us poor people down there in some way. Excepting the government decides to do something with us we have a poor show. We are all, or mostly all, in good health; that is, as far as the men who are at work go.

Q. You do not know anything but mule-spinning, I suppose?—A. That is what I have been doing, but I sometimes do something with pick and shovel. I have worked for a man at that, because I am so put on. I am looking for work in a mill. The way they do there is this: There are about twelve or thirteen men that go into a mill every morning, and they have to stand their chance, looking for work. The man who has a boy with him he stands the best chance, and then, if it is my turn or a neighbor's turn who has no boy, if another man comes in who has a boy he is taken right in, and we are left out. I said to the boss once it was my turn to go in, and now you have taken on that man; what am I to do; I have got two little boys at home, one of them three years and a half and the other one year and a half old, and how am I to find something for them to eat; I can't get my turn when I come here.

He said he could not do anything for me. I says, "Have I got to starve; ain't I to have any work?" They are forcing these young boys into the mills that should not be in mills at all; forcing them in because they are throwing the mules out and putting on ring-frames. They are doing everything of that kind that they possibly can to crush down the poor people—the poor operatives there.

Russell H. Conwell's "Acres of Diamonds" was one of the most popular orations of the late nineteenth century. Its famous assertion: "I say you ought to be rich; you have no right to be poor" seems to have thrilled audiences for a generation. The speech, which goes on from the section below to pile example on example and admonition upon admonition, is as full a statement as one could wish of the idea that everyone in American society has the opportunity to get rich if he will only take it. (From Agnes R. Burr, *Russell H. Conwell,* Philadelphia, 1917.)

RUSSELL H. CONWELL: ACRES OF DIAMONDS

. . . I say you ought to be rich; you have no right to be poor. To live in Philadelphia and not be rich is a misfortune, and it is doubly a misfortune, because you could have been rich just as well as be poor. Philadelphia furnishes so many opportunities. You ought to be rich. But persons with certain religious prejudice will ask, "How can you spend your time advising the rising generation to give their time to getting money—dollars and cents—the commercial spirit?"

Yet I must say that you ought to spend time getting rich. You and I know there are some things more valuable than money; of course, we do. Ah, yes! By a heart made unspeakably sad by a grave on which the autumn leaves now fall, I know there are some things higher and grander and sublimer than money. Well does the man know, who has suffered, that there are some things sweeter and holier and more sacred than gold. Nevertheless, the man of common sense also knows that there is not any one of those things that is not greatly enhanced by the use of money. Money is power. Love is the grandest thing on God's earth, but fortunate the lover who has plenty of money. Money is power; money has powers; and for a man to say, "I do not want money," is to say, "I do not wish to do any good to my fellowmen." It is absurd thus to talk. It is absurd to disconnect them. This is a wonderfully great life, and you ought to spend your time getting money, because of the power there is in money. And yet this religious prejudice is so great that some people think it is a great honor to be one of God's poor. I am looking in the faces of people who think just that way. I heard a man once say in a prayer-meeting that he was thankful that he was one of God's poor, and then I silently wondered what his wife would say to that speech, as she took in washing to support the man while he sat and smoked on the veranda. I don't want to see any more of that kind of God's poor. Now, when a man could have been rich just as well, and he is now weak because he is poor, he has done some great wrong; he has been untruthful to himself; he has been unkind to his fellowmen. We ought to get rich if we can by honorable and Christian methods, and these are the only methods that sweep us quickly toward the goal of riches.

With the slave free and the West tamed by Christianity, many people's philanthropic zeal turned to the cities' poorfolk as suitable objects. The success-oriented culture had a strange fascination with those who had failed. (Selection from Jacob Riis, *How the Other Half Lives*, 1890.)

JACOB RIIS: *HOW THE OTHER HALF LIVES*

In the dull content of life bred on the tenement-house dead level there is little to redeem it, or to calm apprehension for a society that has nothing better to offer its toilers; while the patient efforts of the lives finally attuned to it to render the situation tolerable, and the very success of these efforts, serve only to bring out in stronger contrast the general gloom of the picture by showing how much farther they might have gone with half a chance. Go into any of the "respectable" tenement neighborhoods—the fact that there are not more than two saloons on the corner, nor over three or four in the block will serve as a fair guide—where live the great body of hard-working Irish and German immigrants and their descendants, who accept naturally the conditions of tenement life, because for them there is nothing else in New York; be with and among its people until you understand their ways, their aims, and the quality of their ambitions, and unless you can content yourself with the scriptural promise that the poor we shall have always with us, or with the menagerie view that, if fed, they have no cause of complaint, you shall come away agreeing with me that, humanly speaking, life there does not seem worth the living. Take a random one of these uptown tenement blocks, not of the worst nor yet of the most prosperous kind, within hail of what the newspapers would call a "fine residential section." These houses were built since the last cholera scare made people willing to listen to reason. The block is not like the one over on the East Side in which I actually lost my way once. There were thirty or forty rear houses in the heart of it, three or four on every lot, set at all sorts of angles, with odd, winding passages, or no passage at all, only "runways" for the thieves and toughs of the neighborhood. These yards are clear. There is air there, and it is about all there is. The view between brick walls outside is that of a stony street; inside, of rows of unpainted board fences, a bewildering maze of clothes-posts and lines; underfoot, a desert of brown, hard-baked soil from which every blade of grass, every stray weed, every speck of green, has been trodden out, as must inevitably be every gentle thought and aspiration above the mere wants of the body in those whose moral natures such home surroundings are to nourish. In self-defence, you know, all life eventually accommodates itself to its environment, and human life is no exception. Within the house there is nothing to supply the want thus left unsatisfied. Tenement-houses have no aesthetic resources. If any are to be brought to bear on them, they must come from the outside. There is the common hall with doors opening softly on every landing as the strange step is heard on the stairs, the air-shaft that seems always so busy letting out foul stenches from below that it has no time to earn its name by bringing down fresh air, the squeaking pumps that hold no water, and the rent that is never less than one week's wages out of the four, quite as often half of the family earnings.

Why complete the sketch? It is drearily familiar already. Such as it is, it is the frame in which are set days, weeks, months, and years of unceasing toil, just able to fill the mouth and clothe the back. Such as it is, it is the world, and all of it, to which these weary workers return nightly to feed heart and brain after wearing out the body at the bench, or in the shop. To it come the young with their restless yearnings, perhaps to pass on the threshold one of the daughters of sin, driven to the tenement by the police when they raided her den, sallying forth in silks and fine attire after her day of idleness. These in their coarse garments—girls with the love of youth for beautiful things, with this hard life before them—who shall save them from the tempter? Down in the street the saloon, always bright and gay, gathering to itself all the cheer of the block, beckons the boys. In many such blocks the census-taker found two thousand men, women, and children, and over, who called them home.

The picture is faithful enough to stand for its class wherever along both rivers the Irish brogue is heard. As already said, the Celt falls most readily victim to tenement influences since shanty-town and its original free-soilers have become things of the past. If he be thrifty and shrewd his progress thenceforward is along the plane of the tenement, on which he soon assumes to manage without improving things. The German has an advantage over his Celtic neighbor in his strong love for flowers, which not all the tenements on the East Side have power to smother. His garden goes with him wherever he goes. Not that it represents any high moral principle in the man; rather perhaps the capacity for it. He turns his saloon into a shrubbery as soon as his back-yard. But wherever he puts it in a tenement block it does the work of a dozen police clubs. In proportion as it spreads the neighborhood takes on a more orderly character. As the green dies out of the landscape and increases in political importance, the police find more to do. Where it disappears altogether from sight, lapsing into a mere sentiment, police-beats are shortened and the force patrols double at night. Neither the man nor the sentiment is wholly responsible for this. It is the tenement unadorned that is. The changing of Tompkins Square from a sand lot into a beautiful park put an end for good and all to the Bread or Blood riots of which it used to be the scene, and transformed a nest of dangerous agitators into a harmless, beer-craving band of Anarchists. They have scarcely been heard of since. Opponents of the small parks system as a means of relieving the congested population of tenement districts, please take note.

With the first hot nights in June police despatches, that record the killing of men and women by rolling off roofs and window-sills while asleep, announce that the time of greatest suffering among the poor is at hand. It is in hot weather, when life indoors is well-nigh unbearable with cooking, sleeping, and working, all crowded into the small rooms together, that the tenement expands, reckless of all restraint. Then a strange and picturesque life moves upon the flat roofs. In the day and early evening mothers air their babies there, the boys fly their kites from the housetops, undismayed by police regulations, and the young men and girls court and pass the growler. In the stifling July nights, when the big barracks are like fiery furnaces, their very walls giving out absorbed heat, men and women lie in restless, sweltering rows, panting for air and sleep. Then every truck in the street, every crowded fire-escape, becomes a bedroom, infinitely preferable to any the house affords. A cooling shower on such a night is hailed as a heaven-sent blessing in a hundred thousand homes.

Life in the tenements in July and August spells death to an army of little ones whom the doctor's skill is powerless to save. When the white badge of mourning flutters from every second door, sleepless mothers walk the streets in the gray of the early dawn, trying to stir a cooling breeze to fan the brow of the sick baby. There is no sadder sight than this patient devotion striving against fearfully hopeless odds. Fifty "summer doctors," especially trained to this work, are then sent into the tenements by the Board of Health, with free advice and medicine for the poor. Devoted women follow in their track with care and nursing for the sick. Fresh-air excursions run daily out of New York on land and water; but despite all efforts the grave-diggers in Calvary work over-time, and little coffins are stacked mountain high on the deck of the Charity Commissioners' boat when it makes its semi-weekly trips to the city cemetery.

Under the most favorable circumstances, an epidemic, which the well-to-do can afford to make light of as a thing to be got over or avoided by reasonable care, is excessively fatal among the children of the poor, by reason of the practical impossibility of isolating the patient in a tenement. The measles, ordinarily a harmless disease, furnishes a familiar example. Tread it ever so lightly on the avenues, in the tenements it kills right and left. Such an epidemic ravaged three crowded blocks in Elizabeth Street on the heels of the grippe last winter, and, when it had spent its fury, the death-maps in the Bureau of Vital Statistics looked as if a black hand had been laid across those blocks, over-shadowing in part the contiguous tenements in Mott Street, and with the thumb covering a particularly packed settlement of half a dozen houses in Mulberry Street. The track of the epidemic through these teeming barracks was as clearly defined as the track of a tornado through a forest district. There were houses in which as many as eight little children had died in five months. The records showed that respiratory diseases, the common heritage of the grippe and the measles, had caused death in most cases, discovering the trouble to be, next to the inability to check the contagion in those crowds, in the poverty of the parents and the wretched home conditions that made proper care of the sick impossible. The fact was emphasized by the occurrence here and there of a few isolated deaths from diphtheria and scarlet fever. In the case of these diseases, considered more dangerous to the public health, the health officers exercised summary powers of removal to the hospital where proper treatment could be had, and the result was a low death-rate.

These were tenements of the tall, modern type. A little more than a year ago, when a census was made of the tenements and compared with the mortality tables, no little surprise and congratulation was caused by the discovery that as the buildings grew taller the death-rate fell. The reason is plain, though the reverse had been expected by most people. The biggest tenements have been built in the last ten years of sanitary reform rule, and have been brought, in all but the crowding, under its laws. The old houses that from private dwellings were made into tenements, or were run up to house the biggest crowds in defiance of every moral and physical law, can be improved by no device short of demolition. They will ever remain the worst. . . .

Nellie Bly, the pen name of the journalist Elizabeth Cochrane, answered a newspaper editor's ad for someone willing to dash around the world in 75 days as a publicity stunt. When he indicated he would naturally choose a man, she threatened to go by herself and beat him to the finish line. Miss Bly was best remembered by the public for this exploit though she originally gained fame as a journalistic crusader for the rights of women and child laborers, as well as the insane. (From Elizabeth Cochrane, *Nellie Bly's Book*, 1895.)

NELLIE BLY: AGAINST THE MONSOON

That evening we sailed for Hong Kong. The next day the sea was rough and head winds made the run lower than we had hoped for. Towards noon almost all the passengers disappeared. The roughness increased and the cook enjoyed a holiday. There was some chaffing among the passengers who remained on deck. During dinner the chief officer began to relate the woes of people he had seen suffering from the dire disease that threatened now to even overpower the captain. I listened for quite a while, merely because I could not help hearing; and if there was anything the chief could do well it was relating anecdotes. At last one made me get up and run, it was so vivid, and the moment the doctor, who sat opposite, saw me go he got up and followed. I managed to overcome my faintness without really being sick, but the doctor gave way entirely. I went back to dinner to find the cause of our misery had disappeared. When I saw him later, his face was pale and he confessed contritely that his realistic joke had made even him seasick.

During the roughness that followed the doctor would always say to me pleadingly:

"Don't make a start, for if you do I will have to follow."

The terrible swell of the sea during the Monsoon was the most beautiful thing I ever saw. I would sit breathless on deck watching the bow of the ship standing upright on a wave then dash headlong down as if intending to carry us to the bottom. Some of the men made no secret of being seasick and were stretched out in their chairs on deck where they might hope to catch the first breath of air. Although there was a dreadful swell, still the atmosphere was heavy and close. Sometimes I felt as if I would smother. One man who had been quite attentive to me became seasick. I was relieved when I heard it, still I felt very cruel when I would see his pale face and hear him plead for sympathy. As heartless as I thought it was I could not sympathize with a seasick man. There was an effort on the part of others to tease the poor fellow. When I sat down on deck they would carefully take away all the chairs excepting those occupied by themselves, but it mattered little to the seasick man. He would quietly curl up on his rugs at my feet and there lie, in all his misery, gazing at me.

"You would not think that I am enjoying a vacation, but I am," he said plaintively to me one day.

"You don't know how nice I can look," he said pathetically at another time. "If you would only stay over at Hong Kong for a week you would see how pretty I can look."

"Indeed, such a phenomenon might induce me to remain there six weeks," I said coldly.

At last some one told him I was engaged to the chief officer, who did not approve of my talking to other men, thinking this would make him cease following me about, but it only served to increase his devotion. Finding me alone on deck one stormy evening, he sat down at my feet and holding to the arms of my chair began to talk in a wild way.

"Do you think life is worth living?" he asked.

"Yes, life is very sweet. The thought of death is the only thing that causes me unhappiness," I answered truthfully.

"You cannot understand it or you would feel different. I could take you in my arms and jump overboard, and before they would know it we would be at rest," he said passionately.

"You can't tell. It might not be rest——" I began and he broke in hotly.

"I know, I know. I can show you. I will prove it to you. Death by drowning is a peaceful slumber, a quiet drifting away."

"Is it?" I said, with a pretense of eagerness. I feared to get up for I felt the first move might result in my burial beneath the angry sea.

"You know, tell me about it. Explain it to me," I gasped, a feeling of coldness creeping over me as I realized that I was alone with what for the time was a mad man. Just as he began to speak I saw the chief officer come on deck and slowly advance towards me. I dared not call. I dared not smile, lest he should notice. I feared the chief would go away, but no, he saw me, and with a desire to tease the man who had been so devoted he came up on tip-toe, then, clapping the poor fellow on the back, he said:

"What a very pretty love scene!"

"Come," I shouted, breaking away before the startled man could understand. The chief, still in a spirit of fun, took my hand and we rushed down below. I told him and the captain what had occurred and the captain wanted to put the man in irons but I begged that he be left free. I was careful afterwards not to spend one moment alone and unprotected on deck.

The Parsees, travelling first class, were compelled to go below when a heavy swell was on. We welcomed the storm on that account if on no other, because they had a peculiar habit of dropping off their slippers when they sat down. As they wore no hose, this habit was annoying. The doctor seriously affirmed that every time he sat down anywhere a Parsee was sure to squat alongside, drop his shoes and turn his bare, brown feet up to be gazed upon.

The monkey proved a good seaman. One day when I visited it I found the young men had been toasting its health. It was holding its aching head when I went in, and evidently thinking I was the cause of the swelling, it sprang at me, making me seek safety in flight.

The hurricane deck was a great resort for lovers, so Chief Officer Sleeman told me; and evidently he knew, for he talked a great deal about two American girls who had travelled to Egypt, I believe, on the Thames when he was first officer of it. He had lost their address but his heart was true, for he had lost a philopœna to one and though he did not know her habitation he bought a philopœna and put it in a bank in London where it awaits some farther knowledge of the fair young American's whereabouts. . . .

It is wonderful the amount of whiskey and soda Englishmen consume. They drink it at all times and places. There was an Englishman on the Oriental who drank whiskey and soda all the day, half a dozen different wines at dinner, and then complained, as he invariably staggered away from the table, that the wine list had no variety!

Talk about cranks! One woman told the chief officer one day that she wanted a cabin just over the ship's screw so she could tell that the ship was going! She got it, and she was the worst sea-sick woman I ever saw. Another passenger complained because the berths had spring mattresses! . . .

After the horse and before the automobile came the bicycle. In the 1880s and even more in the '90s when pneumatic tires came in, a bicycle craze swept the United States. Bicycles were hardly considered playthings for children then. As in Europe now, they were a serious means of transportation as well as a device for exercise and amusement. They especially offered a new freedom and mobility to American women and were one of the excuses that liberated women from the constriction of Victorian garments. (From *Outing*, May 1883 and April 1884.)

THE BICYCLE CRAZE

Humanity on Wheels

The hygienic influences of the cycle are thus well set forth:

The bicycle and tricycle are not only enjoyable modes of locomotion, they are also without a peer in their hygienic capacity. By their use the muscular system is exercised and developed, with a uniformity that cannot be achieved by any other means with equal simplicity, and certainty. There is hardly a voluntary muscle that is not called into play, in the varied and complex movements of the bicycle rider. Not only the muscles of the legs are exercised, but those of the arms are called upon to steady and steer the machine, and to add power in propelling up grade, or keeping up rapid motion; while the back and abdominal muscles are on the alert in maintaining the erect position. In fact, with the foot on the pedal as one point, and the hand grasping the handle as another, we have the entire voluntary muscular system operating between those two points; and the force exerted will be little or much, according to the speed or character of the road. The respiration is quickened and deepened. The hands grasping the handles, the arms and shoulders become fixed points, and we are enabled to fill the lungs more fully, and thus the air is more thoroughly changed,—bad air expelled, and fresh air inhaled into the remotest part,—and the lungs thoroughly exercised. This is of incalculable value to those who are shut up all day in close rooms, and to others, who, by reason of quiet occupations, are never called upon to breathe deeply, and contract the habit of superficial respiration. Consequently, a large portion of the lungs are not properly exercised, and, with lowered vitality, become veritable hot-beds, inviting the development and propagation of disease.

Bicycling accelerates and adds force to the heart-beat, whereby the blood is propelled more rapidly through the arteries, conveyed through the capillaries, and carried along the veins. Becoming thoroughly oxygenated in its passage through the now well-aerated lungs, it makes again and again its vitalizing tour throughout the body, stimulating healthful nutrition. The tingle of health is felt throughout the entire system. The pallid cheek assumes a rosy hue, the lips become red, and the eyes sparkle with renewed vigor; the stagnant blood is driven from the nooks and crannies of the brain, the cobwebs brushed away, and mental exaltation and exhilaration take the place of depression and weariness. That must be a very pertinacious "fit of the blues" that can withstand an hour's spin on the bicycle. The very fact of being in motion is enlivening, and the more rapidly we are carried along, the greater the exhilaration produced. Who does not become enthusiastic riding after a fleet pair of horses, and still more so rushing along behind the shrieking locomotive?

"Over the rails a-gleaming,
    Thirty an hour or so,
The engine leaped like a demon,
    Breathing a fiery glow.
But to me ahold of the lever,
    It seemed a child alway,
Trustful, and always ready
    My lightest touch to obey."

With similar emotions, and equal confidence in the docility and obedience of his machine, does the rider of the bicycle whirl along, rejoicing in the glowing tints of the rosy morning, sparkling in the brightness of the noonday sun, or fanned by the breezes of the dewy evening, exulting in the ease and rapidity of his progress; while through crowded thoroughfare to suburban limits, and out into the free air of the open country, does the eye drink in new scenes and survey the ever-changing landscape.

The magazine has a good share of short stories and pleasing sketches. We have room for only this bit of fun:

When our new member joined our circle, we were engaged in animated discussion of that most fascinating pursuit of wheelmen—the taking of "headers." Mr. Slowboy, having been formally but cordially greeted and welcomed by the chief blower or bugler of the club, by its president, and the several vice's and their assistants, and provided with a seat near the fire, begged of us not to allow his entrance to interrupt our conversation; and, with the air of one anxious to improve his mind, prepared to listen to the discussion. Thus encouraged, Mr. Kinlye, who had been talking when the door opened, proceeded as follows:

"Well, gentlemen, as I was saying, he was about twenty years of age, tall and slender, and had been terribly ill, or, as the members of our esteemed contemporary association, The Tile Club, would artistically state it, had been making a gargoyle of himself during the entire first week of the voyage. I was on my return trip from Liverpool to New York, last year, Mr. Slowboy, on the Cunard steamer 'Bicyclia.'

"Two days before we reached New York he appeared at the head of the saloon stairway, looking very pale and feeble; but the fresh air seemed to revive him almost immediately, and he and I took a number of turns up and down the deck together. In course of conversation I discovered him to be an enthusiastic wheelman, and that he had a bicycle on board that he had purchased in Coventry just before leaving England. He had not yet used it, but was very anxious to do so, and before going below declared his intention of trying it on the deck of the steamer the next day.

"On the following morning it was nearly noon before he appeared on deck, and by that time we were in sight of the Highland lights, and all hands were making preparations for going ashore. He had improved so wonderfully in personal appearance since the night before that I hardly recognized him. After congratulating him upon his complete recovery, I again introduced the subject of bicycles, upon which he sent the porter to fetch his new machine. It was a beautiful 55-inch semi-racer, full nickled, and complete in every detail. He invited me to try it; but I declined, giving as an excuse the dangerous roll of the ship. Laughing at my timidity he took a little run, made the most graceful mount I had ever seen, and wheeled away up the deck, meeting every roll of the ship with the utmost skill, and attracting the universal admiration of the passengers. Rounding the forward house, he came spinning, at a fearful pace, down the other side, while the spectators almost held their breath at his temerity and imminent danger. Our fears were, alas! too well founded; for, in making the turn around the after-house, at a moment when the ship rolled in the same direction, he lost control of his machine, and rushed, with frightful velocity, against the rail. In another instant he had taken the most frightful header I ever witnessed, over the side of the ship and into the sea. His bicycle, turning a complete somersault, followed him, flashed for a moment like a meteor in the bright sunlight, and also disppeared beneath the wave."

"Poor fellow!" murmured the second vice-president; and so he lost his bicycle?"

"Not at all," said Mr. Kinlye, "with its hollow backbone, forks, rims, and handle-bar, the machine was as buoyant as a lifeboat, and almost immediately reäppeared on the surface of the water. Its rider, also being hollow down to his boots, by reason of his long sea-sickness, came to the top at the same moment, swam to his machine, vaulted into the saddle, and bending low over the handle-bar, began to work the pedals. And I'm blamed if the rubber tire, which I had noticed was unusually soft, didn't bite hold of the water, and the thing began to move towards us. In a few moments he was alongside; but instead of catching the rope that had been thrown to him, he waved his cap, called out, 'Ta-ta, I'll tell 'em you're coming,' spurted, and was soon far ahead of us, and lost sight of up the bay. We afterwards found that he had dodged the revenue boat, and got his machine safely ashore without paying a cent of duty or royalty."

"Wonderful!" murmured several of the members.

"Gentlemen," said Mr. Slowboy, who had during the preceding narrative stared at Mr. Kinlye, at first with interest, and afterwards with ill-concealed astonishment and indignation,—"gentlemen, *and* Mr. Kinlye, I have the honor to bid you a very good-evening, and shall to-morrow tender, in writing, to your honorable secretary, my resignation as a member of this club."

As he passed from the room, having forgotten his bear-skin shako, and left it behind him in his agitation, those present exchanged glances expressive of deep sorrow and disappointment. Our first new member had failed to pass the final test of the membership committee, of which Mr. Kinyle is chairman, which, under the by-laws of the club, they were obliged to apply. It comes under the head of admission of new members, and reads as follows: "Before being admitted to full membership in the Cantellalie Bicycle Club, applicants must satisfy the membership committee of their ability to listen to the most improbable tales of bicycular prowess, without expressing incredulity."

We must not conclude this hasty review without quoting a few words in relation to the tricycle, by which the use and enjoyment of the wheel are so greatly extended. These are some of the advantages possessed by the tricycle, as noted in an interesting article on the subject:

The tricycle stands alone. It needs no strings, supports, or stands to lean against. In use, the firm seat, with the centre of gravity so low, is priceless. One may cross his legs, read his paper, or carry his umbrella, lunch, and a book, and enjoy all in his seat. Going to many places, his machine at rest is the much-needed seat, with foot-rests.

The tricycle is ridden in ordinary dress. It is very often inconvenient to be dressed in the costume made necessary by the bicycle. Knee-breeches and long stockings are not needed in the tricycle.

It is perfectly adapted to the use of ladies, who are more and more taking it up as the equal in every way of horseback riding, without its expenses, danger, and inconvenience.

The shape and strength allows any needed baggage to be carried readily. Extra clothes, books, samples for commercial travelers, etc., etc., up to one hundred pounds, are practicable, and many tricycles are fitted with an extra seat, on which a child, or even an adult, is carried.

People with one arm, or disqualified in various ways for the bicycle, may use the tricycle with pleasure and safety. Indeed, I have in mind a case where an old bicycle rider broke his arm from a fall, and while carrying it in a sling used a tricycle. The result was his conversion to the newer machine, and abandonment of the bicycle.

The tricycle admits of any seat, with or without back, that the rider prefers, and many have two or more seats, which are attached in a minute's time, to suit the trip or rider.

Another point in favor of the tricycle is that the disagreeable, ridiculous, and often dangerous experiences of learning the bicycle are all escaped; not that a tricycle requires no learning, for after a month one is apt to ride with less than half the effort at first required, but this all comes from actual experience. A new rider may, however, with perfect safety, go at once on the road. The bicycle rider who learned on his own machine, is apt to want a new one soon after.

Wheelman's Song

I.

Good-morning, good Pedestrian,—I'm glad to see you out;
The day is full of healthfulness,—the birds are all about;
There is a quiet breeziness in all the pleasant air;
I hope this happy exercise may drive away our care.
    For I am a pedestrian,—
    A very good pedestrian,—
And all the glowing benefit of walking I can share:
Although I tread the atmosphere and do not touch the ground,
I welcome you fraternally; wherever you are bound.
But my impatient lady-love in yonder vale doth wait;
I wish you better company, and strike a swifter gait.

II.

Good-morning, good Equestrian,—a noble steed you ride;
We do not seem to frighten him,—so here is by your side.
It is a feast of happiness to smoothly bound along,
With sturdy muscles under you, and footing swiftly strong!
    For I am an equestrian,—
    A very fair equestrian,—
With bugle-blast of melody, and unassuming song;
And all the thrilling ecstasy of horsemanship I feel,
Although the steed I ride upon is bred of molten steel.
But his impatience urges me to swifter time than you,
And so I wish you pleasure, sir, and bid a kind adieu.

III.

Good-morning, Mr. Racer,—you've a trotter that is fine:
I never would disparage him, or say too much of mine.
Your horse is full of mettle, sir, and bravely takes his load;
It must be pure deliciousness to speed him on the road.
    For I am quite a racing man,—

A modest, humble, racing man,—
Though slight is my solicitude upon the turf bestowed;
But if you have an anxiousness to try a little race,
I'll undertake, with courtesy, to give you second place;
But if the first you win from me, and fairly it be earned,
I'll hope, in near futurity, the tables may be turned.

IV.

Good-morning, Mr. Carriageer,—you have an easy ride:
Those cushions are luxurious, and pleasantly you glide.
'Tis very nice and fortunate, if one be tired or ill,
To have a carriage to his call, and travel as he will.
 But I, sir, keep my carriage, too,—
 A very pleasant carriage, too;
Though it is not the easy one that your desires would fill,
It carries me in comfort over many a pleasant mile,
And we who ride are satisfied completely with its style
So with a blithe economy establishments are run,
With driver, footman, passenger, and horses all in one.

V.

Good-morning, fellow-wheelmen,—here's a warm fraternal hand,
As, with a rush of victory, we sweep across the land!
If some may be dissatisfied to see the way we ride,
We only wish their majesties could travel by our side!
 For we are pure philanthropists,—
 Unqualified philanthropists;
And would not have this happiness to any one denied;
We claim a great utility that daily must increase;
We claim from inactivity a sensible release;
A constant mental, physical, and moral help we feel,
That bids us turn enthusiasts, and cry, "God bless the wheel!"
      —*Will Carleton.*

Historians have generally considered the saloon as rather beneath their notice. Yet saloons were vital economic, social and especially political institutions. It was not simply a case of paying your money and getting your booze; rather there was the etiquette of the free lunch, of the bartender buying one for a customer after he had downed a fixed amount (3 for 1 or 4 for 1 or whatever), of rounds "on the house," of "treats" for a whole group or the whole bar or the guy next to you. Bars in a variety of ways brought men together: this is why they became natural political centers. And the free lunch counter could in time of depression turn into an informal social welfare agency without tearing at the dignity of a steady patron out of a job. (Selection from George Rector, *The Girl from Rector's*, 1927.)

THE FREE LUNCH

. . . Considine's [Metropole] had three entrances and a man thrown out of one door could always come in another. George Considine was a very husky citizen and usually acted as master of ceremonies in his own barroom. He ejected one intoxicated gentleman who was too boisterous and told him not to come back again. Considine took him on a personally conducted tour to the door and dropped him for a field goal on the sidewalk. Then he walked back, rubbing his hands in the reflective manner of a man who has just done something well worth doing. To his surprise he saw the drunk coming in another door opening on the side street.

Considine grabbed him by the scruff and tossed him out, saying, "Didn't I tell you not to come back?" Five minutes later the same well-lubricated lad staggered through a third door, and as Considine started for him he backed out, exclaiming, "Good heavens, do you own all the places in town?"

Considine and the other café owners experienced great difficulties with the itinerant actors and Broadwayites who came in to sample the free lunch without first going through the formality of sampling the beer. The barkeeps kept an eagle eye on the food show and woe to the man who tried to eat himself fat after buying one or no beers. It was another of those famous unwritten laws that no client could attack the lunch counter until he had purchased two beers at five cents apiece. Having complied with this invisible mandate a man could stroll casually over to the free lunch, pick out a reasonably clean fork, and start stabbing at the tomatoes, scallions, beans, radishes, sausages, and sliced ham. After he got his load he was expected to step back to the bar and contribute another ring to the cash register. You could eat and drink very well for fifteen cents.

There were free lunches served that were famous all over the town. The buffet of the Hotel Knickerbocker paraded a marvelous collection of snicks and snacks on its free-lunch counter. The lunch counter actually had chicken salad, lobster salad, lobster Newburgh, melted cheese on toast, cold corned beef, Virginia ham, and even chafing dishes. Unfortunately the beer in the Knickerbocker café was ten cents a scoop.

This outrageous price was resented by the better class of lunch grapplers, who seemed to consider a five-cent glass the standard price. The Waldorf, Biltmore, and Plaza hotels all supplied free lunches to their bar patrons, and this method of distributing rations seriously interfered with the restaurant business.

Thousands of bachelors subsisted entirely on the free-for-all banquet style of feeding. However, it was then impossible for a man to bring his family into the barroom and have a basket picnic. Rector's didn't suffer much from the two-beer dining. We had no barroom, and if we had, we would have been too smart to give away lunches to prospective patrons. The man who lived on free lunch was the same kind of citizen who will look at a circus procession but will never pay to see the circus itself. He lived from hand to mouth—and got most of it on his vest.

The competition among saloon proprietors grew very keen in their individual efforts to attract bar flies by spreading tremendous repasts on the lunch shelf. The buffets with the most free groceries usually got the biggest play from the crowd. A man could get a New England boiled dinner and two beers for ten cents. It got so bad that six or seven of us restaurant owners had an emergency meeting to decide on ways and means of combating the free-lunch evil.

America was free and united in those days. The lunch was free and the cigar stores were united. We decided that we couldn't find anything in the Constitution that declared generously donated food to be aiding and abetting the enemy, and therefore treasonable. So we adjourned the meeting and went over in a body to the Knickerbocker and sampled the lunch ourselves.

Rector's was connected with free lunch in a very direct manner. One of our patrons complained that any man who had picked up a dinner check in Rector's would be compelled to live on free lunch for the rest of the month. Our charges may have been a trifle high, but were not to be compared with the prices of today. If a man wants to dine frugally nowadays he must go to a feed-and-grain store and do his best. There is no more free lunch. In fact, as I have explained, there never was. You always had to buy the customary two beers before you could stuff yourself like a turkey on Thanksgiving. The hobo who tried to crash the lunch without purchasing the schooners which came sailing over the bar was generally grasped by a husky bouncer and streeted. The process of being streeted meant that you were grasped by the slack of the trousers and the back of the neck and tossed out on the street. Sometimes the uninvited guest turned the tables on the bouncer.

I once saw a burly hobo sneak into Silver Dollar Smith's, a saloon famous for its shining floor of mosaic composed of Uncle Sam's bright dollars. He made a balk motion toward the bar to fool the proprietor and then turned to the lunch, where he wolfed down the entire exhibit, which consisted mostly of American cheese, Schweitzer, and Limburger. He had all the cheese stowed away before the boss woke up and started for him. The hobo grappled the proprietor and tossed him back over the bar. He did the same thing to the bartenders and then threw the bouncer through the window. With all opposition removed, he then proceeded to chase out the patrons and drank their deserted beer. Completely refreshed and invigorated, he watched the owner and his three assistants struggling to their feet and read them a fine piece of advice.

He said, "Don't think that men are mice because they eat cheese."

Football came very close to being outlawed at the turn of the century for "brutality" until reforms in the rules modified the game to put a bit more of a premium on speed and agility and less on the pure brute thrust that it stressed in the nineteenth century. A few years later the forward pass and runners like Red Grange turned football into a very different game. Apparently the emphasis on "hitting" in football—so strong in the present—runs in cycles pretty much the way that warfare moves back and forth between offense and defense. (From James Hopper, "The Fullback Who Got Used to It," *The Saturday Evening Post,* 1904.)

JAMES HOPPER: THE FULLBACK WHO GOT USED TO IT

. . . In the dressing-room, during the ten-minute intermission, Harley lay on the floor, stretched with arms out like a cross, his mind concentrated in keeping relaxed his muscles, twitching with weariness. While the trainers sponged and bandaged, the coach, perched upon a bench, harangued the men fiercely. It was only when the referee's whistle, blowing outside, summoned them to be renewal of the struggle, however, that he addressed Harley. "It's your punting, remember— your punting alone that can save us to-day," he whispered.

"I'll punt!" said Harley, and he trotted out after the team for the long ordeal that was to be the second half.

At first things went a little better. By three long dashes the Blues carried the ball to the Reds twenty-five yard line. But this could not last. The backs, with Harley, were a miserable misfit. They lost the ball, and again the Red team, not to be denied, began its stubborn fight for the last white line. The first time they gained the twenty-yard line before the Blues could stop them and let Harley kick back down the field; the second time they were stopped only on the fifteen-yard line; the third time they pounded to the ten-yard line before the Blues clutched the ball and let Harley punt it out of danger.

The stabbing in Harley's side was piercing him to the very vitals now; but this was not what bothered him most. With a growing, sickening fear he was realizing that his punting was falling off. His right leg, bruised and swollen with the continuous pounding, was refusing to obey the command of his will. His first punt at the beginning of the half had been sixty yards, the second fifty, the third forty, and now it was only with the most bitter effort that he could propel the ball a bare thirty. The Red captain noticed this. They began to punt, and at each exchange they gained shocking distances. Then, when thus they had worked the ball to the forty-yard line, they pounded forward again.

This time there was something new about their advance. They bucked the right side of the line only, always the right side. Again and again, with a repetition that was hypnotizing, they hurled themselves at the same spot. It was the Blues' strong side, and progress was slow. Three times they made the needed five yards only by a few inches. The Blue right end and backs, enticed by this promise held out to them, began to throw themselves recklessly into the breach, and all of a sudden it dawned upon Harley that this was just what the Reds expected them to do. He crouched low, every sense on the alert. Then, suddenly, his suspicion was fulfilled. The next buck of the Reds wavered, was not pushed home, and the two teams stood bunched together for a moment, swaying and heaving, the Blue ends and backs all beneath the pile. There was a queer movement, a faint swirl, and suddenly three red-jerseyed men detached themselves, circled out, swerved back to a straight line, and, with a wonderful burst of speed, made straight for the goal. Harley took a step forward and studied the situation. They were coming straight at him. The two men ahead, side by side, were the interferers. Behind them was the man with the ball. He took another step forward and waited for them, crouched low to the ground. In two seconds they were upon him; just as their heated breath was in his face he sprang to the left. One of the interferers threw himself after him. With a snap Harley threw himself back in his tracks, and he was right in the way of the second man. He danced back before him, warding him off with stiffly outstretched arms, his eye on the man with the ball who, running low behind his human rampart, was swerving now to the right, now to the left, meditating a get-away. Suddenly he made up his mind. Clutching his interferer's jersey to help his start, he made a false movement to the left and burst out to the right. Harley gave one huge leap, slung his whole body out sideways, stretched his arm, and clutched at a flying ankle. The hold was broken as soon as made, but it was enough. With his tremendous impetus this slight check sent the runner sprawling to the ground. The ball flopped out of his arms. With one low dive Harley was upon it, hugging it against his breast.

He lay on it quite a while, for a deadly faintness was upon him. The bark of the quarter, fiercely calling for a punt, recalled him to his inexorable duty. He took his position to kick, and then suddenly he knew he could not do it. Even as the ball was coming back toward him, his arms, in spite of his straining effort, dropped limply to his sides. With a thump the ball struck him on the chest, bounced sideways. A red jersey flashed along the ground and covered it up—and he stood there, stupid, the sense of irretrievable disaster in his heart. The Red team formed for a drop-kick at the goal. There was a thump, and the ball soared gently over Harley's head, between the posts, over the cross-bar. A shriek of exultation came from the stands, pierced his ears, reverberated within his brain like a concussion. The Reds had made a goal from the field—had scored five points.

And the Reds pounded on, fiercely exultant, mad for another taste of success, for an orgy of victory. Five points; they wanted twenty!

And Harley felt that they were likely to have them. An immense weariness pressed upon him; it was as if the earth's attraction had multiplied tenfold, sucking him down like an iron file magnet. His muscles refused to obey him; they twinged, they throbbed, they squeaked, they cried out in agony. Each time his kick was weaker; the ball traveled in smaller and smaller curves. Twice he punted only twenty yards; then he fell to fifteen. The Blues stopped the Reds once more. Then the inevitable moment that he had forseen was present. He kicked, and even as he went down beneath the human ram that had slowly battered him to pieces, he saw the ball shooting straight upward, absolutely straight, without an inch of forward motion.

He rolled weakly to one side and watched it. It seemed to go up an inconceivable distance; when it had reached its height it seemed to stick, as if pasted to the sky. Then swiftly it began to descend. Beneath it two teams were milling like cattle at a round-up; fighting for the better positions, faces tense to the sky, hands clutching convulsively upward. Harley rose to his knees. The ball came down like a meteor. It struck some one with a thump. It rebounded, and suddenly it lay at Harley's feet, spinning like a top.

With a gulp of eagerness he whisked it up and leaped forward. A new life thrilled in his veins. A few yards ahead a red-shirted figure crouched down to intercept him. He made straight for him, then, just as the man left his feet for the tackle, he swerved to the right in a lightning movement, and was past. Another figure was in his path—the Red full-back. He could not afford an attempt to circle him, for already, he knew, they were in pursuit behind. With a new burst of speed he charged toward him. The full-back took a step forward, left his feet, lunged low along the ground. With a tremendous effort Harley leaped straight up in the air, doubled up like a jack-knife, and the red jersey flashed past beneath him. He fell as he lit, but with a twist rolled over and was on his feet again, and then there was no one before him— nothing except white lines, a series of gleaming white lines, and far off the goal-posts, like gallows against the setting sun. But he began to stumble; his legs dragged behind him. Fiercely he jerked up his knees in quick succession toward his chin and put on speed. It was hard. An immense weariness clogged him; his head sank low between his shoulders. It was fearfully far to that goal-post, fearfully far.

And they were in pursuit. Fierce, insistent, nearer, ever nearer, there was a drumming of feet behind him. He stumbled, recovered. He remembered that to run fast he must bring his knees straight up before him; instead they had a tendency to straddle sideways, and his whole mind, his mental force, his character, his whole spiritual self concentrated itself on this: to bring his knees straight toward his chin. It racked him to do so; it tore him. It was a run long as death. The yards were long as miles. The white lines were an inconceivable distance apart.

White lines, white lines, more white lines—no, there weren't any more; they were gone; how funny, there were no more white lines! A hand like a serpent clutched him by the ankle. He pounded the ground with the other leg. That was seized, too. Well, he was tired, anyway. Softly he fell forward on his face, the ball hugged to his breast.

What happened to Harley after that he was always very reluctant to tell. But he did relate it fully once, that very night, at a banquet where, in spite of three broken ribs and several minor ailments, he fairly bubbled over with ecstatic joy and told—well, many things that he had never meant to tell. It seemed that after he fell he soared up into the sky like a balloon, up and up, into regions ever lighter, ever happier. Below him he could see the good old earth, rotund and red-faced like a drunken man. It was mighty fine up there, but still he was not satisfied. He wanted to get back to earth. There was something down there that he had left undone: something of extraordinary importance. He was very unhappy, very much worried over it. After a while he discovered that he was tied to the earthly ball by a string: a tenuous, silken thread. A genial thought came to him. Hand over hand he pulled himself down along that string till he reached the earth again. And once there he readily found what it was he had to do. He had to kick the goal for that touchdown he had made.

And he did. Dripping with the buckets of water thrown upon him, sagging with weariness, he watched the red-headed quarter pat a nice little heap of sand before him. He directed the same quarter as he poised the ball above the little mound—"Seam this way, top to the right, a little more—that's it, put it down." He took a quick step forward, swung his right foot, and the ball soared up square between the posts, scoring the sixth point, which effectively made the five of the Reds look, in the words of the coach, like thirty cents.

entertainment and uplift

Modern critics all agree that *The Adventures of Huckleberry Finn* is Mark Twain's masterpiece. From their natural setting of a raft drifting down the broad river, Huck and slave Jim make forays onto the land and explore the civilization about them. In this episode, they meet some travelling actors and con men and see a circus, two of the most exciting attractions that anyone in "Arkansaw" could imagine. (From Mark Twain, *The Adventures of Huckleberry Finn*, 1884.)

MARK TWAIN: HUCK FINN'S "ARKANSAW DIFFICULTY"

It was after sun-up now, but we went right on and didn't tie up. The king and the duke turned out by and by looking pretty rusty; but after they'd jumped overboard and took a swim it chippered them up a good deal. After breakfast the king he took a seat on the corner of the raft, and pulled off his boots and rolled up his britches, and let his legs dangle in the water, so as to be comfortable, and lit his pipe, and went to getting his "Romeo and Juliet" by heart. When he had got it pretty good him and the duke begun to practise it together. The duke had to learn him over and over again how to say every speech; and he made him sigh, and put his hand on his heart, and after a while he said he done it pretty well; "only," he says, "you mustn't bellow out *Romeo!* that way, like a bull—you must say it soft and sick and languishy, so —R-o-o-meo! that is the idea; for Juliet's a dear sweet mere child of a girl, you know, and she doesn't bray like a jackass."

Well, next they got out a couple of long swords that the duke made out of oak laths, and began to practise the sword-fight—the duke called himself Richard III.; and the way they laid on and pranced around the raft was grand to see. But by and by the king tripped and fell overboard, and after that they took a rest, and had a talk about all kinds of adventures they'd had in other times along the river.

After dinner the duke says:

"Well, Capet, we'll want to make this a first-class show, you know, so I guess we'll add a little more to it. We want a little something to answer encores with, anyway."

"What onkores, Bilgewater?"

The duke told him, and then says:

"I'll answer by doing the Highland fling or the sailor's hornpipe;

and you—well, let me see—oh, I've got it—you can do Hamlet's soliloquy."

"Hamlet's which?"

"Hamlet's soliloquy, you know; the most celebrated thing in Shakespeare. Ah, it's sublime, sublime! Always fetches the house. I haven't got it in the book—I've only got one volume—but I reckon I can piece it out from memory. I'll just walk up and down a minute, and see if I can call it back from recollection's vaults."

So he went to marching up and down, thinking, and frowning horrible every now and then; then he would hoist up his eyebrows; next he would squeeze his hand on his forehead and stagger back and kind of moan; next he would sigh, and next he'd let on to drop a tear. It was beautiful to see him. By and by he got it. He told us to give attention. Then he strikes a most noble attitude, with one leg shoved forwards, and his arms stretched away up, and his head tilted back, looking up at the sky; and then he begins to rip and rave and grit his teeth; and after that, all through his speech, he howled, and spread around, and swelled up his chest, and just knocked the spots out of any acting ever *I* see before. This is the speech—I learned it, easy enough, while he was learning it to the king:

> To be, or not to be; that is the bare bodkin
> That makes calamity of so long life;
> For who would fardels bear, till Birnam Wood do come to Dunsinane,
> But that the fear of something after death
> Murders the innocent sleep,
> Great nature's second course,
> And makes us rather sling the arrows of outrageous fortune
> Than fly to others that we know not of.
> There's the respect must give us pause:
> Wake Duncan with thy knocking! I would thou couldst;
> For who would bear the whips and scorns of time,
> The oppressor's wrong, the proud man's contumely,
> The law's delay, and the quietus which his pangs might take,
> In the dead waste and middle of the night, when churchyards yawn
> In customary suits of solemn black,
> But that the undiscovered country from whose bourne no travel returns,
> Breathes forth contagion on the world,
> And thus the native hue of resolution, like the poor cat i' the adage,
> Is sicklied o'er with care,
> And all the clouds that lowered o'er our housetops.
> With this regard their currents turn awry,
> And lose the name of action.
> 'Tis a consummation devoutly to be wished. But soft you, the fair Ophelia:
> Ope not thy ponderous and marble jaws,
> But get thee to a nunnery—go!

Well, the old man he liked that speech, and he mighty soon got it so he could do it first rate. It seemed like he was just born for it; and when he had his hand in and was excited, it was perfectly lovely the way he would rip and tear and rair up behind when he was getting it off.

The first chance we got the duke he had some show-bills printed; and after that, for two or three days as we floated along, the raft was a most uncommon lively place, for there warn't nothing but sword-fighting and rehearsing—as the duke called it—going on all the time. One morning, when we was pretty well down the state of Arkansaw, we come in sight of a little one-horse town in a big bend; so we tied up about three-quarters of a mile above it, in the mouth of a crick which was shut in like a tunnel by the cypress trees, and all of us but Jim took the canoe and went down there to see if there was any chance in that place for our show.

We struck it mighty lucky; there was going to be a circus there that afternoon, and the country-people was already beginning to come in, in all kinds of old shackly wagons, and on horses. The circus would leave before night, so our show would have a pretty good chance. The duke he hired the courthouse, and we went around and stuck up our bills. They read like this:

Shaksperean Revival ! ! !

Wonderful Attraction!

For One Night Only!

The world renowned tragedians,

David Garrick the younger, of Drury Lane Theatre, London,

and

Edmund Kean the elder, of the Royal Haymarket Theatre

Whitechapel, Pudding Lane, Piccadilly, London, and the

Royal Continental Theatres, in their sublime

Shaksperean Spectacle entitled

The Balcony Scene

in

Romeo and Juliet ! ! !

Romeo . . . . Mr. Garrick

Juliet . . . . Mr. Kean

Assisted by the whole strength of the company!

New costumes, new scenery, new appointments!

Also:

The thrilling, masterly, and blood-curdling

Broad-sword conflict

In Richard III. ! ! !

Richard III . . . . Mr. Garrick

Richmond . . . . Mr. Kean

Also:

(by special request)

Hamlet's Immortal Soliloquy ! !

By the Illustrious Kean!

Done by him 300 consecutive nights in Paris!

For One Night Only,

On account of imperative European engagements!

Admission 25 cents; children and servants, 10 cents.

. . . I went to the circus and loafed around the back side till the watchman went by, and then dived in under the tent. I had my twenty-dollar gold piece and some other money, but I reckoned I better save it, because there ain't no telling how soon you are going to need it, away from home and amongst strangers that way. You can't be too careful. I ain't opposed to spending money on circuses when there ain't no other way, but there ain't no use in *wasting* it on them.

It was a real bully circus. It was the splendidest sight that ever was when they all come riding in, two and two, and gentleman and lady, side by side, the men just in their drawers and undershirts, and no shoes nor stirrups, and resting their hands on their thighs easy and comfortable—there must 'a' been twenty of them—and every lady with a lovely complexion, and perfectly beautiful, and looking just like a gang of real sure-enough queens, and dressed in clothes that cost millions of dollars, and just littered with diamonds. It was a powerful fine sight; I never see anything so lovely. And then one by one they got up and stood, and went a-weaving around the ring so gentle and wavy and graceful, the men looking ever so tall and airy and straight, with their heads bobbing and skimming along, away up there under the tent-roof, and every lady's rose-leafy dress flapping soft and silky around her hips, and she looking like the most loveliest parasol.

And then faster and faster they went, all of them dancing, first one foot out in the air and then the other, the horses leaning more and more, and the ringmaster going round and round the center pole, cracking his whip and shouting "Hi!—hi!" and the clown cracking jokes behind him; and by and by all hands dropped the reins, and every lady put her knuckles on her hips and every gentleman folded his arms, and then how the horses did lean over and hump themselves! And so one after the other they all skipped off into the ring, and made the sweetest bow I ever see, and then scampered out, and everybody clapped their hands and went just about wild.

Well, all through the circus they done the most astonishing things; and all the time that clown carried on so it most killed the people. The ringmaster couldn't ever say a word to him but he was back at him quick as a wink with the funniest things a body ever said; and how he ever *could* think of so many of them, and so sudden and so pat, was what I couldn't no way understand. Why, I couldn't 'a' thought of them in a year. And by and by a drunken man tried to get into the ring—said he wanted to ride; said he could ride as well as anybody that ever was. They argued and tried to keep him out, but he wouldn't listen, and the whole show come to a standstill. Then the people begun to holler at him and make fun of him, and that made him mad, and he begun to rip and tear; so that stirred up the people, and a lot of men begun to pile down off of the benches and swarm toward the ring, saying, "Knock him down! throw him out!" and one or two women begun to scream. So, then, the ringmaster he made a little speech, and said he hoped there wouldn't be no disturbance, and if the man would promise he wouldn't make no more trouble he would let him ride if he thought he could stay on the horse. So everybody laughed and said all right, and the man got on. The minute he was on, the horse begun to rip and tear and jump and cavort around, with two circus men hanging on to his bridle trying to hold him, and the drunken man hanging on to his neck, and his heels flying in the air every jump, and the whole crowd of people standing up shouting and laughing till tears rolled down. And at last, sure enough, all the circus men could do, the horse broke loose, and away he went like the very nation, round and round the ring, with that sot laying down on him and hanging to his neck, with first one leg hanging most to the ground on one side, and then t'other one on t'other side, and the people just crazy. It warn't funny to me, though; I was all of a tremble to see his danger. But pretty soon he struggled up astraddle and grabbed the bridle, a-reeling this way and that; and the next minute he sprung up and dropped the bridle and stood! and the horse a-going like a house afire, too. He just stood up there, a-sailing around as easy and comfortable as if he warn't ever drunk in his life—and then he begun to pull off his clothes and sling them. He shed them so thick they kind of clogged up the air, and altogether he shed seventeen suits. And then, there he was, slim and handsome, and dressed the gaudiest and prettiest you ever saw, and he lit into that horse with his whip and made him fairly hum—and finally skipped off, and made his bow and danced off to the dressing-room, and everybody just a-howling with pleasure and astonishment.

Then the ringmaster he saw how he had been fooled, and he *was* the sickest ringmaster you ever see, I reckon. Why, it was one of his own men! He had got up that joke all out of his own head, and never let on to nobody. Well, I felt sheepish enough to be took in so, but I wouldn't 'a' been in that ringmaster's place, not for a thousand dollars. I don't know; there may be bullier circuses than what that one was, but I never struck them yet. Anyways, it was plenty good enough for *me*; and wherever I run across it, it can have all of *my* custom every time.

Well, that night we had *our* show; but there warn't only about twelve people there—just enough to pay expenses. And they laughed all the time, and that made the duke mad; and everybody left, anyway, before the show was over, but one boy which was asleep. So the duke said these Arkansaw lunkheads couldn't come up to Shakespeare; what they wanted was low comedy—and maybe something ruther worse than low comedy, he reckoned. He said he could size their style. So next morning he got some big sheets of wrapping-paper and some black paint, and drawed off some handbills, and stuck them up all over the village. The bills said:

AT THE COURT HOUSE
FOR 3 NIGHTS ONLY!
The World-Renowned Tragedians
DAVID GARRICK THE YOUNGER!
AND
EDMUND KEAN THE ELDER!
*Of the London and Continental
Theatres,*
In their Thrilling Tragedy of
THE KING'S CAMELEOPARD,
OR
THE ROYAL NONESUCH ! ! !
Admission 50 cents.

Then at the bottom was the biggest line of all, which said:

Ladies and children not admitted

"There," says he, "if that line don't fetch them, I don't know Arkansaw!"

. . . Well, all day him and the king was hard at it, rigging up a stage and a curtain and a row of candles for footlights; and that night the house was jam full of men in no time. When the place couldn't hold no more, the duke he quit tending door and went around the back way and come onto the stage and stood up before the curtain and made a little speech, and praised up this tragedy, and said it was the most thrillingest one that ever was; and so he went on a-bragging about the tragedy, and about Edmund Kean the Elder, which was to play the main principal part in it; and at last when he'd got everybody's expectations up high enough, he rolled up the curtain, and the next minute the king come a-prancing out on all fours, naked; and he was painted all over, ring-streaked-and-striped, all sorts of colors, as splendid as a rainbow. And—but never mind the rest of his outfit; it was just wild, but it was awful funny. The people most killed themselves laughing; and when the king got done capering and capered off behind the scenes, they roared and clapped and stormed and haw-hawed till he come back and done it over again, and after that they made him do it another time. Well, it would make a cow laugh to see the shines that old idiot cut.

Then the duke he lets the curtain down, and bows to the people, and says the great tragedy will be performed only two nights more, on accounts of pressing London engagements, where the seats is all sold already for it in Drury Lane; and then he makes them another bow, and says if he has succeeded in pleasing them and instructing them, he will be deeply obleeged if they will mention it to their friends and get them to come and see it.

Twenty people sings out:

"What, is it over? Is that *all?*"

The duke says yes. Then there was a fine time. Everybody sings out, "Sold!" and rose up mad, and was a-going for that stage and them tragedians. But a big, fine-looking man jumps up on a bench and shouts:

"Hold on! Just a word, gentlemen." They stopped to listen. "We are sold—mighty badly sold. But we don't want to be the laughing-stock of this whole town, I reckon, and never hear the last of this thing as long as we live. *No.* What we want is to go out of here quiet, and talk this show up, and sell the *rest* of the town! Then we'll all be in the same boat. Ain't that sensible?" ("You bet it is!—the jedge is right!" everybody sings out.) "All right, then—not a word about any sell. Go along home, and advise everybody to come and see the tragedy."

Next day you couldn't hear nothing around that town but how splendid that show was. House was jammed again that night, and we sold this crowd the same way. When me and the king and the duke got home to the raft we all had a supper; and by and by, about midnight, they made Jim and me back her out and float her down the middle of the river, and fetch her in and hide her about two mile below town.

The third night the house was crammed again—and they warn't new-comers this time, but people that was at the show the other two nights. I stood by the duke at the door, and I see that every man that went in had his pockets bulging, or something muffled up under his coat—and I see it warn't no perfumery, neither, not by a long sight. I smelt sickly eggs by the barrel, and rotten cabbages, and such things; and if I know the signs of a dead cat being around, and I bet I do, there was sixty-four of them went in. I shoved in there for a minute, but it was too various for me; I couldn't stand it. Well, when the place couldn't hold no more people the duke he give a fellow a quarter and told him to tend door for him a minute, and then he started around for the stage door, I after him; but the minute we turned the corner and was in the dark he says:

"Walk fast now till you get away from the houses, and then shin for the raft like the dickens was after you!"

I done it, and he done the same. We struck the raft at the same time, and in less than two seconds we was gliding down-stream, all dark and still, and edging towards the middle of the river, nobody saying a word. I reckoned the poor king was in for a gaudy time of it with the audience, but nothing of the sort; pretty soon he crawls out from under the wigwam, and says:

"Well, how'd the old thing pan out this time, duke?" He hadn't been uptown at all.

We never showed a light till we was about ten mile below the village. Then we lit up and had a supper, and the king and the duke fairly laughed their bones loose over the way they'd served them people. The duke says:

"Greenhorns, flatheads! *I* knew the first house would keep mum and let the rest of the town get roped in; and I knew they'd lay for us the third night, and consider it was *their* turn now. Well, it *is* their turn, and I'd give something to know how much they'd take for it. I *would* just like to know how they're putting in their opportunity. They can turn it into a picnic if they want to—they brought plenty provisions."

Them rapscallions took in four hundred and sixty-five dollars in that three nights. I never see money hauled in by the wagon-load like that before.

Tarzan, the "apeman with the heart and head and body of an English gentle-man, and the training of a wild beast," became one of the twentieth century's leading popular fiction heroes. In Edgar Rice Burroughs's novels, Tarzan represents a primitivist critique of over-civilized society. Just what he represents in his later movie, comic book, and television incarnations is anyone's guess. (From Edgar Rice Burroughs, *Tarzan of the Apes*, 1906.)

EDGAR RICE BURROUGHS: *TARZAN OF THE APES*

Man and Man

Tarzan of the Apes lived on his wild, jungle existence with little change for several years, only that he grew stronger and wiser, and learned from his books more and more of the strange worlds which lay somewhere outside his primeval forest.

To him life was never monotonous or stale. There was always Pisah the fish, to be caught in the many streams and the little lakes, and Sabor, with her ferocious cousins to keep one ever on the alert and give zest to every instant that one spent upon the ground.

Often they hunted him, and more often he hunted them, but though they never quite reached him with those cruel, sharp claws of theirs, yet there were times when one could scarce have passed a thick leaf between their talons and his smooth hide.

Quick was Sabor, the lioness, and quick were Numa and Sheeta, but Tarzan of the Apes was lightning.

With Tantor, the elephant, he made friends. How? Ask me not. But this is known to the denizens of the jungle, that on many moonlit nights Tarzan of the Apes and Tantor, the elephant, walked together, and where the way was clear Tarzan rode, perched high upon Tantor's mighty back.

All else of the jungle were his enemies, except his own tribe, among whom he now had many friends.

Many days during these years he spent in the cabin of his father, where still lay, untouched, the bones of his parents and the little skeleton of Kala's baby. At eighteen he read fluently and understood nearly all he read in the many and varied volumes on the shelves.

Also could he write, with printed letters, rapidly and plainly, but script he had not mastered, for though there were several copy books among his treasure, there was so little written English in the cabin that he saw no use for bothering with this other form of writing, though he could read it, laboriously.

Thus, at eighteen, we find him, an English lordling, who could speak no English, and yet who could read and write his native language. Never had he seen a human being other than himself, for the little area traversed by his tribe was watered by no great river to bring down the savage natives of the interior.

High hills shut it off on three sides, the ocean on the fourth. It was alive with lions and leopards and poisonous snakes. Its untouched mazes of matted jungle had as yet invited no hardy pioneer from the human beasts beyond its frontier. . . .

Kala had moved slowly along an elephant track toward the east, and was busily engaged in turning over rotted limbs and logs in search of esculent bugs and fungi, when the faintest shadow of a strange noise brought her to startled attention.

For fifty yards before her the trail was straight, and down this leafy tunnel she saw the stealthy advancing figure of a strange and fearful creature.

It was Kulonga.

Kala did not wait to see more, but, turning, moved rapidly back along the trail. She did not run; but, after the manner of her kind when not aroused, sought rather to avoid than to escape.

Close after her came Kulonga. Here was meat. He could make a killing and feast well this day. On he hurried, his spear poised for the throw.

At a turning of the trail he came in sight of her again upon another straight stretch. His spear hand went far back, the muscles rolled, lightning-like, beneath the sleek hide. Out shot the arm, and the spear sped toward Kala.

A poor cast. It but grazed her side.

With a cry of rage and pain the she-ape turned upon her tormentor. In an instant the trees were crashing beneath the weight of her hurrying fellows, swinging rapidly toward the scene of trouble in answer to Kala's scream.

As she charged, Kulonga unslung his bow and fitted an arrow with almost unthinkable quickness. Drawing the shaft far back he drove the poisoned missile straight into the heart of the great anthropoid.

With a horrid scream Kala plunged forward upon her face before the astonished members of her tribe.

Roaring and shrieking the apes dashed toward Kulonga, but that wary savage was fleeing down the trail like a frightened antelope.

He knew something of the ferocity of these wild, hairy men, and his one desire was to put as many miles between himself and them as he possibly could.

They followed him, racing through the trees, for a long distance, but finally one by one they abandoned the chase and returned to the scene of the tragedy.

None of them had ever seen a man before, other than Tarzan, and so they wondered vaguely what strange manner of creature it might be that had invaded their jungle.

On the far beach, by the little cabin Tarzan heard the faint echoes of the conflict and knowing that something was seriously amiss among the tribe he hastened rapidly toward the direction of the sound.

When he arrived he found the entire tribe gathered jabbering about the dead body of his slain mother.

Tarzan's grief and anger were unbounded. He roared out his hideous challenge time and again. He beat upon his great chest with his clenched fists, and then he fell upon the body of Kala and sobbed out the pitiful sorrowing of his lonely heart.

To lose the only creature in all one's world who ever had manifested love and affection for one, is a great bereavement indeed.

What though Kala was a fierce and hideous ape! To Tarzan she had been kind, she had been beautiful.

Upon her he had lavished, unknown to himself, all the reverence and respect and love that a normal English boy feels for his own mother. He had never known another, and so to Kala was given, though mutely, all that would have belonged to the fair and lovely Lady Alice had she lived.

After the first outburst of grief Tarzan controlled himself, and questioning the members of the tribe who had witnessed the killing of Kala he learned all that their meager vocabulary could vouchsafe him.

It was enough, however, for his needs. It told him of a strange, hairless, black ape with feathers growing upon its head, who launched death from a slender branch, and then ran, with the fleetness of Bara, the deer, toward the rising sun.

Tarzan waited no longer, but leaping into the branches of the trees sped rapidly through the forest. He knew the windings of the elephant trail along which Kala's murderer had flown, and so he cut straight through the jungle to intercept the black warrior who was evidently following the tortuous detours of the trail.

At his side was the hunting knife of his unknown sire, and across his shoulders the coils of his own long rope. In an hour he struck the trail again, and coming to earth examined the soil minutely.

In the soft mud on the bank of a tiny rivulet he found footprints such as he alone in all the jungle had ever made, but much larger than his. His heart beat fast. Could it be that he was trailing a MAN—one of his own race?

There were two sets of imprints pointing in opposite directions. So his quarry had already passed on his return along the trail. As he examined the newer spoor a tiny particle of earth toppled from the outer edge of one of the footprints to the bottom of its shallow depression —ah, the trail was very fresh, his prey must have but scarcely passed.

Tarzan swung himself to be trees once more, and with swift noiselessness sped along high above the trail.

He had covered barely a mile when he came upon the black warrior standing in a little open space. In his hand was his slender bow to which he had fitted one of his death dealing arrows.

Opposite him across the little clearing stood Horta, the boar, with lowered head and foam flecked tusks, ready to charge.

Tarzan looked with wonder upon the strange creature beneath him —so like him in form and yet so different in face and color. His books had portrayed the *negro*, but how different had been the dull, dead print to this sleek thing of ebony, pulsing with life.

As the man stood there with taut drawn bow Tarzan recognized in him not so much the *negro* as the *Archer* of his picture book—

A stands for Archer

How wonderful! Tarzan almost betrayed his presence in the deep excitement of his discovery.

But things were commencing to happen below him. The sinewy black arm had drawn the shaft far back; Horta, the boar, was charging, and then the black released the little poisoned arrow, and Tarzan saw it fly with the quickness of thought and lodge in the bristling neck of the boar.

Scarcely had the shaft left his bow ere Kulonga had fitted another to it, but Horta, the boar, was upon him so quickly that he had no time to discharge it. With a bound the black leaped entirely over the rushing beast and turning with incredible swiftness planted a second arrow in Horta's back.

Then Kulonga sprang into a near-by tree.

Horta wheeled to charge his enemy once more, a dozen steps he took, then he staggered and fell upon his side. For a moment his muscles stiffened and relaxed convulsively, then he lay still.

Kulonga came down from his tree.

With a knife that hung at his side he cut several large pieces from the boar's body, and in the center of the trail he built a fire, cooking and eating as much as he wanted. The rest he left where it had fallen.

Tarzan was an interested spectator. His desire to kill burned fiercely in his wild breast, but his desire to learn was even greater. He would follow this savage creature for a while and know from whence he came. He could kill him at his leisure later, when the bow and deadly arrows were laid aside.

When Kulonga had finished his repast and disappeared beyond a near turning of the path, Tarzan dropped quietly to the ground. With his knife he severed many strips of meat from Horta's carcass, but he did not cook them.

He had seen fire, but only when Ara, the lightning, had destroyed some great tree. That any creature of the jungle could produce the red-and-yellow fangs which devoured wood and left nothing but fine dust surprised Tarzan greatly, and why the black warrior had ruined his delicious repast by plunging it into the blighting heat was quite beyond him. Possibly Ara was a friend with whom the Archer was sharing his food.

But, be that as it may, Tarzan would not ruin good meat in any such foolish manner, so he gobbled down a great quantity of the raw flesh, burying the balance of the carcass beside the trail where he could find it upon his return.

And then Lord Greystoke wiped his greasy fingers upon his naked thighs and took up the trail of Kulonga, the son of Mbonga, the king; while in far-off London another Lord Greystoke, the younger brother of the real Lord Greystoke's father, sent back his chops to the club's *chef* because they were underdone, and when he had finished his repast he dipped his finger-ends into a silver bowl of scented water and dried them upon a piece of snowy damask.

All day Tarzan followed Kulonga, hovering above him in the trees like some malign spirit. Twice more he saw him hurl his arrows of destruction—once at Dango, the hyena, and again at Manu, the monkey. In each instance the animal died almost instantly, for Kulonga's poison was very fresh and very deadly.

Tarzan thought much on this wondrous method of slaying as he swung slowly along at a safe distance behind his quarry. He knew that alone the tiny prick of the arrow could not so quickly dispatch these wild things of the jungle, who were often torn and scratched and gored in a frightful manner as they fought with their jungle neighbors, yet as often recovered as not.

No, there was something mysterious connected with these tiny slivers of wood which could bring death by a mere scratch. He must look into the matter.

That night Kulonga slept in the crotch of a mighty tree and far above him crouched Tarzan of the Apes.

When Kulonga awoke he found that his bow and arrows had disappeared. The black warrior was furious and frightened, but more frightened than furious. He searched the ground below the tree, and he searched the tree above the ground; but there was no sign of either bow or arrows or of the nocturnal marauder.

Kulonga was panic-stricken. His spear he had hurled at Kala and had not recovered; and, now that his bow and arrows were gone, he was defenseless except for a single knife. His only hope lay in reaching the village of Mbonga as quickly as his legs would carry him.

That he was not far from home he was certain, so he took the trail at a rapid trot.

From a great mass of impenetrable foliage a few yards away emerged Tarzan of the Apes to swing quietly in his wake.

Kulonga's bow and arrows were securely tied high in the top of a giant tree from which a patch of bark had been removed by a sharp knife near to the ground, and a branch half cut through and left hanging about fifty feet higher up. Thus Tarzan blazed the forest trails and marked his caches.

As Kulonga continued his journey Tarzan closed up on him until he traveled almost over the black's head. His rope he now held coiled in his right hand; he was almost ready for the kill.

The moment was delayed only because Tarzan was anxious to ascertain the black warrior's destination, and presently he was rewarded, for they came suddenly in view of a great clearing, at one end of which lay many strange lairs.

Tarzan was directly over Kulonga, as he made the discovery. The forest ended abruptly and beyond lay two hundred yards of planted fields between the jungle and the village.

Tarzan must act quickly or his prey would be gone; but Tarzan's life training left so little space between decision and action when an emergency confronted him that there was not even room for the shadow of a thought between.

So it was that as Kulonga emerged from the shadow of the jungle a slender coil of rope sped sinuously above him from the lowest branch of a mighty tree directly upon the edge of the fields of Mbonga, and ere the king's son had taken a half dozen steps into the clearing a quick noose tightened about his neck.

So quickly did Tarzan of the Apes drag back his prey that Kulonga's cry of alarm was throttled in his windpipe. Hand over hand Tarzan drew the struggling black until he had him hanging by his neck in mid-air; then Tarzan climbed to a larger branch drawing the still threshing victim well up into the sheltering verdure of the tree.

Here he fastened the rope securely to a stout branch, and then, descending, plunged his hunting knife into Kulonga's heart. Kala was avenged.

Tarzan examined the black minutely, never had he seen any other human being. The knife with its sheath and belt caught his eye; he appropriated them. A copper anklet also took his fancy, and this he transferred to his own leg.

He examined and admired the tattooing on the forehead and breast. He marveled at the sharp filed teeth. He investigated and appropriated the feathered headdress, and then he prepared to get down to business, for Tarzan of the Apes was hungry, and here was meat; meat of the kill, which jungle ethics permitted him to eat.

How may we judge him, by what standards, this apeman with the heart and head and body of an English gentleman, and the training of a wild beast?

Tublat, whom he had hated and who had hated him, he had killed in fair fight, and yet never had the thought of eating Tublat's flesh entered his head. It would have been as revolting to him as is cannibalism to us.

But who was Kulonga that he might not be eaten as fairly as Horta, the boar, or Bara, the deer? Was he not simply another of the countless wild things of the jungle who preyed upon one another to satisfy the cravings of hunger?

Of a sudden, a strange doubt stayed his hand. Had not his books taught him that he was a man? And was not The Archer a man, also?

Did men eat men? Alas, he did not know. Why, then, this hesitancy! Once more he essayed the effort, but of a sudden a qualm of nausea overwhelmed him. He did not understand.

All he knew was that he could not eat the flesh of this black man, and thus hereditary instinct, ages old, usurped the functions of his untaught mind and saved him from transgressing a world-wide law of whose very existence he was ignorant.

Quickly he lowered Kulonga's body to the ground, removed the noose, and took to the trees again.

Owen Wister's *The Virginian*, since its appearance in 1902, has sold about 2,000,000 copies and been the basis of four movies and a television serial. Wister created an image of the cowboy as nature's nobleman that influenced two generations of western writers and fixed for half a century the standard image of the movie western hero. (Excerpts from Owen Wister, *The Virginian: A Horseman of the Plains*, 1902.)

OWEN WISTER: *THE VIRGINIAN*

Lounging there at ease against the wall was a slim young giant, more beautiful than pictures. His broad, soft hat was pushed back; a loose-knotted, dull-scarlet handkerchief sagged from his throat; and one casual thumb was hooked in the cartridge-belt that slanted across his hips. He had plainly come many miles from somewhere across the vast horizon, as the dust upon him showed. His boots were white with it. His overalls were gray with it. The weather-beaten bloom of his face shone through it duskily, as the ripe peaches look upon their trees in a dry season. But no dinginess of travel or shabbiness of attire could tarnish the splendor that radiated from his youth and strength. The old man upon whose temper his remarks were doing such deadly work was combed and curried to a finish, a bridegroom swept and garnished; but alas for age! Had I been the bride, I should have taken the giant, dust and all. . . .

Then I heard a fellow greet my Virginian. He came rollicking out of a door, and made a pass with his hand at the Virginian's hat. The Southerner dodged it, and I saw once more the tiger undulation of body, and knew my escort was he of the rope and the corral.

"How are yu', Steve?" he said to the rollicking man. And in his tone I heard instantly old friendship speaking. With Steve he would take and give familiarity.

Steve looked at me, and looked away—and that was all. But it was enough. In no company had I ever felt so much an outsider. Yet I liked the company, and wished that it would like me.

"Just come to town?" inquired Steve of the Virginian.

"Been here since noon. Been waiting for the train."

"Going out to-night?"

"I reckon I'll pull out to-morro'."

"Beds are all took," said Steve. This was for my benefit.

"Dear me!" said I.

"But I guess one of them drummers will let you double up with him." Steve was enjoying himself, I think. He had his saddle and blankets, and beds were nothing to him.

"Drummers, are they?" asked the Virginian.

"Two Jews handling cigars, one American with consumption killer, and a Dutchman with jew'lry."

The Virginian set down my valise, and seemed to meditate. "I did want a bed to-night," he murmured gently.

"Well," Steve suggested, "the American looks like he washed the oftenest."

"That's of no consequence to me," observed the Southerner.

"Guess it'll be when yu' see 'em."

"Oh, I'm meaning something different. I wanted a bed to myself."

"Then you'll have to build one."

"Bet yu' I have the Dutchman's."

"Take a man that won't scare. Bet yu' drinks yu' can't have the American's."

"Go yu'," said the Virginian. "I'll have his bed without any fuss. Drinks for the crowd."

"I suppose you have me beat," said Steve, grinning at him affectionately. "You're such a son-of-a —— when you get down to work. Well, so-long! I got to fix my horse's hoofs."

I had expected that the man would be struck down. He had used to the Virginian a term of heaviest insult, I thought. I had marvelled to hear it come so unheralded from Steve's friendly lips. And now I marvelled still more. Evidently he had meant no harm by it, and evidently no offence had been taken. Used thus, this language was plainly complimentary. I had stepped into a world new to me indeed, and novelties were occurring with scarce any time to get breath between them. . . .

So far my hours at Medicine Bow had seemed to glide beneath a sunshine of merriment, of easy-going jocularity. This was suddenly gone, like the wind changing to north in the middle of a warm day. But I stayed, being ashamed to go.

Five or six players sat over in the corner at a round table where counters were piled. Their eyes were close upon their cards, and one seemed to be dealing a card at a time to each, with pauses and betting between. Steve was there and the Virginian; the others were new faces.

"No place for amatures," repeated the voice; and now I saw that it was the dealer's. There was in his countenance the same ugliness that his words conveyed.

"Who's that talkin'?" said one of the men near me, in a low voice.

"Trampas."

"What's he?"

"Cow-puncher, bronco-buster, tin-horn, most anything."

"Who's he talkin' at?"

"Think it's the black-headed guy he's talking at."

"That ain't supposed to be safe, is it?"

"Guess we're all goin' to find out in a few minutes."

"Been trouble between 'em?"

"They've not me before. Trampas don't enjoy losin' to a stranger."

"Fello's from Arizona, yu' say?"

"No. Virginia. He's recently back from havin' a look at Arizona. Went down there last year for a change. Works for the Sunk Creek outfit." And then the dealer lowered his voice still further and said something in the other man's ear, causing him to grin. After which both of them looked at me.

There had been silence over in the corner; but now the man Trampas spoke again.

"*And* ten," said he, sliding out some chips from before him. Very strange it was to hear him, how he contrived to make those words a personal taunt. The Virginian was looking at his cards. He might have been deaf.

"*And* twenty," said the next player, easily.

The next threw his cards down.

It was now the Virginian's turn to bet, or leave the game, and he did not speak at once.

Therefore Trampas spoke. "Your bet, you son-of-a ———."

The Virginian's pistol came out, and his hand lay on the table, holding it unaimed. And with a voice as gentle as ever, the voice that sounded almost like a caress, but drawling a very little more than usual, so that there was almost a space between each word, he issued his orders to the man Trampas:—

"When you call me that, *smile*." And he looked at Trampas across the table.

Yes, the voice was gentle. But in my ears it seemed as if somewhere the bell of death was ringing; and silence, like a stroke, fell on the large room. All men present, as if by some magnetic current, had become aware of this crisis. In my ignorance, and the total stoppage of my thoughts, I stood stock-still, and noticed various people crouching, or shifting their positions.

"Sit quiet," said the dealer, scornfully to the man near me. "Can't you see he don't want to push trouble? He has handed Trampas the choice to back down or draw his steel."

Then, with equal suddenness and ease, the room came out of its strangeness. Voices and cards, the click of chips, the puff of tobacco, glasses lifted to drink,—this level of smooth relaxation hinted no more plainly of what lay beneath than does the surface tell the depth of the sea.

For Trampas had made his choice. And that choice was not to "draw his steel." If it was knowledge that he sought, he had found it, and no mistake! We heard no further reference to what he had been pleased to style "amatures." In no company would the black-headed man who had visited Arizona be rated a novice at the cool art of self-preservation.

One doubt remained: what kind of a man was Trampas? A public back-down is an unfinished thing,—for some natures at least. I looked at his face, and thought it sullen, but tricky rather than courageous.

Something had been added to my knowledge also. Once again I had heard applied to the Virginian that epithet which Steve so freely used. The same words, identical to the letter. But this time they had produced a pistol. "When you call me that, *smile!*" So I perceived a new example of the old truth, that the letter means nothing until the spirit gives it life.

Arthur Sarsfield Ward, writing under the pen name of Sax Rohmer, caught many themes in the American imagination in his very successful series of books about "The Insidious Dr. Fu-Manchu." From the 1890s on, people talked in vague terms of "the Yellow Peril." Rohmer combined these fears with a popular literary device, the scientifically oriented detective, added generous doses of soft-to-positively-mushy core pornography, and created a formula that remains popular down to the present day of agent .007 and his compeers. (Selection from Sax Rohmer, *The Insidious Dr. Fu-Manchu*, 1917.)

SAX ROHMER: *THE INSIDIOUS DR. FU-MANCHU*

It was the night following that of the double tragedy at Rowan House. Nayland Smith, with Inspector Weymouth, was engaged in some mysterious inquiry at the docks, and I had remained at home to resume my strange chronicle. And—why should I not confess it?—my memories had frightened me.

I was arranging my notes respecting the case of Sir Lionel Barton. They were hopelessly incomplete. For instance, I had jotted down the following queries:—(1) Did any true parallel exist between the death of M. Page le Roi and the death of Kwee, the Chinaman, and of Strozza? (2) What had become of the mummy of Mekara? (3) How had the murderer escaped from a locked room? (4) What was the purpose of the rubber stopper? (5) Why was Kwee hiding in the conservatory? (6) Was the green mist a mere subjective hallucination—a figment of Croxted's imagination—or had he actually seen it?

Until these questions were satisfactorily answered, further progress was impossible. Nayland Smith frankly admitted that he was out of his depth. "It looks, on the face of it, more like a case for the Psychical Research people than for a plain Civil Servant, lately of Mandalay," he had said only that morning.

"Sir Lionel Barton really believes that supernatural agencies were brought into operation by the opening of the high priest's coffin. For my part, even if I believed the same, I should still maintain that Dr. Fu-Manchu controlled those manifestations. But reason it out for yourself and see if we arrive at any common center. Don't work so much upon the datum of the green mist, but keep to the *facts* which are established."

I commenced to knock out my pipe in the ashtray; then paused, pipe in hand. The house was quite still, for my landlady and all the small household were out.

Above the noise of the passing tramcar I thought I had heard the hall door open. In the ensuing silence I sat and listened.

Not a sound. Stay! I slipped my hand into the table drawer, took out my revolver, and stood up.

There *was* a sound. Someone or something was creeping upstairs in the dark!

Familiar with the ghastly media employed by the Chinaman, I was seized with an impulse to leap to the door, shut and lock it. But the rustling sound proceeded, now, from immediately outside my partially opened door. I had not the time to close it; knowing somewhat of the horrors at the command of Fu-Manchu, I had not the courage to open it. My heart leaping wildly, and my eyes upon that bar of darkness with its gruesome potentialities, I waited—waited for whatever was to come. Perhaps twelve seconds passed in silence.

"Who's there?" I cried. "Answer, or I fire!"

"Ah! no," came a soft voice, thrillingly musical. "Put it down—that pistol. Quick! I must speak to you."

The door was pushed open, and there entered a slim figure wrapped in a hooded cloak. My hand fell, and I stood, stricken to silence, looking into the beautiful dark eyes of Dr. Fu-Manchu's messenger—if her own statement could be credited, slave. On two occasions this girl, whose association with the Doctor was one of the most profound mysteries of the case, had risked—I cannot say what; unnameable punishment, perhaps—to save me from death; in both cases from a terrible death. For what was she come now?

Her lips slightly parted, she stood, holding her cloak about her, and watching me with great passionate eyes.

"How—" I began.

But she shook her head impatiently.

"*He* has a duplicate key of the house door," was her amazing statement. "I have never betrayed a secret of my master before, but you must arrange to replace the lock."

She came forward and rested her slim hands confidingly upon my shoulders. "I have come again to ask you to take me away from him," she said simply.

And she lifted her face to me.

Her words struck a chord in my heart which sang with strange music, with music so barbaric that, frankly, I blushed to find it harmony. Have I said that she was beautiful? It can convey no faint conception of her. With her pure, fair skin, eyes like the velvet darkness of the East, and red lips so tremulously near to mine, she was the most seductively lovely creature I ever had looked upon. In that electric moment my heart went out in sympathy to every man who had bartered honor, country, all for a woman's kiss.

"I will see that you are placed under proper protection," I said firmly, but my voice was not quite my own. "It is quite absurd to talk of slavery here in England. You are a free agent, or you could not be here now. Dr. Fu-Manchu cannot control your actions."

"Ah!" she cried, casting back her head scornfully, and releasing a cloud of hair, through whose softness gleamed a jeweled head-dress. "No? He cannot? Do you know what it means to have been a slave? Here, in your free England, do you know what it means—the *razzia*, the desert journey, the whips of the drivers, the house of the dealer, the shame. Bah!"

How beautiful she was in her indignation!

"Slavery is put down, you imagine, perhaps? You do not believe that to-day—*to-day*—twenty-five English sovereigns will buy a Galla girl, who is brown, and"—whisper—"two hundred and fifty a Circassian, who is white. No, there is no slavery! So! Then what am I?"

She threw open her cloak, and it is a literal fact that I rubbed my eyes, half believing that I dreamed. For beneath, she was arrayed in gossamer silk which more than indicated the perfect lines of her slim shape; wore a jeweled girdle and barbaric ornaments; was a figure fit for the walled gardens of Stamboul—a figure amazing, incomprehensible, in the prosaic setting of my rooms.

"To-night I had no time to make myself an English miss," she said, wrapping her cloak quickly about her. "You see me as I am."

Her garments exhaled a faint perfume, and it reminded me of another meeting I had had with her. I looked into the challenging eyes.

"Your request is but a pretense," I said. "Why do you keep the secrets of that man, when they mean death to so many?"

"Death! I have seen my own sister die of fever in the desert—seen her thrown like carrion into a hole in the sand. I have seen men flogged until they prayed for death as a boon. I have known the lash myself. Death! What does it matter?"

She shocked me inexpressibly. Enveloped in her cloak again, and with only her slight accent to betray her, it was dreadful to hear such words from a girl who, save for her singular type of beauty, might have been a cultured European.

"Prove, then, that you really wish to leave this man's service. Tell me what killed Strozza and the Chinaman," I said.

She shrugged her shoulders.

"I do not know that. But if you will carry me off"—she clutched me nervously—"so that I am helpless, lock me up so that I cannot escape, beat me, if you like, I will tell you all I do know. While he is my master I will never betray him. Tear me from him—by force, do you understand, *by force,* and my lips will be sealed no longer. Ah! but you do not understand, with your 'proper authorities'—your police. Police! Ah, I have said enough."

A clock across the common began to strike. The girl started and laid her hands upon my shoulders again. There were tears glittering among the curved black lashes.

"You do not understand," she whispered. "Oh, will you never understand and release me from him! I must go. Already I have remained too long. Listen. Go out without delay. Remain out—at a hotel, where you will, but do not stay here."

"And Nayland Smith?"

"What is he to me, this Nayland Smith? Ah, why will you not unseal my lips? You are in danger—you hear me, in danger! Go away from here to-night."

She dropped her hands and ran from the room. In the open doorway she turned, stamping her foot passionately.

"You have hands and arms," she cried, "and yet you let me go. Be warned, then; fly from here—" She broke off with something that sounded like a sob.

I made no move to stay her—this beautiful accomplice of the arch-murderer, Fu-Manchu. I heard her light footsteps pattering down the stairs, I heard her open and close the door—the door of which Dr. Fu-Manchu held the key. Still I stood where she had parted from me, and was so standing when a key grated in the lock and Nayland Smith came running up.

"Did you see her?" I began.

But his face showed that he had not done so, and rapidly I told him of my strange visitor, of her words, of her warning.

"How can she have passed through London in that costume?" I cried in bewilderment. "Where can she have come from?"

Smith shrugged his shoulders and began to stuff broad-cut mixture into the familiar cracked briar.

"She might have traveled in a car or in a cab," he said; "and undoubtedly she came direct from the house of Dr. Fu-Manchu. You should have detained her, Petrie. It is the third time we have had that woman in our power, the third time we have let her go free."

"Smith," I replied, "I couldn't. She came of her own free will to give me a warning. She disarms me."

"Because you can see she is in love with you?" he suggested, and burst into one of his rare laughs when the angry flush rose to my cheek. "She is, Petrie—why pretend to be blind to it? You don't know the Oriental mind as I do; but I quite understand the girl's position. She fears the English authorities, but would submit to capture by you! If you would only seize her by the hair, drag her to some cellar, hurl her down and stand over her with a whip, she would tell you everything she knows, and salve her strange Eastern conscience with the reflection that speech was forced from her. I am not joking; it is so, I assure you. And she would adore you for your savagery, deeming you forceful and strong!"

"Smith," I said, "be serious. You know what her warning meant before."

"I can guess what it means now," he rapped. "Hallo!"

Someone was furiously ringing the bell.

"No one at home?" said my friend. "I will go. I think I know what it is."

A few minutes later he returned, carrying a large square package.

"From Weymouth," he explained, "by district messenger. I left him behind at the docks, and he arranged to forward any evidence which subsequently he found. This will be fragments of the mummy."

"What! You think the mummy was abstracted?"

"Yes, at the docks. I am sure of it; and somebody else was in the sarcophagus when it reached Rowan House. A sarcophagus, I find, is practically airtight, so that the use of the rubber stopper becomes evident —ventilation. How this person killed Strozza I have yet to learn."

"Also, how he escaped from a locked room. And what about the green mist?"

Nayland Smith spread his hands in a characteristic gesture.

"The green mist, Petrie, can be explained in several ways. Remember, we have only one man's word that it existed. It is at best a confusing datum, to which we must not attach a fictitious importance."

He threw the wrappings on the floor and tugged at a twine loop in the lid of the square box, which now stood upon the table. Suddenly the lid came away, bringing with it a lead lining, such as in usual in tea-chests. This lining was partially attached to one side of the box, so that the action of removing the lid at once raised and tilted it.

Then happened a singular thing.

Out over the table billowed a sort of yellowish-green cloud—an oily vapor—and an inspiration, it was nothing less, born of a memory and of some words of my beautiful visitor, came to me.

"*Run, Smith!*" I screamed. "The door! the door, for your life! Fu-Manchu sent that box!"

I threw my arms round him. As he bent forward the moving vapor rose almost to his nostrils. I dragged him back and all but pitched him out on to the landing. We entered my bedroom, and there, as I turned on the light, I saw that Smith's tanned face was unusually drawn, and touched with pallor.

"It is a poisonous gas!" I said hoarsely; "in many respects identical with *chlorine,* but having unique properties which prove it to be something else—God and Fu-Manchu, alone know what! It is the fumes of chlorine that kill the men in the bleaching powder works. We have been blind—I particularly. Don't you see? There was no one in the sarcophagus, Smith, but there was enough of that fearful stuff to have suffocated a regiment!"

Smith clenched his fists convulsively.

"My God!" he said, "how can I hope to deal with the author of such a scheme? I see the whole plan. He did not reckon on the mummy case being overturned, and Kwee's part was to remove the plug with the aid of the string—after Sir Lionel had been suffocated. The gas, I take it, is heavier than air."

"Chlorine gas has a specific gravity of 2.470," I said; "two and a half times heavier than air. You can pour it from jar to jar like a liquid—if you are wearing a chemist's mask. In these respects this stuff appears to be similar; the points of difference would not interest you. The sarcophagus would have emptied through the vent, and the gas have dispersed, with no clew remaining—except the smell."

"I did smell it, Petrie, on the stopper, but, of course, was unfamiliar with it. You may remember that you were prevented from doing so by the arrival of Sir Lionel? The scent of those infernal flowers must partially have drowned it, too. Poor, misguided Strozza inhaled the stuff, capsized the case in his fall, and all the gas—"

"Went pouring under the conservatory door, and down the steps, where Kwee was crouching. Croxted's breaking the window created sufficient draught to disperse what little remained. It will have settled on the floor now. I will go and open both windows."

Nayland raised his haggard face.

"He evidently made more than was necessary to dispatch Sir Lionel Barton," he said; "and contemptuously—you note the attitude, Petrie? —contemptuously devoted the surplus to me. His contempt is justified. I am a child striving to cope with a mental giant. It is by no wit of mine that Dr. Fu-Manchu scores a double failure."

. . . a man entered, carrying a lantern. Its light showed my surmise to be accurate, showed the slime-coated walls of a dungeon some fifteen feet square—shone upon the long yellow robe of the man who stood watching us, upon the malignant, intellectual countenance.

It was Dr. Fu-Manchu.

At last they were face to face—the head of the great Yellow Movement, and the man who fought on behalf of the entire white race. How can I paint the individual who now stood before us—perhaps the greatest genius of modern times?

Of him it had been fitly said that he had a brow like Shakespeare and a face like Satan. Something serpentine, hypnotic, was in his very presence. Smith drew one sharp breath, and was silent. Together, chained to the wall, two mediæval captives, living mockeries of our boasted modern security, we crouched before Dr. Fu-Manchu.

He came forward with an indescribable gait, cat-like yet awkward, carrying his high shoulders almost hunched. He placed the lantern in a niche in the wall, never turning away the reptilian gaze of those eyes which must haunt my dreams forever. They possessed a viridescence which hitherto I had supposed possible only in the eye of the cat—and the film intermittently clouded their brightness—but I can speak of them no more.

I had never supposed, prior to meeting Dr. Fu-Manchu, that so intense a force of malignancy could radiate—from any human being. He spoke. His English was perfect, though at time his words were oddly chosen; his delivery alternately was guttural and sibilant.

"Mr. Smith and Dr. Petrie, your interference with my plans has gone too far. I have seriously turned my attention to you."

He displayed his teeth, small and evenly separated, but discolored in a way that was familiar to me. I studied his eyes with a new professional interest, which even the extremity of our danger could not wholly banish. Their greenness seemed to be of the iris; the pupil was oddly contracted—a pin-point.

Smith leaned his back against the wall with assumed indifference.

"You have presumed," continued Fu-Manchu, "to meddle with a world-change. Poor spiders—caught in the wheels of the inevitable! You have linked my name with the futility of the Young China Movement —the name of Fu-Manchu! Mr. Smith, you are an incompetent meddler— I despise you! Dr. Petrie, you are a fool—I am sorry for you!"

He rested one bony hand on his hip, narrowing the long eyes as he looked down on us. The purposeful cruelty of the man was inherent; it was entirely untheatrical. Still Smith remained silent.

"So I am determined to remove you from the scene of your blunders!" added Fu-Manchu.

"Opium will very shortly do the same for you!" I rapped at him savagely.

Without emotion he turned the narrowed eyes upon me.

"That is a matter of opinion, Doctor," he said. "You may have lacked the opportunities which have been mine for studying that subject

—and in any event I shall not be privileged to enjoy your advice in the future."

"You will not long outlive me," I replied. "And our deaths will not profit you, incidentally; because—" Smith's foot touched mine.

"Because?" inquired Fu-Manchu softly. "Ah! Mr. Smith is so prudent! He is thinking that I have *files!*" He pronounced the word in a way that made me shudder. "Mr. Smith has seen a *wire jacket!* Have you ever seen a wire jacket? As a surgeon its functions would interest you!"

I stifled a cry that rose to my lips; for, with a shrill whistling sound, a small shape came bounding into the dimly lit vault, then shot upward. A marmoset landed on the shoulder of Dr. Fu-Manchu and peered grotesquely into the dreadful yellow face. The doctor raised his bony hand and fondled the little creature, crooning to it.

"One of my pets, Mr. Smith," he said, suddenly opening his eyes fully so that they blazed like green lamps. "I have others, equally useful. My scorpions—have you met my scorpions? No? My pythons and hamadryads? Then there are my fungi and my tiny allies, the bacilli. I have a collection in my laboratory quite unique. Have you ever visited Molokai, the leper island, Doctor? No? But Mr. Nayland Smith will be familiar with the asylum at Rangoon! And we must not forget my black spiders, with their diamond eyes—my spiders, that sit in the dark and watch—then leap!"

He raised his lean hands, so that the sleeve of the robe fell back to the elbow, and the ape dropped, chattering, to the floor and ran from the cellar.

"O God of Cathay!" he cried, "by what death shall these die—these miserable ones who would bind thine Empire, which is boundless!"

Like some priest of Tezcat he stood, his eyes upraised to the roof, his lean body quivering—a sight to shock the most unimpressionable mind.

"He is mad!" I whispered to Smith. "God help us, the man is a dangerous homicidal maniac!"

Nayland Smith's tanned face was very drawn, but he shook his head grimly.

"Dangerous, yes, I agree," he muttered; "his existence is a danger to the entire white race which, now, we are powerless to avert."

Dr. Fu-Manchu recovered himself, took up the lantern and, turning abruptly, walked to the door, with his awkward, yet feline gait. At the threshold he looked back.

"You would have warned Mr. Graham Guthrie?" he said, in a soft voice. "To-night, at half-past twelve, Mr. Graham Guthrie dies!"

Smith sat silent and motionless, his eyes fixed upon the speaker.

"You were in Rangoon in 1908?" continued Dr. Fu-Manchu—"you remember the Call?"

From somewhere above us—I could not determine the exact direction—came a low, wailing cry, an uncanny thing of falling cadences, which in that dismal vault, with the sinister yellow-robed figure at the door, seemed to pour ice into my veins. Its effect upon Smith was truly extraordinary. His face showed grayly in the faint light, and I heard him draw a hissing breath through clenched teeth.

"It calls for you!" said Fu-Manchu. "At half-past twelve it calls for Graham Guthrie!"

The door closed and darkness mantled us again.

"Smith," I said, "what was that?" The horrors about us were playing havoc with my nerves.

"It was the Call of Siva!" replied Smith hoarsely.

"What is it? Who uttered it? What does it mean?"

"I don't know what it is, Petrie, nor who utters it. But it means death!"

The author of "Trees," Joyce Kilmer, died in World War I, lending a certain romance to his ever-popular ode. The poem itself is a metaphorical monstrosity: truly it would require a special act of God to construct a tree to Kilmer's specification, with its "mouth" to the ground, its "hair" up where the robins nest, and its eyes and arms directed upward. (From Joyce Kilmer, *Trees and Other Poems*, 1914.)

JOYCE KILMER, **TREES**

(For Mrs. Henry Mills Alden)

I think that I shall never see
A poem lovely as a tree.

A tree whose hungry mouth is prest
Against the earth's sweet flowing breast;

A tree that looks at God all day,
And lifts her leafy arms to pray;

A tree that may in Summer wear
A nest of robins in her hair;

Upon whose bosom snow has lain;
Who intimately lives with rain.

Poems are made by fools like me,
But only God can make a tree.

This song, which apparently dates from right after the Civil War, became a favorite during the campaign of 1884. The unsuccessful Republican presidential candidate, James G. Blaine, had years before been implicated in a financial scandal. Democrats, embarrassed by revelations that their own Grover Cleveland had fathered an illegitimate child, gladly branded Blaine a "dodger."

THE DODGER

1 Oh, the candidate's a dodger, yes, a well-known dodger,
Oh, the candidate's a dodger, yes, and I'm a dodger, too.
He'll meet you and treat you and ask you for your note,
But look out, boys, he's a-dodging for a note!

Chorus

Oh, we're all dodging, a-dodging, dodging, dodging,
Oh, we're all dodging our way through the world.

2 Oh, the lawyer he's a dodger, yes, a well-known dodger,
Oh, the lawyer he's a dodger, yes, and I'm a dodger, too.
He'll plead your case and claim you for a friend,
But look out boys, he's easy for to bend!

3 Oh, the preacher he's a dodger, yes, a well-known dodger,
Oh, the preacher he's a dodger, yes, and I'm a dodger, too.
He'll preach you the gospel and tell you of your crimes,
But look out, boys, he's a-dodging for your dimes!

4 Oh, the merchant he's a dodger, yes, a well-known dodger,
Oh, the merchant he's a dodger, yes, and I'm a dodger, too.
He'll sell you goods at double the price
And when you go to pay him, you'll have to pay him twice!

5 Oh, the farmer he's a dodger, yes, a well-known dodger,
Oh, the farmer he's a dodger, yes, and I'm a dodger, too.
He'll plow his cotton, he'll hoe his corn,
And he'll make a living just as sure as you're born!

6 Oh, the lover he's a dodger, yes, a well-known dodger,
Oh, the lover he's a dodger, yes, and I'm a dodger, too.
He'll hug you and kiss you and call you his bride,
But look out, girls, he's a-telling you a lie!

Thomas Dixon, Jr.'s *The Clansman* stirred excitement as a novel, as a play, and then as one of the first great motion pictures, *The Birth of a Nation*—the form in which modern audiences know it best. The history of this one piece of popular literature is a painfully apt symbol of the low point that black American efforts toward civil rights had reached in the period from about 1890 to 1910. (Thomas Dixon, Jr., "Why I Wrote *The Clansman*," *The Theatre* (Magazine), January 1900.)

THOMAS DIXON, JR.: WHY I WROTE THE CLANSMAN

The remarkable reception which has been given "The Clansman" in the South was in many respects a revelation to me.

As a novelist it was rather a stunning shock to find that the drama is so much more powerful a form of expression.

My ideas in narrative had met with an interesting reception from a large number of folks who read books, but the great masses of the people had not been reached by them. The same ideas translated into dramatic action and placed on the stage sweep entire communities off their feet. And this occurs without exception in every town and city in which the play is presented.

The performance has excited a great controversy in the Southern press. Long editorials are written on its motif and its probable effects on society and politics. Many of these editors have attacked the play with unrestrained fury—not by reason of its immorality or untruthfulness, but upon the remarkable ground that it stirs the audience to depths of emotion which obliterate reason and will cause riot and bloodshed.

Such a contention is, of course, childish twaddle, and yet the persistence with which this declaration is repeated by editors in nearly all the cities of the Black Belt of the South is but another pointer to the fact that the drama is by far the most powerful of all forms of art.

Why it has been apparently neglected by men who seek to revolutionize society can perhaps be accounted for in this country only by remembering that its technique is so difficult. And yet the very immensity of its difficulties should challenge the soul of genius to the highest reach of capacity.

To me the writing and production of this, my first play, has been the most thrilling work of my life, and I have had some stirring hours in other fields of labor.

As a student of higher mathematics in college I learned to calculate the horizontal parallax of the sun, fix the date of an eclipse of the moon, and find the position of a ship at sea from the chart of the stars. All this was child's play compared to the problems involved in the translation of the ideas of two volumes of narrative into a single unified swift action on the stage within the limits of three hours. After two years of systematic study of dramatic technique, it took me three months, working steadily sixteen hours a day, to accomplish this, a month to select the cast to interpret it and five weeks of rehearsals to condense the dialogue. . . .

Every step of this work has been supremely fascinating, and no single moment of it all quite so exciting as the first night in Norfolk when I stood in the wings with the manuscript in hand and watched with bated breath the actors feel for their lines and heard the thunder of the explosions of emotional dynamite in the hearts of my audience. I knew it was stored there if I could only reach it with a spark across those footlights.

Whether I actually found the hearts of my hearers can perhaps be best judged from the following words from the correspondent of the New York *Evening Post*, my bitterest enemy in the newspaper world. He is reporting the performance in Charleston, S. C., a month later, October 25, and says:

"As a potent factor in determing the future treatment of the gravest problem with which the country has to concern itself, and as a means of sowing the seed of revulsion for the black man, this play cannot well be ignored.

"Already 'The Clansman' is almost the sole subject of conversation in every Southern home where the news of its presentation has come. In the city of Charleston, the day following the two performances, press reports and published criticisms were eagerly read. The Southern newspapers are flooded with letters from prominent men who could not be induced to so advertise a dramatic production which had not as its issue a question of tremendously vital importance. Mr. Dixon has his audience. To those who have the future harmony of the two races at heart, the presentation of 'The Clansman' must come as a crushing blow.

"Picture, if you will, a Southern playhouse crowded to the doors on a sultry night with whites. There are no negroes in the gallery, which is unusual. The audience is of the best and the worst. There are present those to whom the ghastly picture of a land rent with race feud, aggravated by prejudice and by political buccaneering and chicanery, is little obscured by time. The younger generation, which had no part in the war and its disastrous sequel, is as bitter as the fathers. There is the spirit of the mob. There is something in the stolidness of the crowd, before the rise of the curtain, that is out of keeping with the temperament of the people. It is as if they were awaiting the return of the jury, knowing already what the verdict will be. They know, but they must hear it again, and again. The orchestra is playing a lively air—but an orchestra is superfluous. The people have not come to be amused—and that is a feature which is startlingly evident to every close observer.

"There is comedy, or what passes for comedy, in the play. True, there are laughs, but it is not hearty, wholesome laughter. There is an hysterical note in that laughter; and it hushes as if by common consent. Every reference to the maintenance of the power of the white race is greeted with a subdued roar.

"It is now many years since the first ill-advised production of Mrs. Stowe's 'Uncle Tom's Cabin.' Something like the tremendous wave of passion which that play wrought in the North, at a time when passion ran high, is being reproduced by 'The Clansman' in the South at a time when passion sleeps, but sleeps restlessly. In 'Uncle Tom's Cabin' the negro was shown at his best. In 'The Clansman' the negro is shown at his worst. The glamour of his love of humor, his songs and pleasures, his faithfulness, is stripped from him. True, there is a 'good nigger' in the play, and he evokes little interest. The daring pen of Mr. Dixon has presumed to place before the eyes of a Southern audience a picture approaching as nearly as possible to the 'unspeakable crime.'

"When the cause of the carpet-baggers and the Black League seemed in the ascendant there was hissing. But it was not such hissing as one hears directed toward the eyebrows of the villain in the ordinary melodrama. The whole house, from pit to roof, seethed. At times the actors could not go on."

The following extract from *The Times*, reporting the Chattanooga performance, gives a more friendly accent to the same message:

"Two audiences, which were by far the most demonstrative and sincerely enthusiastic that have ever witnessed a production at the Opera House, saw last night 'The Clansman,' laughed and cried, hissed and cheered, screamed and applauded as sensible men and women have never been known to do while witnessing a performance in Chattanooga.

"It is not within the province of a dramatic criticism to discuss the result upon a people of the production of a certain play, and nothing of this character will be attempted. We are concerned here merely with the strength of the play, the excellence of the cast and the enthusiasm with which the audience received it.

"If there has ever been produced in this country a play of such intense dramatic qualities, a play which holds the attention of the audience so closely, and one which excites to an almost inconceivable pitch, it has never been seen in Chattanooga. 'The Clansman' is so intense that one feels almost exhausted after witnessing the production and it produces an excitement so real as to almost breed violence."

When the success of the play was assured beyond a doubt on the first night the supreme consciousness of power over an audience was something I had never experienced before. For fifteen years I have lectured—often to crowds of 5,000 people. I know the feeling of an orator who holds an audience breathless on every word, and yet it was nothing compared to the joy of watching those two thousand people in that theatre live with me in laughter and tears, in hisses and cheers, the scenes of my play. I dreamed myself a musician, the fifty actors on the stage the living strings of a great harp which throbbed in unison with my own pulse-beat as I swept the souls of my listeners.

The accusation that I wrote "The Clansman" to appeal to prejudice or assault the negro race is, of course, the silliest nonsense. For the negro I have only the profoundest pity and the kindliest sympathy.

My play is a demonstration of the truth of Abraham Lincoln's words: "*There is a physical difference between the white and black races which will forever forbid them living together on terms of political and social equality.*" Believing this with his whole soul, Lincoln, up to the day of his death, urged Congress to colonize the negroes.

This nation must yet return to Lincoln's plan, or, within fifty years face a civil-racial war, the most horrible and cruel that ever blackened the annals of the world. I have given twenty years of patient study to this problem and I can see no other possible solution.

In my play I have sought National Unity through knowledge of the truth.

The Southern people vainly imagine they have solved the negro question by Jim Crow cars and Grandfather Clauses for the temporary disfranchisement of the blacks. They have overlooked the fundamental fact that this Nation is a democracy, not an aristocracy, and that equality—absolute equality, without one lying subterfuge—is the supreme law of our life.

When Mr. Roosevelt, whom I helped elect President, recently rode through the crowded streets of the South, the center of admiring eyes, a black shadow brooded over the fairest sky—a dark host lined one side of the street—a white host the other. With what different emotions they gazed on this wonderful man! At every banquet table of his triumphal tour an unbidden guest was there, grim, black, silent, nameless, yet seen by every eye! What of the future! This is the question I am trying to put to the American people North and South—reverently and yet boldly. I believe that the stage is the best medium for placing this tremendously vital question plainly before the whole people. My play cannot be misunderstood. In the fierce white glare of the footlights its purpose and the lesson it conveys become clear to every man and woman in this broad fair land of our. It is, indeed, the "writing on the wall." Will the American people heed its warning?

When Carry Nation published her oddly titled memoirs in 1908, the crusade for which she had fought thirty years, the prohibition of alcoholic beverage sales, was nearing its fruition. Actually dramatic tactics like Carry Nation's played less of a role in getting prohibition written into the Constitution than the quiet political lobbying of the Anti-Saloon League of America. (From Carry A. Nation, *The Use and Need of the Life of Carry A. Nation*, 1908.)

CARRY A. NATION: AUTOBIOGRAPHY

. . . I took a valise with me, and in that valise I put a rod of iron, perhaps a foot long, and as large around as my thumb. I also took a cane with me. I found out by smashing in Kiowa that I could use a rock but once, so I took the cane with me. I got down to Wichita about seven o'clock in the evening, that day, and went to the hotel near the Santa Fe depot and left my valise. I went up town to select the place I would begin at first. I went into about fourteen places, where men were drinking at bars, the same as they do in licensed places. The police standing with the others. This outrage of law and decency was in violation of the oaths taken by every city officer, including mayor and councilmen, and they were as much bound to destroy these joints as they would be to arrest a murderer, or break up a den of thieves, but many of these so-called officers encouraged the violation of the law and patronized these places. I have often explained that this was the scheme of politicians and brewers to make prohibition a failure, by encouraging in every way the violation of the constitution. I felt the outrage deeply, and would gladly have given my life to redress the wrongs of the people. As Esther said: "How can I see the desolation of my people? If I perish, I perish." (Esther 4:16.) As Patrick Henry said: "Give me liberty or give me death."

I finally came to the "Carey Hotel," next to which was called the Carey Annex or Bar. The first thing that struck me was the life-size picture of a naked woman, opposite the mirror. This was an oil painting with a glass over it, and was a very fine painting hired from the artist who painted it, to be put in that place for a vile purpose. I called to the bartender; told him he was insulting his own mother by having her form stripped naked and hung up in a place where it was not even decent for a woman to be in when she had her clothes on. I told him he was a law-breaker and that he should be behind prison bars, instead of saloon bars. He said nothing to me but walked to the back of his saloon. It is very significant that the picture of naked women are in saloons. Women are stripped of everything by them. Her husband is torn from her, she is robbed of her sons, her home, her food and her virtue, and then they strip her clothes off and hang her up bare in these dens of robbery and murder. Truly does a saloon make a woman bare of all things! The motive for doing this is to suggest vice, animating the animal in man and degrading the respect he should have for the sex to whom he owes his being, yes, his Savior also!

I decided to go to the Carey for several reasons. It was the most dangerous, being the finest. The low doggery will take the low and keep them low, but these so-called respectable ones will take the respectable, make them low, then kick them out. A poor vagabond applied to a bartender in one of these hells glittering with crystallized tears and fine fixtures. The man behind the bar said: "You get out, you disgrace my place." The poor creature, who had been his mother's greatest treasure, shuffled out toward the door. Another customer came in, a nice looking young man, with a good suit, a white collar, and looking as if he had plenty of money. The smiling bar-tender mixed a drink and was handing it to him. The poor vagabond from the door called out. "Five years ago, I came into your place, looking just like that young man. You have made me what you see me now. Give that drink to me and finish your work. Don't begin on him."

I went back to the hotel and bound the rod and cane together, then wrapped paper around the top of it. I slept but little that night, spending most of the night in prayer. I wore a large cape. I took the cane and walked down the back stairs the next morning, and out into the alley, I picked up as many rocks as I could carry under my cape. I walked into the Carey barroom, and threw two rocks at the picture; then turned and smashed the mirror that covered almost the entire side of the large room. Some men drinking at the bar ran out; the bar-tender was wiping a glass and he seemed transfixed to the spot and never moved. I took the cane and broke up the sideboard, which had on it all kinds of intoxicating drinks. Then I ran out across the street to destroy another one. I was arrested at 8:30 A.M., my rocks and cane taken from me, and I was taken to the police headquarters, where I was treated very nicely by the Chief of Police, Mr. Cubbin, who seemed to be amused at what I had done. This man was not very popular with the administration, and was soon put out. I was kept in the office until 6:30 P.M. Gov. Stanley was in town at that time, and I telephoned to several places for him. I saw that he was dodging me, so I called a messenger boy and sent a note to Gov. Stanley, telling him that I was unlawfully restrained of my liberty; that I wished him to call and see me, or try to relieve me in some way. The messenger told me, when he came back, that he caught him at his home, that he read the message over three times, then said: "I have nothing to say," and went in, and closed the door. This is the man who taught Sunday school in Wichita for twenty years, where they were letting these murder shops run in violation of the law. Strange that this man should pull wool over the eyes of the voters of Kansas. I never did have any confidence in him.

Kansas has learned some dear lessons, and she will be wise indeed when she learns that only Prohibitionists will enforce prohibition laws.

At 6:30 P.M., I was tried and taken to Wichita jail; found guilty of malicious mischief, Sam Amidon being the prosecuting attorney, and the friend of every joint keeper in the city. He called me a "spotter," when I wanted to give evidence against the jointists.

The legislature was to convene in a few days and it was understood that the question of re-submitting the Prohibition Amendment would come up. Being a part of the constitution, the people had to vote on it, and it was frustrating their plans to have such agitation at this time, and these republican leaders were determined to put a quietus upon me, if possible. The scheme was to get me in an insane asylum, and they wished to increase my insanity, as they called my zeal, so as to have me out of their way, for I was calling too much attention to their lawlessness, at this time, when it might prove disastrous to their plots. Two sheriffs conducted me to my cell. The sensation of being locked in such a place for the first time is not like any other, and never occurs the second time. These men watched me after the door was locked. I tried to be brave, but the tears were running down my face. I took hold of the iron bars of my door, and tried to shake them and said: "Never mind, you put me in here a cub, but I will go out a roaring lion and I will make all hell howl." I wanted to let them know that I was going to grow while in there.

Ward McAllister, distinguished hanger-on of high society, once remarked that there were only about 400 people worth knowing. This gave birth to the idea of "the 400," the social register that any city with social pretensions publishes to this day. In the late nineteenth century, the doings of "high society" made the front page. (From Ward McAllister, *Society as I Have Found It*, 1890.)

WARD MC ALLISTER: THE 400

I would now make some suggestions as to the proper way of introducing a young girl into New York society, particularly if she is not well supported by an old family connection. It is cruel to take a girl to a ball where she knows no one,

"And to subject her to
The fashionable stare of twenty score
Of well-bred persons, called the world."

Had I charged a fee for every consultation with anxious mothers on this subject, I would be a rich man. I well remember a near relative of mine once writing me from Paris, as follows: "I consign my wife and daughter to your care. They will spend the winter in New York; at once give them a ball at Delmonico's, and draw on me for the outlay." I replied, "My dear fellow, how many people do you know in this city whom you could invite to a ball? The funds you send me will be used, but not in giving a ball." The girl being a beauty, all the rest was easy enough. I gave her theatre party after theatre party, followed by charming little suppers, asked to them the *jeunesse dorée* of the day; took her repeatedly to the opera, and saw that she was there always surrounded by admirers; incessantly talked of her fascinations; assured my young friends that she was endowed with a fortune equal to the mines of Ophir, that she danced like a dream, and possessed all the graces, a sunbeam across one's path; then saw to it that she had a prominent place in every cotillion, and a fitting partner; showed her whom to smile upon, and on whom to frown; gave her the *entrée* to all the nice houses; criticised severely her toilet until it became perfect; daily met her on the Avenue with the most charming man in town, who by one pretext or another I turned over to her; made her the constant subject of conversation; insisted upon it that she was to be the belle of the coming winter; advised her parents that she should have her first season at Bar Harbor, where she could learn to flirt to her heart's content, and vie with other girls. Her second summer, when she was older, I suggested her passing at Newport, where she should have a pair of ponies, a pretty trap, with a well-gotten-up groom, and Worth to dress her. Here I hinted that much must depend on her father's purse, as to her wardrobe. As a friend of mine once said, to me, "Your pace is charming, but can you keep it up?" I also advised keeping the young girl well in hand and not letting her give offense to the powers that be; to see to it that she was not the first to arrive and the last to leave a ball, and further, that nothing was more winning in a girl than a pleasant bow and a gracious smile given to either young or old. The fashion now for women is to hold themselves erect. The modern manner of shaking hands I do not like, but yet it is adopted. Being interested in the girl's success, I further impressed upon her the importance of making herself agreeable to older people, remembering that much of her enjoyment would be derived from them. If asked to dance a cotillion, let it be conditional that no bouquet be sent her; to be cautious how she refused the first offers of marriage made her, as they were generally the best.

A word, just here, to the newly married. It works well to have the man more in love with you than you are with him. My advice to all young married women is to keep up flirting with their husbands as much after marriage as before; to make themselves as attractive to their husbands after their marriage as they were when they captivated them; not to neglect their toilet, but rather improve it; to be as coquettish and coy after they are bound together as before, when no ties held them. The more they are appreciated by the world, the more will their husbands value them. In fashionable life, conspicuous jealousy is a mistake. A woman is bound to take and hold a high social position. In this way she advances and strengthens her husband. How many women we see who have benefited their husbands, and secured for them these advantages.

A young girl should be treated like a bride when she makes her *début* into society. Her relatives should rally around her and give her entertainments to welcome her into the world which she is to adorn. It is in excessive bad taste for such relatives to in any way refer to the cost of these dinners, balls, etc. Every one in society knows how to estimate such things. Again, at such dinners, it is not in good taste to load your table with *bonbonnières* and other articles intended to be taken away by your guests. This reminds me of a dear old lady, who, when I dined with her, always insisted on my putting in my dress coat pocket a large hothouse peach, which never reached home in a perfect state.

The launching of a beautiful young girl into society is one thing; it is another to place her family on a good, sound social footing. You can launch them into the social sea, but can they float? "Manners maketh man," is an old proverb. These they certainly must possess. There is no society in the world as generous as New York society is; "friend, parent, neighbor, all it will embrace," but once embraced they must have the power of sustaining themselves. The best quality for them to possess is modesty in asserting their claims; letting people seek them rather than attempting to rush too quickly to the front. The Prince of Wales, on a charming American young woman expressing her surprise at the cordial reception given her by London society, replied, "My dear lady, there are certain people who are bound to come to the front and stay there; you are one of them." It requires not only money, but brains, and, above all, infinite tact; possessing the three, your success is assured. If taken by the hand by a person in society you are at once led into the charmed circle, and then your own correct perceptions of what should or should not be done must do the rest. As a philosophical friend once said to me, "A gentleman can always walk, but he cannot afford to have a shabby equipage." Another philosopher soliloquized as follows: "The first evidence of wealth is your equipage." By the way, his definition of aristocracy in America was, the possession of hereditary wealth.

If you want to be fashionable, be always in the company of fashionable people. As an old beau suggested to me, If you see a fossil of a man, shabbily dressed, relying solely on his pedigree, dating back to time immemorial, who has the aspirations of a duke and the fortunes of a footman, do not cut him; it is better to cross the street and avoid meeting him. It is well to be in with the nobs who are born to their position, but the support of the swells is more advantageous, for society is sustained and carried on by the swells, the nobs looking quietly on and accepting the position, feeling they are there by divine right; but they do not make fashionable society, or carry it on. A nob can be a swell if he chooses, i.e. if he will spend the money; but for his social existence this is unnecessary. A nob is like a poet,—*nascitur non fit;* not so a swell,—he creates himself.

The influence of black music on American popular culture is deep and continuous. When W. E. B. DuBois wrote about "The Sorrow Songs" this influence ran the full gamut from the most "spiritual" to the earthiest, from the religious slave songs to the atrocious and raucous "coon" songs of the nineties. (From W. E. B. DuBois, *The Souls of Black Folk,* 1903.)

W. E. B. DU BOIS: BLACK MUSIC

The Sorrow Songs

I walk through the churchyard
    To lay this body down;
I know moon-rise, I know star-rise;
I walk in the moonlight, I walk in the starlight;
I'll lie in the grave and stretch out my arms,
I'll go to judgment in the evening of the day,
And my soul and thy soul shall meet that day,
    When I lay this body down.

NEGRO SONG.

They that walked in darkness sang songs in the olden days—Sorrow Songs—for they were weary at heart. And so before each thought that I have written in this book I have set a phrase, a haunting echo of these weird old songs in which the soul of the black slave spoke to men. Ever since I was a child these songs have stirred me strangely. They came out of the South unknown to me, one by one, and yet at once I knew them as of me and of mine. Then in after years when I came to Nashville I saw the great temple builded of these songs towering over the pale city. To me Jubilee Hall seemed ever made of the songs themselves, and its bricks were red with the blood and dust of toil. Out of them rose for me morning, noon, and night, bursts of wonderful melody, full of the voices of my brothers and sisters, full of the voices of the past.

Little of beauty has America given the world save the rude grandeur God himself stamped on her bosom; the human spirit in this new world has expressed itself in vigor and ingenuity rather than in beauty. And so by fateful chance the Negro folk-song—the rhythmic cry of the slave—stands to-day not simply as the sole American music, but as the most beautiful expression of human experience born this side of the seas. It has been neglected, it has been, and is, half despised, and above all it has been persistently mistaken and misunderstood; but notwithstanding, it still remains as the singular spiritual heritage of the nation and the greatest gift of the Negro people. . . .

What are these songs, and what do they mean? I know little of music and can say nothing in technical phrase, but I know something of men, and knowing them, I know that these songs are the articulate message of the slave to the world. They tell us in these eager days that life was joyous to the black slave, careless and happy. I can easily believe this of some, of many. But not all the past South, though it rose from the dead, can gainsay the heart-touching witness of these songs. They are the music of an unhappy people, of the children of disappointment; they tell of death and suffering and unvoiced longing toward a truer world, of misty wanderings and hidden ways.

The songs are indeed the siftings of centuries; the music is far more ancient than the words, and in it we can trace here and there signs of development. My grandfather's grandmother was seized by an evil Dutch trader two centuries ago; and coming to the valleys of the Hudson and Housatonic, black, little, and lithe, she shivered and shrank in the harsh north winds, looked longingly at the hills, and often crooned a heathen melody to the child between her knees. . . .

The child sang it to his children and they to their children's children, and so two hundred years it has travelled down to us and we sing it to our children, knowing as little as our fathers what its words may mean, but knowing well the meaning of its music.

This was primitive African music; it may be seen in larger form in the strange chant which heralds "The Coming of John":

"You may bury me in the East,
You may bury me in the West,
But I'll hear the trumpet sound in that morning,"

—the voice of exile.

Ten master songs, more or less, one may pluck from this forest of melody—songs of undoubted Negro origin and wide popular currency, and songs peculiarly characteristic of the slave. One of these I have just mentioned. Another whose strains begin this book is "Nobody knows the trouble I've seen." When, struck with a sudden poverty, the United States refused to fulfil its promises of land to the freedmen, a brigadier-general went down to the Sea Islands to carry the news. An old woman on the outskirts of the throng began singing this song; all the mass joined with her, swaying. And the soldier wept.

The third song is the cradle-song of death which all men know, —"Swing low, sweet chariot,"—whose bars begin the life story of "Alexander Crummell." Then there is the song of many waters, "Roll, Jordan, roll," a mighty chorus with minor cadences. There were many songs of the fugitive like that which opens "The Wings of Atalanta," and the more familiar "Been a-listening." The seventh is the song of the End and the Beginning—"My Lord, what a mourning! when the stars begin to fall"; a strain of this is placed before "The Dawn of Freedom." The song of groping—"My way's cloudy"—begins "The Meaning of Progress"; the ninth is the song of this chapter—"Wrestlin' Jacob, the day is a-breaking"—a paean of hopeful strife. The last master song is the song of songs —"Steal away,"—sprung from "The Faith of the Fathers."

There are many others of the Negro folk-songs as striking and characteristic as these, as, for instance, the three strains in the third, eighth, and ninth chapters; and others I am sure could easily make a selection on more scientific principles. There are, too, songs that seem to me a step removed from the more primitive types: there is the maze-like medley, "Bright sparkles," one phrase of which heads "The Black Belt"; the Easter carol, "Dust, dust and ashes"; the dirge, "My mother's took her flight and gone home"; and that burst of melody hovering over "The Passing of the First-Born"—"I hope my mother will be there in that beautiful world on high."

These represent a third step in the development of the slave song, of which "You may bury me in the East" is the first, and songs like "March on (chapter six) and "Steal away" are the second. The first is African music, the second Afro-American, while the third is a blending of Negro music with the music heard in the foster land. The result is still distinctively Negro and the methods of blending original, but the elements are both Negro and Caucasian. One might go further and find a fourth step in this development, where the songs of white America have been distinctively influenced by the slave songs or have incorporated whole phrases of Negro melody, as "Swanee River" and "Old Black Joe." Side by side, too, with the growth has gone the debasements and imitations—the Negro "minstrel" songs, many of the "gospel" hymns, and some of the contemporary "coon" songs,—a mass of music in which the novice may easily lose himself and never find the real Negro melodies. . . .

Let us cheer the weary traveller,
Cheer the weary traveller,
Let us cheer the weary traveller,
Along the heavenly way.

And the traveller girds himself, and sets his face toward the Morning, and goes his way.

The Boll Weevil

1   The boll weevil is a little black bug
Come from Mexico they say,
Come all the way to Texas
Just a-lookin' for a place to stay.

Chorus
Just a-lookin' for a home,
Just a-lookin' for a home,
Just a-lookin' for a home,
Just a-lookin' for a home.

2   The first time I seen the boll weevil,
     He was settin' on the square;
     The next time I seen the boll weevil,
     He had all his family there.

3   The farmer took the boll weevil
     And buried him in hot sand;
     The boll weevil say to the farmer,
     "I'll stand it like a man."

4   Then the farmer took the boll weevil
     And left him on the ice;
     The boll weevil say to the farmer,
     "This is mighty cool and nice."

5   The farmer took the boll weevil
     And fed him on paris green;
     The boll weevil say to the farmer,
     "It's the best I ever seen."

6   The boll weevil say to the farmer
     "You better let me alone;
     I et up all your cotton
     And now I'll start on the corn."

7   The merchant got half the cotton,
     The boll weevil got the rest;
     Didn't leave the poor old farmer
     But one old cotton dress.

8   The farmer say to the merchant,
     "I ain't made but one bale,
     But before I'll give you that one,
     I'll fight and go to jail."

9   If anyone should ask you
     Who was it made this song,
     Tell him 'twas a poor farmer
     With a pair of blue duckin's on.

Swing Low, Sweet Chariot

Chorus
Swing low, sweet chariot,

Coming for to carry me home,
Swing low, sweet chariot,
Coming for to carry me home.

1 I looked over Jordan, and what did I see,
Coming for to carry me home?
A band of angels coming after me,
Coming for to carry me home.

2 If you get there before I do,
Coming for to carry me home?
To all my friends I'm coming too,
Coming for to carry me home.

3 The brightest day that ever I saw,
Coming for to carry me home?
When Jesus wash'd my sins away,
Coming for to carry me home.

4 I'm sometimes up and sometimes down.
Coming for to carry me home?
But still my soul feels heavenly bound,
Coming for to carry me home.

Loveless Love

1 Love is like a gold brick in a bunco game
Like a banknote with a bogus name
Both have caused many downfalls
Love has done the same
Love has for its emblem Cupid with his bow
Loveless love has lots and lots of dough
So carry lots of Jack and pick'em as you go
For Love, oh love, oh loveness love
Has set our hearts on goalless goals
From milkless milk, and silkless silk
We are growing used to soulless souls
Such grafting times we never saw
That's why we have a pure food law,
In ev'rything we find a flaw,
Even love, oh love, oh loveless love.

2 Love is like a hydrant—it turns off and on
Like some friendships when your money's gone
Love stands in with the loan sharks
when your hearts in pawn

If I had some strong wings like an aeroplane
Had some broad wings like an aeroplane
I would fly away forever ne'er to come again
For Love, oh love, oh loveless love.
You set our hearts on goalless goals,
With dreamless dreams and schemeless scheme,
We wreck our love boats on the shoals,
We S.O.S. by wireless wire
And in the wreckage of desire,
We sigh for wings like Noah's dove
Just to fly away from loveless love.

Of all the musical fads revolving around the peculiarities of white Americans' responses to blacks, the crudest and one of the best known was the "Coon Songs" that were such a rage in the 1890s until they were replaced by the far more genuine cultural article, ragtime. "All Coons Look Alike to Me," perhaps the most offensive of the lot, was written by a black man, Ernest Hogan. He received the denunciation he deserved from other blacks. "Nigger, Nigger Never Die" is interesting because behind all the vile racism of the song is a demand for dignity and a call to militancy.

COON SONGS

Nigger, Nigger Never Die

1   When I was a Pickaninny, my mamma sent me to school,
She said, Boy, your old enough to go and learn the golden rule
At the Branch school where she sent me all the other Kids were white,
Every morning noon and evening, with these Kids I had to fight,
If at study I should whisper, someone would be sure to tell
When we went to play at recess, all the white Kids at me yell, Oh,

Chorus
Nigger, Nigger, never die, black face and a china eye,
Mouth as big as a steamboat slip, Indian rubber nose and a liver lip
Eny, meny, miny, mo, catch a nigger by the toe
Nigger eat scrap iron, nigger chew glue.

2   And when I grew up to manhood, I took unto myself a wife,
    The prettiest little black gal, that you ever seen in all your life
    After years of love an happiness, we had pickaninnys too,
    That used to play and fight the white Kids, like their daddy used
        to do,
    If I'd catch them I would scold them, I would make the youngsters
        tell
    They'd say daddy while we are playing, all the white Kids at us
        yell, Oh,

Chorus
Nigger, Nigger, never die, black face and a china eye,
Mouth as big as a steamboat slip, Indian rubber nose and a liver lip
Eny, meny, miny, mo, catch a nigger by the toe
Nigger eat scrap iron, nigger chew glue.

All Coons Look Alike To Me

1   Talk about a coon a having trouble,
    I think I have enough of ma own,
    Its all about ma Lucy Janey Stubbles,
    And she has caused my heart to mourn,
    Thar's another coon barber from Virginia,
    In soci'ty he's the leader of the day,
    And now ma honey gal is gwine to quit me,
    Yes she's gone and drove this coon away,
    She'd no excuse, to turn me loose,
    I've been abused, I'm all confused,
    Cause these words she did say . . .

Chorus
All coons look alike to me,
I've got another beau, you see,
And he's just as good to me
As you, nig! ever tried to be,
He spends his money free,
I know we can't agree
So I don't like you no how,
All coons look alike to me.

2   Never said a word to hurt her feelings,
    I always bou't her presents by the score,
    And now my brain with sorrow am a reeling,
    Cause she won't accept them any more,

If I treated her wrong she may have loved me,
Like all the rest she's gone and let me down,
If I'm lucky I'm a gwine to catch my policy,
And win my sweet thing way from town,
For I'm worried, Yes, I'm desp'rate,
I've been Jonahed, and I'll get dang'rous,
If these words she says to me . . .

Chorus
All coons look alike to me,
I've got another beau, you see,
And he's just as good to me
As you, nig! ever tried to be,
He spends his money free,
I know we can't agree
So I don't like you no how,
All coons look alike to me.

the movies

Heroes, villains, manners, morals, hopes, dreams, truth, and fantasy: this is the heady broth of the sights and sounds of the movies. Exhibited at the turn of the century in nickelodeons (literally five-cent theaters), movies became longer in duration, greater in cultural importance, and certainly higher in cost for both producer and viewer. By the 1970s some exhibitors charged $5.00 for reserved seats. Yet there are still inexpensive movies—turn on the television; all you pay is time out for advertisements.

The film stills and commentary in this collection are meant to give an indication of the range of visual styles and thematic materials in American movies. The importance of "stars" in movie history is only briefly indicated. The audience does not only ogle idols in movie theaters; it observes itself, its desires, and its realities.

To order films for classroom use, consult: James L. Limbacher, compiler. *Feature Films on 8 mm and 16 mm: A Directory of Feature Films Available for Rental, Sale and Lease in the United States, 3rd ed.* New York: R. R. Bowker Co., 1971.

The Musketeers of Pig Alley, 1912. Filmed on real city streets as well as in a studio, this story of struggling slum dwellers indicates the appetite of audiences for social realism.

The Perils of Pauline, 1914. Pearl White, the Queen of the Serial Adventure—a form which flourished well into the 1940s—is making things perilous for an anonymous villain. The serials were exhibited in weekly installments, usually twelve, and done as damsel-in-distress, crime, Western, war and science-fiction stories.

The Birth of A Nation, 1915. D. W. Griffith's film of the Civil War and Reconstruction was the first "epic"; the grandeur of the battle scenes and the grace of camera movements and editing combine to make it a still absorbing drama. Unfortunately much of the plot is rooted in racial prejudice; one of the NAACP's early activities was protest marches against its exhibition. Censorship of the movies, which came about intermittently and mostly through industry self-policing, was always directed against sex, occasionally violence, but almost never against racial prejudice or political beliefs.

Easy Street, 1917. Charlie Chaplin ingeniously subdues the bully with gas from the street lamp. Slapstick short movies were so popular that several companies profited through producing only one- and two-reel comedies.

Cleopatra, 1917. Theda Bara demonstrating why men were supposed to go mad with desire for the "vamp." Woman-as-vampire destroyed men through sex. This sort of story flourished at the height of the women's rights movement.

The Little American, 1917. Mary Pickford projected quite a different image of the female, here menaced by the Kaiser's minions. Pickford was the foremost of the actresses who portrayed child-women, dependent on heroic men to protect and, particularly, marry them.

Don't Change Your Husband, 1918. Gloria Swanson in a moment of domestic distress. Directed by Cecil B. De Mille, this was one of the first dramas of middle class life. De Mille's grandiose notions of interior decoration influenced other film makers and probably popular taste as well.

The Four Horsemen of the Apocalypse, 1921. A publicity shot of Rudolph Valentino in the role that made him a star. The Latin Lover type remained popular into the 1930s and reflected the influence of women as ticket buyers.

Safety Last, 1923. Harold Lloyd in an interesting predicament. Lloyd specialized in playing the ordinary fellow who got into hilarious and often hair-raising situations. This type of comedy, later dubbed "sitcoms," would be the dominant comedy of radio and television.

The Thief of Bagdad, 1924. Douglas Fairbanks, right, created the athletic adventure film. He was the personification of the swashbuckler. Fairy-tale fantasies were popular in the 1920s; the wedding of Arabian Nights' lore and athleticism was the best of this type.

William S. Hart in a typical pose as the lone Westerner. In the 1920s Hart was the preeminent star of Westerns, a form which has always been a staple of movie production. Hart's films contributed to the mythology of the cowboy, but the physical details of the settings and some of the plot elements had a gritty reality which would reappear only much later. The stylized Western with its laundered and ironed cowboys dominated the form.

Our Dancing Daughters, 1928. Joan Crawford and friends show what "flaming youth" was all about. Crawford is the theatrically longest-lived star; her roles are near to a micro-history of the position and aspirations of middle-class women in America.

Little Caesar, 1930. Edward G. Robinson, as the gangster boss, receives a calling card from a rival gang. While flaming youth was being extinguished by the deepening Depression, the suppliers of their fuel, the bootleggers, became the movie rage. Gangsters confused the categories of hero and villain: they made money on sound things like cupidity, greed, and fear—things not subject to business cycles.

I Am A Fugitive From A Chain Gang, 1932. Paul Muni played an unjustly imprisoned man (based on a true story) in a drama that symbolized the fate of thousands caught not in legal toils but in social and economic forces they were helpless to combat. At the end, asked how he lives, Muni replies, "I steal!"

Dracula, 1930. The true escapist films, which require the audience to work up a self-induced fright, are the horror and monster fantasies. Originally produced for the general market, they were increasingly made for the developing youth audience.

The Mask of Fu-Manchu, 1932. Boris Karloff as the insidious Dr. Fu-Manchu is about to work his will on the drugged youth. Fu Manchu was a comic-strip racist story, but it typifies attitudes toward Asians in a period when many movies were set in the European colonies of Asia. Hollywood profitably shouldered the White Man's Burden. Sessue Hayakawa had been the hero of a number of American films for a few years after the First World War, but by the 1930s Asians were almost exclusively coolies or cruel villains. Equally pernicious was the treatment of blacks; they were presented as lovable idiots or loyal servants to white masters; if "natives" in Africa, they were fools, totally manipulated by whites.

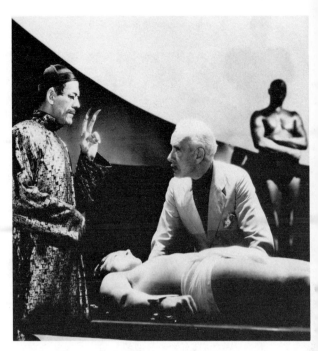

A shot of a human kaleidoscope from a Busby Berkeley musical of the 1930s. Berkeley's musicals usually were stories of backstage life, silly but enjoyable. He was the only movie maker successfully to commercialize surrealism by disguising it as a production number.

Fred Astaire and Ginger Rogers danced through the 1930s in gay, romantic, and elegant musicals. Astaire's diffident grace was the musical version of the 1930s model lover.

A Night At the Opera, 1935. The Marx Brothers' anarchic mayhem was the sound movies' equivalent of silent slapstick: self-importance, pomposity, and supposed expertise were always the objects of Marxian ridicule.

Twentieth Century, 1934. Carole Lombard gapes at John Barrymore as she catches him in another fantastic lie. This film and *It Happened One Night* (1934) began a cycle of movies known as "screwball comedies." Eccentricity and upper-class manners were the genial plot-mix in these stories.

Mr. Deeds Goes to Town, 1936. Gary Cooper, center, played a man who gave away his unexpected inheritance to needy farmers despite the legal machinations of those who claimed he was insane to give up twenty million dollars. This and other social comedies created by Frank Capra proclaimed the ultimate triumph of goodness and individuality over institutional and social pressures.

Wee Willie Winkie, 1937. The greatest child star was Shirley Temple. In this film she helped her grandfather's regiment protect the British Empire. The Empire was the subject of numerous costume adventure films in the 1930s; needless to say British soldiers were inevitably the heroes of these stories.

Dead End, 1937. This publicity shot shows of the Dead End kids at their boyish recreations. In their initial appearance, these slum dwellers were the object of pity and reform, but their tough-talking urban juvenile spunk was popular enough to launch a series of films that lasted to the late 1940s. The middle-class teenage films such as Andy Hardy and Henry Aldrich appealed principally to adults. The Bowery Boys, as the Kids were later called, made heroes of teenagers and appealed to the Saturday matinee audience.

Confessions of a Nazi Spy, 1939. Based on an exposé of the German-American Bund and the Nazi spy organization in the United States, the film aroused protests from America First and other isolationist groups. It was only the forerunner of a number of anti-Nazi films that appeared before America entered the Second World War.

Gone With the Wind, 1939. The Civil War and Reconstruction was the setting for perhaps the most entertaining film made in America. History, costumes, indirect social commentary, and, above all, romance, made a dazzling mixture. The South depicted in the film was not entirely the stuff of myths, as the still indicates, but Scarlett, Rhett, Ashley, and Melanie, the principal characters, were the perfect embodiments of Romance.

Edison the Man, 1940. The Great Man's Life pictures which flourished in the 1930s and 1940s are typified by this film about the Wizard of Menlo Park, starring Spencer Tracy. Edison is the only American, excepting Lincoln, to be the subject of two full-dress biographies. The year before, Mickey Rooney had played *Edison the Boy.* Biographical subjects ranged from medical heroes to political leaders to sports figures to show business personalities and included a handful of businessmen. Their plot lines went little beyond Horatio Alger explanations of what led to success and renown. *Patton* (1970) demonstrated that audiences could grasp more sophisticated ideas about a public man's behavior.

The Grapes of Wrath, 1940. The plight of tenant farmers during the Depression and Dust Bowl of the 1930s, the bitter lives of migrant agricultural workers and the dauntless strength of the American family were the themes of this film. Social criticism as a movie subject vanished until after the War, then returned not as protests against economic inequalities but as attacks on racial and ethnic prejudice.

Citizen Kane, 1941. The technical audacity of twenty-six-year-old Orson Welles in presenting the thinly disguised story of William Randolph Hearst made this the single most influential film since *Birth of A Nation.* By purposefully fictionalizing biography, *Citizen Kane* convincingly exposed the egomania, greed and finally sentimentality that were the well-springs of a supposedly great man's life.

Yankee Doodle Dandy, 1942. This biography of stage star George M. Cohan, played by James Cagney, emphasized Cohan's unreserved flag-waving patriotism. Variations on its plot were the substance of the endless musicals produced during the War. 1940s musicals added the fillip of provocatively clad females to satisfy the public appetite for pin-up girls.

Casablanca, 1942. Humphrey Bogart and Dooley Wilson inside "Rick's Cafe." *Casablanca* merged romance with contemporary history; anti-Nazism was not only morally necessary, it was glamorous. Americans found their twentieth century hero in the wary, grave face of Bogie. What Ernest Hemingway and later Norman Mailer defined as heroism, Bogart personified in this and most of his subsequent roles.

The North Star, 1943. An anxious group of our brave Russian allies face the Nazi menace. Several war time movies celebrated the resistance groups in occupied Europe and even the good, i.e., anti-Nazi, Germans; those movies that praised the Russians would be the starting point for the anti-communist Hollywood witch hunt in the late 1940s.

Guadalcanal Diary, 1943. Based on a journalist's account of the Marine Corps victory in the Pacific, this movie typified the semi-documentary war story. The plot embodied an important convention of World War II films: it followed the fortunes of one platoon and extolled the heroism of an ethnically mixed group.

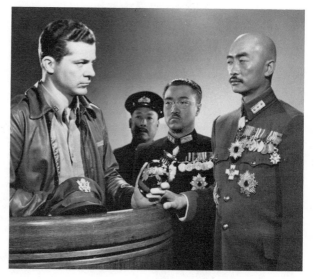

The Purple Heart, 1944. Prisoner of war Dana Andrews stoically resists his cruel captors. "Japs" in the movies were as fanatic and brutal as Nazis. After 1945 the Japanese were presented more sympathetically in American films than the Germans, but not until *Go For Broke!* (1951), the story of the Nisei combat group that fought in Europe, was the existence of Japanese Americans approvingly pictured.

Wonder Man, 1945. Danny Kaye stifles S. Z. "Cuddles" Sakall's splutterings. Kaye began in the mid-war years to create a type of comedy somewhere between that of the Marx Brothers and Harold Lloyd; he was nutty but presentable enough to be a romantic suitor. Chaplin, Buster Keaton, and Kaye are the unique clowns. They combined sweetness and poignancy with laughter.

Meet Me In Saint Louis, 1945. Margaret O'Brien and Judy Garland entertain the family circle. Set in the St. Louis World Fair at the turn of the century, this musical was the best of the numerous movies marked by nostalgia for the good old days. This sanitized view of the past, which was very popular through the early 1950s, appealed to family audiences. When television became the family entertainment, the motion picture industry increasingly made films to cater to varying audiences representing fragmented age and social groupings.

The Best Years of Our Lives, 1946. Harold Russell, Dana Andrews, and Fredric March played three vets returning to their small city. The difficulties of readjustment for vets and civilians were presented soberly, especially in the rôle played by Russell, a real veteran who had lost both hands in combat. Dana Andrews's rôle suggested that the war, which broke the social and economic constraints of the past, might itself have been the best years of some lives: status then depended upon a uniform and medals, not a bank account.

Gentlemen's Agreement, 1947. Gregory Peck and John Garfield were the principals in this attack on anti-Semitism. In the immediate post-war years a number of films about racial and ethnic prejudice appeared, but the form petered out owing to audience lack of interest. New enemies of American well-being, the Communists, absorbed public attention.

Fort Apache, 1948. John Ford's films of the West fixed a legend of American history forever. The awesome scenery of the Southwest joined to exaltation of military virtues, duty, honor, obedience, and the superiority of white civilization created an epic, if false, view of American continental expansion. Henry Fonda and John Wayne, the principal players, specialized in American types. Fonda has played more real and fictional political figures than any other leading actor; he was the intelligent Liberal. Wayne played the rough and ready man who used violence to good or necessary ends; he was the Patriot.

All the King's Men, 1949. Political demagoguery was the subject in this study of a career not unlike the career of Huey Long in Louisiana. Few American films have been as convincing in their depiction of the realities and frightening possibilities of our political system. Broderick Crawford, slouched in the chair, holds court.

The Day the Earth Stood Still, 1951. The first widely popular science fiction film was an anti-atomic weapons fable. Mars sent a representative to Earth with a warning that the "other planets" would not tolerate atomic warfare: peaceful coexistence was mandatory. Science fiction movies subsequently were either adventure stories about "monsters," or, less often, comments on politics and social structure. Atomic-disaster stories, such as *On the Beach* (1959), took up the political message of the 1951 movie with grimly realistic pictorial detail.

The Robe, 1953. Moviemakers attempted to boost the waning attendance at theaters by many means; wide-screens and "spectacle" seemed to succeed best. Spectacle was suited to lavish musicals or costume dramas. *The Robe* exemplifies the Bible or Christian epic that was particularly popular in the 1950s and 1960s. Both *Ben Hur* and *The Ten Commandments* had been filmed previously as silents. *Spartacus* (1960) and *Cleopatra* (1963) were unusual epics because they attempted political commentary and sought historical accuracy.

Night People, 1954. Gregory Peck as an Army Intelligence officer fought the Communists in occupied Berlin. Cold War stories explicitly showed that devious means were the only successful tactics in fighting the Communist Menace. The moral implications of such behavior were ignored.

Blackboard Jungle, 1955. Juvenile delinquency and rebellious youth furnished themes for many films in the 1950s and after. This movie, centering on the experiences of an urban slum school teacher, paid tribute also to the developing youth culture. It was the first major film to have a rock'n'roll musical score. The definitive statement of hostility to established norms was uttered by Marlon Brando in *The Wild One* (1953). Asked what he is rebelling against, the chieftain of the "Black Rebels Motorcycle Club" replies, "Whaddaya got?"

The Defiant Ones, 1958. Tony Curtis and Sidney Poitier played escaped convicts chained together. The story implied that blacks and whites could survive only through co-operation. Poitier's career illustrates the changing position of blacks in American society. He started in anti-prejudice films and ultimately became the first black romantic hero.

Pollyanna, 1960. The sentimental 1912 novel about a "Glad Girl" who helped all the crusty adults see the bright side of life was ideal material for the company which brought to perfection the family movie. Walt Disney's financial success—from mouse to millions—was based on a P. T. Barnum-like ability to delight the public.

Dr. Strangelove, or, How I Stopped Worrying and Learned to Love the Atomic Bomb, 1964. A bitter satire of American politics and the Cold War, *Dr. Strangelove* put the blame for atomic disaster on the fathomless idiocy of humans. Other films in the genre declared technology the culprit. *The Bedford Incident* (1965) also blamed human fallibility, but as the title suggests implied that "error" was controllable.

Beach Blanket Bingo, 1965. Movies catering to the teenage audience were so lucrative in the 1960s that one production company, American Independent, became a great success by aiming exclusively at the teen market. The AIP film *Wild In the Streets* (1968) exploited youthful political protest activities in a weak satire about a teenager elected President of the United States.

Who's Afraid of Virginia Woolf?, 1966. Adults could still be drawn into theaters, as the popularity of this film demonstrated. If the movie's message about the moral rot of the middle class was ignored, the verbal freedom of the dialog excited public interest. Within a few years censorship, in the form of ratings to determine the suitability of films for different age groups, was again established by the motion picture industry.

Easy Rider, 1969. The glorification of youth and a seemingly foot-loose "life style" made *Easy Rider* enormously profitable. It was the teen movie raised to the level of art, for it suggested that the true radicalism of youth was not direct political protest but different attitudes toward material possessions and sexuality. *Easy Rider* was about the domestic Cold War: the war between the "generations."

part 2 the electronic age: since 1910

In the years immediately before World War I American culture began to assume its characteristic modern form. Movies, phonograph records, and radio initiated the age of electronic media in which we continue to live.

New styles of life indicated a revolt against Victorian conventions. The divorce rate climbed toward the level it has since maintained. The first novels and psychological studies about adolescence suggested that a new character was entering the American consciousness—the teenager. The city meant home to millions of Americans, and popular culture began to reflect the triumph of urban values as apartments began to compete with houses. The automobile started to nibble away at the American environment like a colony of soldier ants beginning their hectic multiplication. Hemlines commenced their ascent, and women started to shorten ("bob") their hair and discard their corsets. Mrs. Ida Rosenthal, an enterprising New York seamstress, invented the uplift brassiere in the early 1920s and American women—literally—assumed their definitive modern form.

The new age took a more complex and ambiguous view of life than had the confident nineteenth century. While much of the anxiety that infused high culture bypassed the merrier popular mind, still popular styles and interests assuredly had lost some of their artlessness. The how-to-do-it industry boomed on every front, but the advice deluging the public suggested a world of hard decisions and complicated choices. Childrearing became something to learn from a book and thanks to government agencies such knowledge filtered down into mass society. An age that made Albert Einstein a popular hero and model for young boys (far less often for young girls) to imitate must have known that the world was a deep and hard place to fathom. Similarly, the image of World War I with its trench warfare and clouds of mustard gas contrasted sharply with the visions of daring that had emerged from the Civil War. Only the aviators offered the hint that some new world of individual heroism still remained open to venturesome men and women, a hint that men like Charles A. Lindbergh and women like Amelia Earhart took.

This more complicated world nurtured an increasingly elaborate set of mechanisms for escaping from it. Movies, radio, phonographs, although they offered more than just escape and entertainment, made these their principal commodity. Forms developed in the age of vaudeville set the tone for the electronic media that followed; radio and television especially owed much to the old comics, singers, specialty acts, pretty girls, and trained animals that travelled the old vaudeville circuits. The movies relied rather more on the form they replaced: the popular melodramas of the nineteenth century. Yet all these media soon outgrew their perhaps dubious parentage. The ancestry of Amos 'n' Andy, rooted in vaudeville and even further back in coon and minstrel shows, soon became diffused through long-term identification with the characters of Amos, Andy and the Kingfish by radio listeners and television audiences after them; this process demonstrated the power of the new medium. The panic induced by Orson Welles's presentation of "The War of the Worlds" offers a vivid illustration of the way Americans made radio a part of their imaginations. Similarly, radio—rising above escapist functions—gave a new immediacy to international news, notably in the crises of the 1930s and of World War II that H. V. Kaltenborn and Edward R. Murrow covered "live." And people who had never seen a crew race or a football game thrilled to the play-by-play radio broadcasts of Bill Stern, Ted Husing, or Red Barber.

Television proved an even more powerful medium. Sponsors studied closely the "rating" that shows received; and commercials, sometimes quite entertaining, consumed larger and larger chunks of available talent. Overall television introduced a new sophistication into American life, bringing distant events and new trends instantly into living rooms, along with situation comedies, canned laughter, children's cartoons, soap operas, and talk shows. The rest of American culture—high, low, and middle brow—scrambled to catch up with this remarkable new audience.

In some ways, however, movies entered most deeply into the imagination of modern America. The "star" system reached its apex in Hollywood. Radio, television, sports, even politics only followed imitatively. Movies probably fixed the picture of America overseas more than any other single force. Americans seemed to learn their manners and their new styles from the movies. And, as the fan magazines illustrate, they learned to fix their desires on fantasies created by faceless technicians and photogenic foils, to identify with the special unrealities of the screen. Movies loosened the American psyche just as automobiles did: in the darkened theater or behind the wheel of some fabulous machine one's vision of self could soar beyond the confines of daily life. In these places Americans could feel themselves genuinely free, in moments when they could believe that the old inheritance of America was theirs.

The power of the media constantly threatened to overwhelm all perceptions of the other forms of popular culture. But the world of evolving popular institutions, humor, and ritual went on always a step ahead of the media, which almost instantly picked up each new fad and projected it on a vast national screen. The labor movement produced a rich output of songs, as did the civil rights movement and the foot soldiers of two wars. The language was enriched as much as debased by the racy speech of the cities, the ethnic subcultures, teenagers, beats, the underworld. And American life continued to show fertility in inventing new rituals: the little league, the family dinner at the highway fast-food palace, the television football weekend, frisbie playing, student demonstrations. Electronic media continued to record far more than they created. A charming, variegated, dopey world of relaxation continued to flourish beneath and around the anxious public spectacles of modern history.

growing up

The Department of Labor began publishing manuals on infant and child care in the 1920s. Note the emphasis on discipline and habit in this 1935 edition. No wonder Dr. Spock seemed revolutionary a few years later. (Selections from *Infant Care*, Bureau Publication No. 8, U.S. Department of Labor, Children's Bureau, 1935.)

U.S. GOVERNMENT: INFANT CARE

Habits, Training, and Discipline

Habits are the result of repeated actions. A baby, like a grown person, has a tendency to do again something that he has done before, if he has found satisfaction in doing it the first time. The health, happiness, and efficiency of the older child and of the adult depend largely on the habits formed in early childhood. The habits of the little child are begun in the first year of life, some of them directly after birth. The parents can not postpone planning the child's training until he is "old enough to understand." If the child is to have desirable habits of health and of behavior and grow into a healthy, happy, useful adult, training must begin immediately after birth and be regular throughout infancy so that certain attitudes and acts may become habitual.

Though some habits seem to relate more closely to health and others to behavior the principles that underlie them are the same. Desirable habits must be established consciously by the efforts of the parents and undesirable habits replaced by better ones. The problems of discipline in infancy are part of the general program of habit formation. The important habits that may be established in the first year have to do with eating, sleeping, and elimination. Good habits in all these aspects of the baby's life may be built up if perfect regularity is observed in the performance of each act, if the parents are consistent and logical in their demands and absolutely honest with the baby, and if the baby can find some satisfaction in the act. . . .

Toilet Habits—Training the bowels.

Training of the bowels may be begun as early as the end of the first month. It should always be begun by the third month and may be completed during the eighth month.

The first essential in bowel training is absolute regularity. The task of training is one that requires patience, but the result is well worth the effort involved. Almost any baby can be so trained that there are no more soiled diapers to wash after he is 6 to 8 months old.

To begin the training the mother should notice at what time the baby soils his diaper. The next day at that hour she should hold him over the chamber, using a soap stick, if necessary, to start the movement, and continue this day after day, not varying the time by five minutes, until the baby is fixed in this habit. As the baby grows older he can be taught to grunt, to bear down a little, or to show his desire by some other sign. A convenient time for a stool is just before the baby is undressed for bathing. By the time the baby is 8 months old he should have learned to have a stool regularly each morning.

One method of training the little baby in regular bowel habits is as follows:

Hold the baby in your lap or lay him on a table with his head toward your left, in the position for changing his diaper. Lift the feet with the left hand and with the right insert a soap stick into the rectum to act as a suppository. Still holding the feet up, press a small chamber gently against the buttocks with the right hand and hold it there until the stool is passed. The first time the soap stick is used the stool will come in 5 or 10 minutes. Later the time will be shortened. After the first three or four days or as soon as the baby's bowels will move without a suppository, give up the soap stick.

A method for babies 3 months old who can hold up their heads is as follows: Hold the chamber in your lap and place the baby over it with his back against your chest. This makes it possible for the mother to support the young baby before he is strong and able to sit alone.

As soon as a baby is able to sit up alone (about 6 to 8 months) he should be taught to use the nursery chair.

Training the bladder.

When the baby is 10 months old begin training him to control his bladder. It takes longer to teach the baby the control of his bladder than of his bowels, but the method to be followed is the same. The baby should be given the chamber regularly, at first once an hour while awake, and gradually the periods between should be lengthened. Some one simple word should be used each time he is given the chamber so that he may associate the word with the act and learn to use it himself a little later.

Most babies should learn daytime control of the bladder by the time they are 2 years of age. By this time also the baby may have learned to indicate his need. He should be put into drawers instead of diapers as soon as he can stand. This will help in his training. Many babies continue to wet their clothes only as long as they wear diapers.

The mother must remember that as she is trying to establish a "dry" habit it will not help to let the baby keep on wet clothing. If the child wets himself by accident the drawers or diaper should be changed at once. He should be praised when he keeps dry but not scolded when he has an accident. As a rule a child will not learn to control his bladder at night until between the second and third birthdays, after control during the day is well established. (See The Child from One to Six; his care and training, p. 35, for control of bladder in older child; also Child Management, p. 11, for treatment of bed wetting.)

The philosopher George Santayana called an American an idealist working on matter. To raise material pursuits to the level of an ideal has always been the thrust of the "self-help" literature that Americans have been reading since the days of Benjamin Franklin. Nixon Waterman, "Boy Wanted" (1920.)

NIXON WATERMAN: "BOY WANTED"

The Awakening

Ho, my brave youth! There's a "Boy Wanted," and—how fortunate!—you are the very boy!

Who wants you?

The big, busy, beautiful world wants you, and I really do not see how it is going to get on well without you. It has awaited your coming so long, and has kept in store so many golden opportunities for you to improve, it will be disappointed if, when the proper time arrives, you do not smilingly lay hold and do something worth while.

When are you to begin?

Oh, I sincerely hope that you have already begun to begin; that is, that you have already begun to train your hand and head and heart for making the most of the opportunities that await you. In

Nothing is impossible to the man who can will.—Mirabeau.

You will find poetry nowhere unless you bring some with you. —Joubert.

Things don't turn up in this world until somebody turns them up.—Garfield.

fact, if you are so fortunate as to own thoughtful, intelligent parents, the work of fitting you for the victories of life was begun before you were old enough to give the subject serious consideration.

"When shall I begin to train my child?" asked a young mother of a wise physician.

"How old is the child?" inquired the doctor.

"Two years."

"Then you have already lost just two years," was his serious response.

Oliver Wendell Holmes, when asked the same question, said: "You must begin with the child's grandmother."

But no matter what has or has not been done for you up to the present time, you and I know that from now on your future welfare will be largely of your own making and in your own keeping. If you will thoughtfully plan your purpose as definitely as conditions will permit and then learn to stick to it through thick and thin, your success in life is quite well assured, and you need not fear that at the end of the journey you will have to say, as does many a man while retrospectively viewing his years:

O'er life's long and winding pathway,
Looking backward, I confess
I have not at looking forward
Been a genuine success.

What is there for you to do?

Everything and anything you can do or care to do. You are to take your pick of all the trades, professions, and vocations of mankind. Look about you and note the thousand and one things now being done by the men of to-day. It will not be so very long till all of these men will be old enough to retire from active service, and then you and the other boys, who in the meantime have grown to man's estate, will be called upon to perform every one of the tasks these men are now doing. Doesn't it look as if there would be plenty of honest, earnest, wholesome toil for hand and head in store for you as soon as you are ready to undertake it? You

Work has made me what I am. I never ate a bit of idle bread in my life.—DANIEL WEBSTER.

In the blackest soils grow the fairest flowers, and the loftiest and strongest trees spring heavenward among the rocks.—HOLLAND.

Without courage there cannot be truth; and without truth there can be no other virtue.—WALTER SCOTT.

Vigilance in watching opportunity; tact and daring in seizing upon opportunity; force and persistence in crowding opportunity to its utmost of possible achievement —these are the martial virtues which must command success.—PHELPS.

Work is the inevitable condition of human life, the true source of human welfare.—TOLSTOI.

cannot wonder that the busy old world is ever and always hanging out its notice—

"Boy Wanted"

"Wanted—A Boy" How often we
This quite familiar notice see.
Wanted—a boy for every kind
Of task that a busy world can find.
He is wanted—wanted now and here;
There are towns to build; there are paths
      to clear;
There are seas to sail; there are gulfs to span,
In the ever onward march of man.

Wanted—the world wants boys to-day
And it offers them all it has for pay.
'T will grant them wealth, position, fame,
A useful life, and an honored name.
Boys who will guide the plow and pen;
Boys who will shape the ways for men;
Boys who will forward the tasks begun,
For the world's great work is never done.

The world is eager to employ
Not just one, but every boy
Who, with a purpose stanch and true,
Will greet the work he finds to do.
Honest, faithful, earnest, kind,—
To good, awake; to evil, blind,—
A heart of gold without alloy,—
Wanted—the world wants such a boy.

No, the world does not insist that you are to accept a position and begin work with your hands at once, but it wishes you to begin to think right things. "As he thinketh in his heart, so is he." What you think will have much to do in determining what you are to become.

The mind is master of the man,
And so "they can who think they can."

This influence of the mind in thus shaping

People do not lack strength; they lack will.—VICTOR HUGO.

You cannot dream yourself into a character; you must hammer and forge one yourself.—FROUDE.

The truest wisdom is a resolute determination.—NAPOLEON.

While we are considering when to begin, it is often too late to act.—QUINTILIAN.

the man is very well set forth by James Allen, who says: "A man's mind may be likened to a garden, which may be intelligently cultivated or allowed to run wild; but whether cultivated or neglected, it must, and will, bring forth. If no useful seeds are put into it, then an abundance of useless weed-seeds will fall therein, and will continue to produce their kind. Just as a gardener cultivates his plot, keeping it free from weeds, and growing the flowers and fruits which he requires, so may a man tend the garden of his mind, weeding out all the wrong, useless, and impure thoughts, and cultivating toward perfection the flowers and fruits of right, useful, and pure thoughts. By pursuing this process, a man sooner or later discovers that he is the master-gardener of his soul, the director of his life. He also reveals, within himself, the laws of thought, and understands, with ever-increasing accuracy, how the thought-forces and mind-elements operate in the shaping of his character, circumstances, and destiny."

So it is not too early for you to begin to think bravely and resolutely and hopefully upon the life you intend to live, and to cultivate the mental and physical strength that shall help you later on to put your good thoughts into permanent good deeds. Certainty of victory goes far toward winning battles before they are fought. The boy who thinks "I can" is much more likely to succeed in life than is the one who thinks "I can't."

"Could n't" and "Could"

"Could n't" and "Could" were two promising
     boys
Who lived not a great while ago.
They had just the same playmates and just
     the same toys,
And just the same chances for winning
     life's joys
And all that the years may bestow.

And "Could" soon found out he could fashion
his life

Where boasting ends, there dignity begins.—YOUNG.

Impossible is a word found only in the dictionary of fools.—NAPOLEON.

I am in earnest. I will not equivocate. I will not excuse. I will not retreat a single inch; and I will be heard.—GARRISON.

While you stand deliberating which book your son shall read first, another boy has read both.—DR. JOHNSON.

Dost thou love life? Then do not squander time, for that is the stuff life is made of.—FRANKLIN.

On lines very much as he planned;
He could cultivate goodness and guard
    against strife;
He could have all his deeds with good cheer
    to be rife,
    And build him a name that would stand.

But poor little "Could n't" just could n't pull
    through
    All the trials he met with a sigh;
When a task needed doing, he could n't, he
    knew;
And hence, when he could n't, how could he?
    Could you,
    If you could n't determine you'd try?

> When passion is on the throne, reason is out of doors.—MATTHEW HENRY.

So "Could" just kept building his way to
    success,
    Nor clouding his sky with a doubt,
But "Could n't" strayed into the slough of
    Distress,
Alas! and his end it is easy to guess—
    Strayed in, but he could n't get out.

> I wasted time, and now time doth waste me.—SHAKESPEARE.

And that was the difference 'twixt "Could n't"
    and "Could";
    Each followed his own chosen plan;
And where "Could n't" just would n't "Could"
    earnestly would.
And where one of them weakened the other
    "made good,"
    And won with his watchword, "I can!"

> Weak men wait for opportunities, strong men make them.—MARDEN.

By reading between the lines we can infer
from the foregoing that what the world really
wants is men—good men. But the world is old
enough and wise enough to know that if it does
not train up some good boys, there will be no good
men, by and by. "As the twig is bent the tree is
inclined." "The child is father of the man."

So the world simply wishes to inform you,
here and now, that it will count on your assistance
as soon as you have had sufficient time and opportunity to prepare properly for the many chances

> Give me insight into to-day, and you may have the antique and future worlds.—EMERSON.

it has in store for you. It notifies you in good season of the important use it hopes to make of you. It does not wish you to be confronted suddenly with a life problem you cannot solve intelligently. You must be so well equipped that you will not make life a "fizzle."

A "fizzle," as defined by the dictionaries, is a bungling, unsuccessful undertaking.

Life is, or ought to be, a splendid undertaking. Some make a success of it; some make a "fizzle;" some make a sort of half-and-half. Every one who lives his or her life must make something of it. What that "something" is depends very largely on the individual person. Heredity has something to do with it; yet we like to think it is the individual who has most to do with the finished product.

All men are to some degree "self-made," although they are slow to admit it except in instances where the work has been well done.

> The loser declares it is Fate's hard plan,
> But the winner—oh, ho!—he's a "self-made" man.

It is unfair for the loser to blame others for his deficiencies and delinquencies. No one's reputation is likely to suffer much lasting injury as long as he keep his character unspotted. What others may say of us is not of so much moment; the important question is, "Is it true?"

> Of strife others make us, we've little to fear
> Because we can surely defeat it;
> Few persons get into hot water, 't is clear,
> But they furnish the fuel to heat it.

On the other hand the winner is ungrateful when he credits to his own ability the help and good influence he has derived from his associates and his surroundings. No one lives by, to, or for himself, alone. A great man adds to his greatness by generously praising those who have aided in his advancement.

When I don't know whether to fight or not, I always fight.—NELSON.

What is a gentleman? I'll tell you: a gentleman is one who keeps his promises made to those who cannot enforce them. —HUBBARD.

When one begins to turn in bed it is time to turn out.—WELLINGTON.

When I found I was black, I resolved to live as if I were white, and so force men to look below my skin.—ALEXANDRE DUMAS.

Impossible? I trample upon impossibilities!—PITT.

We are, most of us, selfishly slow to confess
How much others aid us in winning success;
But the Fourth of July and the oyster must see
What failures, without any crackers, they 'd be.

This timely notice telling you what the world is going to ask you to perform is as if you were told to prepare to take an extended and important journey. It would require some time for you to procure a trunk and a traveling-bag and to select wearing apparel suitable for the undertaking. Then, too, you would need to study maps and time-tables so as to select the best lines of travel and to make advantageous connections with trains and steamships. Furthermore, it would be for your best interests to read books describing the countries through which you were to pass, and to learn as much as possible regarding their peoples and customs.

As a matter of fact you *are* preparing to start on an extended and important journey. You are going out into the big world, by and by, to do business. You are going into partnership with the world, after a fashion. You are to put into the business your honesty, industry, integrity, and ability, and in return for your contributions, the world is to bestow upon you all the honor, fame, goodwill, and happiness of mind that your manner of living your life shall merit. The world is only too willing to bargain for the highest and noblest and best products of the human mind with any one who can

When all is holiday, there are no holidays. —LAMB.

Let's take the instant by the forward top.—SHAKESPEARE.

I have generally found that the man who is good at an excuse is good for nothing else.—FRANKLIN.

I feel and grieve, but, by the grace of God, I fret at nothing.—JOHN WESLEY.

Deliver the Goods

The world will buy largely of any one who
    Can deliver the goods.
It is ready and eager to barter if you
    Can deliver the goods.
But don't take its order and make out the bill
Unless you are sure you 'll be able to fill
Your contract, because it won't pay you until
    You deliver the goods.

The world rears its loftiest shafts to the men
    Who deliver the goods.

We can sing away our cares easier than we can reason them away.—BEECHER.

With plow, lever, brush, hammer, sword, or
      with pen
   They deliver the goods.
And while we their eloquent epitaphs scan
That say in the world's work they stood in
      the van,
We know that the meaning is, "Here lies a
      man
Who delivered the goods."

And rude or refined be your wares, still be
      sure
   To deliver the goods.
Though a king or a clown, still remember that
      you 're
   To deliver the goods.
If you find you are called to the pulpit to
      preach,
To the grain-fields to till, to the forum to teach;
Be you poet or porter, remember that each
      Must deliver the goods.

Trifles make per-
fection, but perfection
is no trifle.—MICHAEL
ANGELO.

Anxiety never yet
successfully bridged
over any chasm.—
RUFFINI.

Dr. Hollick's *The Origin of Life and Process of Reproduction in Plants and Animals,
with the Anatomy and Physiology of the Human Generative System, Male and
Female, and the Causes, Prevention and Cure of the Special Diseases to Which
It Is Liable* was, in various editions, in print for a generation after 1878. He was
rather a liberal on sexual matters, as in his acceptance of female sexuality as
normal and natural, and his prescription of Cannabis for "restoring sexual power
and desire." Where his Victorianism still showed, however, was in the discussions
of "solitary Vice," "Self abuse"—in short, masturbation. Much that he says sur-
vives today in old wives' tales or street talk. (Selection from F. Hollick, *The
Origin of Life*, 1878.)

DR. HOLLICK: THE SOLITARY VICE

On Cannabis

There is one drug, brought from the East Indies, the *Cannabis
Indica*, which is the most regular in its action, and produces the most
constant beneficial effects of anything yet tried. It appears to act as a spe-

cial nervous stimulant, exciting those parts of the brain, which influence the sexual organs, so that they feel directly an increase of power. It also causes great mental activity, disposes to cheerfulness, and induces a feeling of warmth and comfort over the whole system. Those who have taken it, in a proper manner, are delighted with its effects, and never complain of any after-depression or reaction in any way. If given improperly, however, or in too heavy a dose, it first causes excitement of the wildest character, with an uncontrollable disposition to bodily activity, and afterward a complete mental and physical prostration. In short, it is most powerful, either for good or for evil, according as it is used, and is the only means we possess, in numerous cases, of restoring sexual power and desire. In the East Indies it is commonly used, like opium in China, for the purpose of producing pleasurable excitement, and also for removing impotence.

Medicines that excite the sexual organs are called *aphrodisiacs* and in various parts of the world they are in great demand, though but seldom administered so as to be of any real service. As I have already remarked, some of these medicines, when properly used, have undoubted aphrodisiac powers, but they are by no means applicable in all cases. They may frequently fail of producing any good effects whatever, and sometimes may even cause irretrievable mischief. Their successful administration, therefore, requires a perfect knowledge of their properties, and an extensive observation of their effects under all circumstances. It is for this reason I have not given any recipes for these drugs, for no one can tell when they should or should not be used unless they know something about them, and the effects of taking them improperly may be so serious that experiment with them is dangerous.

Medicines that *decrease* the sexual powers are called *anaphrodisiacs.*

Every young man should read attentively the remarks upon the influence of *tobacco* and *alcohol,* further on. The real power of these drugs is but little known, and the mischief they do to the sexual organs is unsuspected. Married persons should also be acquainted with many of the facts there given, as they will show that in many instances the most temperate use of these articles is hurtful, and that they often cause impotence and sterility, as well as insanity.

These remarks were intended to apply more especially to the male, but they are equally applicable to the female also. In fact, to females they may often be of more importance than to males, because the female system is more easily affected by many of these drugs, and they act upon them with more intensity. I have known little girls affected in a most deplorable manner by having such drugs given to them, and I am confident that the practice is productive of more mischief than is generally suspected. . . .

On Solitary Vices, and Other Abuses

It is seldom the case that this subject is broached to females in any form, but every person at all acquainted with it will admit that it *ought* to be so, and perhaps more especially to them than to other persons.

It is not only necessary on account of females themselves being often the victims of these vices, but also because, as *mothers*, they of necessity exercise a supervision over the conduct of their children of *both sexes,* and they therefore ought to be acquainted with every matter of importance to their welfare.

I am convinced that much of the evil we see arising from this cause, in children, would be prevented if *mothers* were better informed about it, and had their attention properly awakened in time.

Some persons suppose that solitary abuse is altogether confined to *males;* but this is a great mistake. It is doubtless most *frequent* with them, and in general affects them most injuriously; but it is useless to deny that it is extremely prevalent even with the other sex, and likewise leads in them to the most serious consequences.

The nature of my professional experience necessarily brings me much in contact with peculiar cases of this kind, and I feel it my duty to refer to this subject in the most emphatic manner, more especially as it has hitherto been generally overlooked.

In no other place could it be so appropriately treated upon as in a work of this kind, intended for the special *instruction* and *warning* of both males and females.

From various causes, many of which have been alluded to in our previous articles, and others which will be as we proceed, the sexual instinct or desire is often awakened at too early a period, or excited to a most immoderate degree. Sometimes, even in mere *children* it is strongly developed, so as to lead to unnatural practices at the most tender age, and at other times it becomes so ungovernably intense that everything is forgotten or disregarded in the blind craving for its indulgence.

In our *boarding schools* for young females, it is well known to medical men that these vices are fearfully common, though from their nature they are seldom alluded to. The physician contents himself with treating the *effects,* but never alludes to the *cause!* I have known cases where *every pupil* in such establishments has been led astray in this manner, and to the most alarming detriment of their health.

From vicious association, or some other cause, one among the number learns the habit and teaches the others, till all become contaminated, and usually without suspecting either any great *impropriety* or any injurious result.

I know that many of the most pure-minded and virtuous young females have been thus led astray, and when made aware, either by proper instruction or by dear-bought experience, that they have been doing wrong, they often experience the most poignant remorse. It is their fault, however, in only a slight degree, for most of them are kept so entirely *ignorant* of all they ought to know respecting *themselves*, that the wonder would be if they kept in the right path. Parents have much to blame themselves for in connection with this subject, particularly mothers; and I trust these few remarks will awaken their attention to a matter of such momentous importance.

Some time ago, I made an allusion to this subject in one of my lectures to females, and was surprised at the number who afterward spoke to me corroborating my statements. Many aged persons, and mothers of experience, voluntarily testified to the truth and value of what I had said, and *urged* me to press this matter still more than I had done.

One venerable lady, particularly, confessed to me that when she went to a boarding school, in her young days, these vices were so prevalent, and the effects upon the health of the scholars were so alarming, that it was thought some epidemic disease must prevail, and they all went home.

Another lady informed me, with the greatest agony of feeling, that her daughter came home from school to *die* from these practices, and confessed it to her parent on her death-bed.

I have also received numbers of *letters*, from females of all ages, making similar confessions, and asking what they must do to recover from the effects of their thoughtless practices. Among them, I select the following one, as the writer is now no more, and I know that no one can even suspect who she was, nor indeed would any of her numerous friends and admirers believe the *possibility* of her ever having been the victim she was:

"Dear Friend:—

It is with feelings of deep shame and remorse that I sit down to make this confession; but in the hope that it may save others from the abyss into which I have fallen, and also be the means of some little good to my own unworthy self, I feel that I ought not to fail in doing so. *You,* I know, can both sympathize with and excuse me—perhaps more so than I deserve; and I will, therefore, unburden my mind of a terrible weight which has lain heavily upon it for years.

I am now advanced in life, being fifty-one years of age, and the mother of two children—one, alas ! a sufferer from his mother's folly while she was yet a child.

I was first taught the nature of sexual feelings, and how to excite them, by a servant girl, when only eleven years of age ; and being naturally of a warm and excitable temperament, the gratification was very great, and was frequently indulged in. I had not the slightest idea, when first commencing this disgusting practice, that it was wicked or hurtful, nor did I even suspect so till my health began to fail. Fortunately, an old medical book fell in my way, which spoke upon these matters, and that first opened my eyes to the sin of my conduct. Oh ! that such books as yours had then been written, and that one had fallen in my way; years of suffering and mental anguish might have been spared me, and my dear child would not have been a living memento of his mother's folly.

The symptoms which I first began to experience when about fourteen or fifteen years of age, and which increased as I advanced in life, were of the most distressing character. Extreme languor and weakness, with a disinclination to either bodily or mental exertion, accompanied by a miserable lowness of spirits that nothing alleviated, were my constant attendants. I hated myself—I could not enjoy life—and I feared death. My head was always heavy and full, and my eyes often red as if with constant weeping, while my judgment became gradually weaker, and my memory failed, till I could neither decide what to do in future, nor remember what I had done. Fortunately, I was so circumstanced that others took care of me, or I know not what I should have done.

My physicians attributed my sinking health to dyspepsia, to the change of life, and various other causes, and prescribed medicines and change of air, but not one seemed to suspect the real cause of the evil.

For years I struggled on in this way, striving against the demon of strong desire with all the strength I had, but only to fall at last. Each act of gratification seemed to become more urgent than the former, and also to prostrate me, both bodily and mentally, still lower than before. At last I became utterly prostrated, and lay for many weeks at the point of death, from mere weakness and exhaustion. Providentially this was the means of my salvation. The bodily exhaustion seemed to weaken my morbid excitability, and my fear that I really should die gave me new courage, so that with returning strength I broke the shackles which had hitherto bound me, and became free. From that time I never once debased myself with the degrading practice again, and my health and appearance so improved, that my friends could scarcely believe it was me they saw.

I, however, still suffered from a shattered nervous system, and though well, compared with what I had been, felt that, more or less, the consequences of my fault would follow me to the grave. At times I would be attacked with fits of melancholy and extreme depression of spirits, without any apparent cause, and would become so wretched that death would have been a relief. My old weakness of the limbs would also come on occasionally, and my mind, I feel convinced had not its natural power.

At twenty-two years of age I was married, and lived happily with my husband for twenty-one years, having during that time three children, of whom one died. The youngest of those living, from his birth, exhibited the same unfortunate tendency of the nervous system as his mother, and, with horror I confess it, was evidently born with a disposition to the same evil habits. Oh ! the hours of watching and intense mental agony I endured while rearing up that dear child, and oh ! the bitter accusations my own heart brought up against me, for I could not doubt that his moral infirmity was inherited from myself.

As soon as he could understand, I hesitated not to speak to him openly and candidly about it, and by gaining his confidence and love, was enabled to save him from certain destruction, though not altogether from suffering.

For myself, I still suffer, though none suspect the cause, and I daily see, among my dear young friends, many bright buds of promise withering away, as I did, and no one dreaming why.

Wherever I can I speak on this matter, in such cases; but the ignorance of parents is so great, it is not always possible to do so with advantage. I have the satisfaction, however, of knowing that many have been saved by my efforts in this way, and thus my own fall has perhaps been the means of keeping others in the right path.

Oh, with what delight I first heard your lectures, and read your books ! At last, said I, a better day has dawned, and females will no longer be compelled to suffer and die from mere ignorance. May you be spared to complete your work, and may the satisfaction of feeling that you do good, ever attend you.

Most truly yours,

——————.”

This letter is but one out of a large number equally interesting and instructive, but from the private nature of most of them, and also because the writers are still living, I do not deem their publication to be proper.

The symptoms arising from solitary vice are well sketched in the above letter, though they are often much more severe, and many are experienced which are not there mentioned.

The *hospital*, the *lunatic asylum*, and the *grave* would tell fearful tales respecting this habit, if their records were truly written.

The immediate effects of this vice are, great lassitude and depression of spirits. This is followed, after a time, by other symptoms, many of which are never suspected to arise from this cause. Most generally the memory soon begins to fail, and the mind cannot be directed to one thing for any length of time, but wanders continually; sometimes it even becomes unsettled altogether, and complete fatuity results. The senses are very apt to fail, particularly the eyes, which become affected in various ways, from mere weakness to every degree of inflammation, and even blindness. The hearing will often become affected, and the head will be subject to a distressing fullness, with dizziness, noises, and soreness all over. The individual becomes excessively nervous, full of apprehension, irritable, and wretched. He dislikes society, from mere incapability of exertion, becomes at last melancholy, or mad, and often terminates his existence by suicide. The different organs become more or less deranged, and perform their functions imperfectly: this is particularly the case with the digestive apparatus, the kidneys, and bladder. In males, the genital organs themselves begin to fail; they shrink away, the gratification becomes less, and finally complete impotence and aversion follow.

All these symptoms are, it is true, seldom found in one person, but more or less they characterize every case. Some persons will begin to experience them very soon, while others will not for a long time. It is but rare, however, that any one who practices abuse will miss them altogether.

I do not hesitate to say that a very large portion of the human race are guilty of this excess, probably the great majority, and that a large portion of the evils and suffering which afflict society are produced by it. Indeed, I believe that licentiousness, in one form or other, is the cause of nearly all the disease, both of body and mind, which exists!

Solitary vice, however, is much more prevalent than any other form of licentiousness, and much worse in its effects. Dreadful as are the consequences of excess, in the natural way, they are but trivial compared with those which follow from solitary vice; nor do I think they can, under any circumstances, equal them.

Most persons are aware that this practice prevails, and that it is injurious, but it is only those who have long been familiar with it, as a subject of practice and study, that can be aware of its great extent and fearful effects. The truth, in fact, can scarcely be believed by those not familiar with it. My own opportunities for acquiring information have been very great, so as to make me acquainted with this terrible evil in every particular, and I do not hesitate to say that it is *the master evil* of the present day ! I am firmly convinced that it leads to more disease of body and mind, more suffering and premature decay, *than all other causes put together !* Here I make no reservation, nor do I exaggerate, but, on the contrary, I feel convinced that my statement is under rather than over the truth.

This vice is *almost universal,* the exceptions to it being very rare, particularly in the rising generation. I believe it may be safely asserted that *ninety-nine out of every hundred are addicted to it !* And such are the circumstances in which young people are now placed, that, instead of its decreasing, it is every day becoming more confirmed and extended.

I have reason to suppose that it is as general in the one sex as the other. If there be any difference, it is possible that females practice it most; but simply because they less frequently have natural indulgence in their power.

It is often commenced in extreme youth—nay, even in childhood. I have known instances of children not more than eight years of age, and even younger, being addicted to it. In most of these cases no such thing was suspected, and the poor victims were fast hurrying to an untimely grave. Even when told, their guardians could scarcely believe the statement, till their own observation convinced them it was true. They were then extremely anxious to have the evil removed, which, fortunately, was in most cases accomplished. It is not merely an error of youth, however, but becomes a confirmed and growing habit, to which the individual is a victim all his days. I have known middle-aged, and even old persons, who had never been able to emancipate themselves from it.

With regard to the commencement of this practice, some persons have supposed that it must always be learned from another, or at least that some intimation must be had of its nature before it is begun. This, however, I know is not always necessary. From various causes, most of which we have stated in a former part of this work, the genital organs become precociously developed, and highly sensitive. This produces slight irritation and uneasiness, to relieve which the hand is directed to them, the friction of which produces a new and pleasant sensation before unknown. When once this has been experienced, the desire to create it again becomes irresistible, and with each new indulgence the habit strengthens and becomes more confirmed. In most cases the individual is completely ignorant of the nature of this new indulgence, and knows nothing of its probable consequences. This knowledge, if given in time, would often destroy the habit, but it is seldom given till too late to be of service; indeed, in most cases, the victim has to find it out by dear-bought experience.

Nevertheless, this practice is most generally acquired from others, and for this reason prevails in nearly all institutions where young persons are congregated; nor can this be prevented under present arrangements. Many conductors of these establishments are unacquainted with the existence of the evil; others use every means they can devise to prevent or suppress it, though often without success. From the nature of the practice it cannot be prevented, when there is a disposition to it, unless the offender is kept under *constant surveillance !*

In my public lectures I have always made this a special topic, speaking the truth upon it without reserve, but in charity, and with a sincere desire to do good. This has made me the confidant of hundreds, who would never have disclosed their failings to any one else, and has enabled me to gather more facts bearing on the subject than, perhaps, ever came in the way of any one individual before. It is neither useful nor just, however, to expose the weaknesses of human nature, more than is necessary for their correction: I shall, therefore, only make use of the information I have thus acquired in a general way, and for that purpose.

When in New York City, a few years ago, I was accosted, after my lecture on this subject, by an old gentleman, who desired to speak with me in private. When we were alone, he said to me : "Doctor, you are the first person I ever heard speak plainly on this evil practice, and as I am, unfortunately, aware, by sad experience, of the truth of your assertions, I felt much interested in your discourse, and resolved, if you thought fit, to communicate the details of a case with which I am but too familiar." I thanked him for his confidence, and he gave me the following particulars:

He had a son, a fine, healthy, lively child, about eleven years old, whom he sent to a celebrated academy for young gentlemen, in the suburbs of a neighboring city. For the first six months he continued to receive the most flattering accounts of his son's progress, and was highly pleased with him when he returned home at the vacation. In a short time after he was surprised and grieved to hear that his health was failing, and that he was much more backward than formerly. Medical advice was sought immediately, and the assurance was given that there was nothing serious the matter, and that he would probably rally in a short time. The child kept on in this manner for twelve months longer, gradually becoming worse, until at last he was brought home. The father described his condition at this time as most distressing. He was thin as a skeleton, weak in body and mind, and completely sunk in a deep despondency, from which nothing seemed permanently to rouse him. At last he took to his bed, and died before he was thirteen. One night, however, while he was sick, the father was sitting up with him, and, being weary, leaned back in his chair, with his eyes closed, as if asleep. While in this state, some motion of his son partially roused him, and through his half-open eyes, he saw him in a situation which left no doubt that he was practicing masturbation. The feelings of the father can better be conceived than described. Being a man of information, he partly knew the consequences of this vice, and immediately the idea rushed upon him that this was the cause of his son's sickness, and he at once resolved to discover if his suspicions were true. In the morning after, he began to talk with his child about his schoolfellows, asking him as to their practices in play, etc.; and at last fixing his eyes upon him, he asked him if any ever practiced this habit before him ? The child burst into tears, and laid his head in his bosom. By a little gentle management he led him to confess that he had been addicted to this vice ever since he went to school, having been taught it by a playmate. Sometimes he practiced it three or four times in a day. He also assured his father that there was not one he knew in the school but what did the same, it being considered a meritorious thing, and one which every boy should aim at. The poor fellow had become partly aware, himself, that it was causing his misery, and wished he had not done it; but it had become so much a part of his nature, he could not refrain. The father felt as if a thunderbolt had broken upon him. Here was his only child stricken before his eyes, and nobody suspecting the cause till it was too late. Said he to me—"I hope my sad experience may enlighten some one else in time."

A short time after, while lecturing at the city where his son was sent, I was introduced to the principal of the very school, whom he had already mentioned to me by name. Finding him a man of intelligence, I commenced talking on the subject of solitary vice, and observed that he appeared much interested. As confidence became established, he at last confessed that the prevalence of this practice among his pupils was a constant annoyance to him.

"I know," said he, "that my establishment is only like others, for I do not think there is one in which it does not prevail more or less; but as I know how baneful it is, I am deeply concerned about it. I find it impossible to prevent it altogether, do what I will. All our scholars sleep separate, and we keep a constant eye upon them, but still I know the evil exists; and by some accident or other, each new-comer becomes tainted with it. I am firmly convinced that there is no institution where young people are brought together but in which the practice may be found, and I have no faith in any means preventing it but such as you propose."

Numerous indeed are the melancholy instances of this kind daily to be met with. Many a youth, robust with health, and with every indication of the highest talents, is sent by his parents to some seminary to complete his education, and returns after a time debilitated in mind and body, and without either hope, energy, or capability. They mourn over his ruin, but never dream of what caused it; and even if told, could not, in many cases, understand how it had been brought about. I have a case of this kind in my mind now. It is that of a young man who had made the highest attainments, and who gave promise of being one day among the first and greatest in the land. His friends looked upon him with pride and confidence, and gloried in the prospect of his future exaltation. But alas ! a blight came over their hopes; he began to fade, his mind became imbecile, and at last he sank far below the ordinary standard, without even the desire to rise. He was pointed out to me by a relative, who also told me that it was the practice of solitary vice, learnt at college, which had made him the melancholy wreck he was.

On another occasion, an old man spoke to me after my lecture, and told me that he had a son who had long been in a desperate condition, whose cause of complaint he had never been able to ascertain. "But," said he, "from what you say of the effects of this practice, I think that must be it; I will, however, ascertain if possible immediately." The next week I saw him again, and he told me that he had asked the medical man, who had his son in charge, whether he thought such was the case, and he immediately replied, "Yes ! now you have asked me I can tell you. It is that practice, and nothing else, which has brought your son to his present pitiable condition. I did not like to mention it to you before, for fear you might be, like many others, merely offended with me for speaking the truth; but since you ask, I presume you desire to know." The young man was then so weak he could scarcely stand, and so much affected in his mind that a person was kept with him continually, to prevent him committing suicide. I saw the father, a little time after, again, and he told me, with tears in his eyes, that his son had died in the mean time. "Had it not been for you," said he, "I should never have known what killed him. I have now another child, much younger, who might have died in the same way ; but now I know the evil, I trust I shall be able to prevent it."

Another case, somewhat similar, came under my notice of a little girl, who had been taught the practice by a female servant with whom she slept. The mother fortunately discovered it before the evil was gone too far, and by a proper course of moral and medical treatment it was soon suppressed altogether, and she perfectly recovered.

In one instance I knew a boarding-school where fourteen young females resided, which had to be entirely broken up on account of this practice. One after another fell sick, and all eventually were sent home; previous to which, the principal ascertained, from the confession of one among them, that for a length of time they had all been addicted to this vice. Nine out of these fourteen died in less than five years after!

"Dating" as a formal institution with a fixed etiquette seems to have been fading all through the 1960s, but early in the decade it was certainly flourishing. (Selection from "How to Bait a Date." Reprinted from SEVENTEEN®. Copyright © 1960 by Triangle Communications Inc. All rights reserved.)

"HOW TO BAIT A DATE"

Delightful sight that first day of school: six feet or more of well-muscled masculinity draped across the high school steps. Want to make friends with an athlete? The obvious solution (often the wrong one) is to go in for athletics yourself. Unless you are ready to play tackle on the football team, you won't get to know him. Better prospects lie in convincing your school paper editor that the sports page needs a woman's touch. This way you can interview your hero and make a play for him at the same time. If you can't write, read. Take Ring Lardner to English class with you. Ask your athlete if he's familiar with this great sports writer. Carry the newspaper sports section or one of the more esoteric sports publications and display it prominently. When he does take you out, don't expect late, late dates—he's in training, remember? And now a word to the wise: just because he's beautifully athletic, it doesn't follow that he's conventionally dumb. Ever heard of Bob Mathias? *Not for every girl, this complicated type—cool, aloof, unapproachable on the surface, eager and adventurous inside.* If you like challenge (and who doesn't once in a while?) try captivating the rebel. Carry a copy of a Kerouac novel under your arm. Use very little lipstick, wear a pair of espadrilles as a variation to sneakers. Learn to sit in the lotus position, legs crossed, feet propped on your knees as Zen Buddhists do while contemplating. If all this fails, complain that your eyelashes hurt (ultra-sensitivity pushed to the ludicrous will tickle his offbeat sense of humor). *All the other boys try in vain to copy his style.* Where other boys' hair When the bait is taken, the fun is ready to begin. Lots of new experiences in store for you: rockclimbing, cups and cups of coffee (*espresso,* naturally), with hours and hours of philosophical conversation. Cool jazz, poetry reading, Lenny Bruce, Thoreau's ideas—never a dull moment! All the other boys try in vain to copy his style. Where other boys' hair is too neat or too untidy, his is always just so. You know the type. If you don't, you've read about him in F. Scott Fitzgerald. Because he seems to have been born knowing just what to do, he's sometimes a little awe-inspiring. What's your best move? First, check your appearance. You'll need smooth hair, perfect make-up, neat dresses with just a touch of dash to please this fastidious soul. Looking this way, you won't have to grope for conversational openings: he'll bite. But in holding up your end of the conversation, be prepared to comment knowingly on: foreign movies, gourmet food, what's in, what's out and why. When on a date he's in his native element: completely at ease with your parents, a pleasure at a party and, most satisfying, a great caretaker—of you. *Wherever he goes, his reputation as a Heartbreaker precedes him.* He's got the last word on clothes, cars, girls, what's going. His self-assurance *appears* to be boundless. So suppose you want to dig beneath the shiny veneer? You can join his crowd of admirers (and maybe get lost in it) or get to know him on your own terms. Get him talking, keep him talking. One opener that works is: "You look as if you'd know about (just about anything from people to philosophy)." A bolder tack is to ask him to your next party—perfectly permissible even if you're only on nodding terms. The trick here is in your party planning. Try a little oneupmanship and build your own reputation as a smoothie: dance the Lambeth Walk instead of the cha-cha-cha. Serve shishkebab instead of the usual. Life with Smoothie is filled with glitter. If you have a little of the smoothie in you, no one could be more fun. But, if you haven't, watch out! This egotistical male can be a real *bore! Keen, alert, self-absorbed, and currently enjoying great prestige as a type, the Intellectual is an exciting conquest.* Give him something to think about and he'll give you plenty in return. Making friends is easier than it looks, opportunities are rife for any girl with a smidge of poise: start an intellectual argument with him in class, sit next to him at the library and ask him what he's reading, borrow a book from him, get him to help you with your homework. If he's a joiner, you join up too: become a member of the Science Club, get him to help you organize a Chess Club (learn the moves first, please!), contribute to the literary magazine. Don't make the mistake of stereotyping him. Just because he's a whiz in class doesn't mean he's *all* mental. Chances are he'll put all the vitality at his command into his leisure time. Or if he doesn't know how to play, you can have the fun of teaching him—a pastime that is good for your ego as well as his! *Leaning rather tentatively against the pillar here, sitting in the back seat of the classroom, often observed cracking his knuckles at a party is the Shy Boy.* He may be the best-looking boy in class, or the smartest or the sweetest: only *he* doesn't think so. If you think there is hidden gold here, it's your project to mine it. If he's wearing a sloppy old sweater, say, "Do you know, you remind me so much of Mort Sahl." Vary your compliment to suit his appearance. Another ego-building gambit is "Aren't you the boy who . . ." fill in something spectacular like "won the track meet events?" He didn't, but the fact that you might think he did makes all the difference. Once he's snared, you've made a real coup. Rewards run very high: here's the boy who becomes the giver of a dozen roses, is a born book-carrier. But most important is the pleasure of discovery, for shy people, once unthawed, are often found to possess untapped *supplies* of humor, warmth *and friendship.*

Edgar A. Guest was the most popular versifier (he did not call himself a poet) in America during the first half of the twentieth century. His verse, written for the Detroit *Free Press* from 1891 to 1959, combined sentimentality, idealism, and patriotism into a sweet paste that Americans found as irresistible as ice cream. (From Edgar A. Guest, *A Heap O' Living*, 1917.)

HOME

It takes a heap o' livin' in a house t' make it home,
A heap o' sun an' shadder, an' ye sometimes have t' roam
Afore ye really 'preciate the things ye lef' behind,
An' hunger fer 'em somehow, with 'em allus on yer mind.
It don't make any differunce how rich ye get t' be,
How much yer chairs an' tables cost, how great yer luxury;
It ain't home t' ye, though it be the palace of a king,
Until somehow yer soul is sort o' wrapped round everything.

Home ain't a place that gold can buy or get up in a minute;
Afore it's home there's got t' be a heap o' livin' in it;
Within the walls there's got t' be some babies born, and then
Right there ye've got t' bring 'em up t' women good, an' men;
And gradjerly, as time goes on, ye find ye wouldn't part
With anything they ever used—they've grown into yer heart:
The old high chairs, the playthings, too, the little shoes they wore
Ye hoard; an' if ye could ye'd keep the thumbmarks on the door.

Ye've got t' weep t' make it home, ye've got t' sit an' sigh
An' watch beside a loved one's bed, an' know that Death is nigh;
An' in the stillness o' the night t' see Deaths angel come,
An' close the eyes o' her that smiled, an' leave her sweet voice dumb.
Fer these are scenes that grip the heart, an' when yer tears are dried,
Ye find the home is dearer than it was, an' sanctified;
An' tuggin' at ye always are the pleasant memories
O' her that was an' is no more—ye can't escape from these.

Ye've got t' sing an' dance fer years, ye've got t' romp an' play,
An' learn t' love the things ye have by usin' 'em each day;

169

Even the roses 'round the porch must blossom year by year
Afore they 'come a part o' ye, suggestin' someone dear
Who used t' love 'em long ago, an' trained 'em jes' t' run
The way they do, so's they would get the early mornin' sun;
Ye've got t' love each brick an' stone from cellar up t' dome:
It takes a heap o' livin' in a house t' make it home.

A PATRIOTIC WISH

I'd like to be the sort of man the flag could boast about;
I'd like to be the sort of man it cannot live without;
I'd like to be the type of man
That really is American:
The head-erect and shoulders-square,
Clean-minded fellow, just and fair,
That all men picture when they see
The glorious banner of the free.

I'd like to be the sort of man the flag now typifies,
The kind of man we really want the flag to symbolize;
The loyal brother to a trust,
The big, unselfish soul and just,
The friend of every man oppressed,
The strong support of all that's best,
The sturdy chap the banner's meant,
Where'er it flies, to represent.

I'd like to be the sort of man the flag's supposed to mean,
The man that all in fancy see wherever it is seen,
The chap that's ready for a fight
Whenever there's a wrong to right,
The friend in every time of need,
The doer of the daring deed,
The clean and generous handed man
That is a real American.

Extraordinary to note how long Casey Stengel has been amusing the American public! (From *Low and Inside*, A Book of Baseball Anecdotes, Oddities, and Curiosities, by Ira L. Smith and H. Allen Smith, pp. 212-213. Copyright, 1949, by Ira L. Smith and H. Allen Smith. Garden City, New York: Doubleday & Co., Inc.)

CASEY STENGEL AND THE SPARROW

The story of Casey Stengel and the sparrow has been told in many variations. Usually it is warped around so that it becomes a piece of deliberate screwball behavior on the part of Stengel. Newspaper accounts of the incident, written in 1918 right after it occurred, would seem to contradict these versions.

Stengel was a great hero in the few years he played with the Dodgers; then he was traded to the Pirates. On that day in 1918 he came back to Brooklyn as a member of the Pittsburgh club. Technically he had now gone over to the enemy, yet the Brooklyn fans held him in such high esteen that it was a sure thing they would salute him with cheers on his return.

He did not bat in the top of the first, but was the first man scheduled to hit for Pittsburgh at the beginning of the second. He walked out of the dugout when the time came, selected a bat, and strode to the plate. The Brooklyn fans got to their feet and cheered him mightily. Arriving at the plate, Casey turned and faced the stands and lifted his cap from his head in acknowledgment of the salute, and a bird flew out of his hair, circled the diamond once, and then disappeared into the sky. A great roar went up from the multitude—old Casey hadn't disappointed 'em!

The fact appears to be that Mr. Stengel was as greatly startled as the fans had been when a bird flew out of his thatch. For the moment, however, he made no effort to disillusion his admirers, being content to let them think he had rigged the bird trick in their honor.

Later on he told his story of what had happened. When he had gone to his position in right field in the first inning, he saw an injured sparrow wobbling along at the base of the wall. He walked over and picked it up and was trying to decide what to do with it when he noticed that the ball game had been resumed and he needed to get down to business. He quickly placed the stunned bird under his cap and went to work as an outfielder. He swore later on that he had completely forgotten about the sparrow when he came in from the field and went to bat. Nonetheless, the bird story has been widely repeated as an example of Stengel's showmanship.

Each war generates its own favorite songs, endlessly resung, with more and more verses, usually topical. Without question, "Mad'moiselle from Armentières" was the most popular song of the American Expeditionary Force in World War I. (From *The Songs My Mother Never Taught Me*, according to John J. "Jack" Niles, Douglas S. "Doug" Moore, A. A. "Wally" Wallgren, 1920.)

MAD'MOISELLE FROM ARMENTIÈRES

40,000 Marines Can't Be Wrong

A mad'moiselle from Armentières,
   Parlez-vous.
A mad'moiselle from Armentières,
   Parlez-vous.
A mad'moiselle from Armentières,
She hadn't been hugged for a thousand years,
   Hinky-dinky, parlez-vous.

Mad'moiselle from Armentières,
   Parlez-vous.
Mad'moiselle from Armentières,
   Parlez-vous.
She got the palm and the croix de guerre,
For washin' soldiers' underwear,
   Hinky-dinky, parlez-vous.

Mad'moiselle was dressed in blue,
   Parlez-vous.
Mad'moiselle was dressed in blue,
   Parlez-vous.
Mad'moiselle was dressed in blue,
The souvenir was in blue too,
   Hinky-dinky, parlez-vous.

The tin hat, he's a totin' his pack,
We hope to Christ it breaks his back.

The open shop can't get me sore,
It's closed saloons that rile me more.

The "Pretoria" passed a ship to-day,
For the ship was going the other way.

If you'd get hold of a friend to talk,
'Phones are there, but it's quicker to walk.

If they should make me President,
I wouldn't have to pay no rent.

They say home brew is puny stuff,
But mine would make a lambkin rough.

When shoes cost twenty bucks a pair,
My dog-gone feet are going bare.

With her I flirted, I confess,
But she got revenge when she said yes.

The bonus didn't last me long,
So that is why I write this song.

My Yankee sweetheart looks askance,
At all the mail I get from France.

The doughboy he had beaucoup jack,
'Till mademoiselle got on his track.

But there's a way if there's a will,
We'll run a little private still.

The doughboy he went over the top,
Because he had no place to stop.

From gay Paree he heard guns roar,
And all he learned was "je t'adore."

The day we sailed away from Brest,
I said, "Good-bye" and thought the rest.

The yellow peril was worse than flu,
But now it's reds that make me blue.

"C'mon, sign up for three years, bo,"
He'll be around in a month or so.

Twelve long, rainy months or more,
I spent hunting for that war.

The boys in the 5th Marines, they were the nuts,
They had the damndest kind of guts.

The bonus may come to us some day,
But taxes will take it right away.

Hoover rates a croix de guerre,
He left the goldfish over there.

Bergdoll's lesson is easy to see,
When the draft comes around, R. S. V. P.

I didn't care what became of me,
That's why I joined the Infantry.

He won the war but didn't get much,
Now Bill's in Holland, God help the Dutch.

Dempsey helped to build the ships,
But couldn't see the ocean trips.

The Indian is a good old race,
His nose is red, so is his face.

Oh, I ain't got no power of will,
And all I want's a moonshine still.

Where are the girls who used to swarm,
About me in my uniform?

I'm going bugs with the cost of clothes,
I'd like to be Adam and dress même chose.

The door to my cellar's locked and barred,
I sit with a gun all night on guard.

The M. P. asked me for my pass,
A thing I did not have, alas!

The poor old vine we'll have to drape,
With ribbons fine and dull black crepe.

To find a buddy in a crowd,
Sing "Hinky-dinky" right out loud.

The old red cow left one good pelt,
But they threw the bull for the Sam Browne belt.

'Twas a Hell of a war, as we recall,
But still 'twas better than none at all.

Oh, the 77th Division went over the top,
A sous lieutenant, a Jew and a Wop.

Our General, he got the croix de guerre,
But the poor old bozo never was there.

My Froggie girl was true to me,
She was true to me, she was true to you,
She was true to the whole damned army too,
    Hinky-dinky, Parlez-vous.

The Peace Commissioners drink and talk,
They never had a post to walk.

The Yanks are havin' a Hell of a time,
Wadin' around in the mud and the slime.

Americans marched off to World War I with high hearts singing George M. Cohan's "Over There" as they went. Here are some glimpses of what they found. (Selections from Elmer W. Sherwood, *Diary*, 1921.)

ELMER W. SHERWOOD, *DIARY*

July 21 [1918]

"Black Jack" [Pershing] has given us training in open warfare because he thinks a victory can be obtained only by attack, not merely by defensive tactics.

July 25

The odor of dead things permeates the atmosphere everywhere, but we have become used to the stench—used to almost everything sickening.

July 28

Airplanes have many battles above us. An enemy plane came over today and swooped down upon Battery E. The pilot turned his machine gun loose on the battery and bumped off two more of our men. An American plane evened up the score today by bringing down a German from over our heads. It was a pretty battle.

30

One company captured eight German nests today and turning the machine guns the other way gave the Germans a dose of their own medicine. The war cry is "guts and bayonets" and believe me, they are using both. Sergeant Joyce Kilmer, the poet, was one of the Rainbows who fell today with a bullet through his brain.

August 3

Hundreds of bodies of our brave boys lie on Hill 212, captured with such a great loss of blood. We will never be able to explain war to our loved ones back home even if we are permitted to live and return. It is too gigantic and awesome for expression through words.

September 3

We agreed upon one thing—that a great majority of the men in the Rainbow Division are fatalists. As they express it, "There is a shell in Germany that has my number on it, and when it comes over I will be pushing up daisies."

4

Some cynic pacifists say, "They do not know what they are fighting for." Perhaps our fellows could not tell you in concise terms just what the reasons are. After all, it is left to a few poets and thinkers to express the innermost thoughts and hopes of nations and peoples.

Many of us will not live to know the results, but those who do will see America enshrined as the first power of the world.

8

We hiked all last night, pulling into our present position on this (St. Mihiel) front at 2:30 A.M.

We worked like blazes camouflaging our position and placing our guns until 5 A.M.

After this we turned into blankets and slept until 8:30.

Three and a half hours after an all-night hike isn't much, but perhaps tonight I can get more; at any rate, we have the satisfaction of knowing that all communications are in good order, and that is the main job I have to perform in this man's army.

I have just come back from the front-line trenches where we located an O.P. (Observation Post) for our battery. The first soldier I ran across in the trenches was just over from the U. S. and didn't know "what it is all about." I asked where the enemy was located, and he didn't know. Then I asked him if there had been much excitement up here. He said, "Lord, yes! A fellow out of G Company was killed by a shell last night." He seems to think this bloody warfare. I just wonder what he would say if he could see the fields before Chateau-Thierry as they were when we were up there, literally covered with corpses. Well, all hell will soon break loose here too.

9

This will be the first battle of the war in which the participating troops of our side are to be commanded by Pershing personally, according to the snow [rumor] and it will be the first big all-American drive.

The command may be endeavoring to keep the plans secret. If so, it has not altogether succeeded, because it seems to me everybody in France surmises that we are going to fight to flatten the St. Mihiel salient. Even the French peasants spoke of it as we came up to the front.

This projection of the battlefront is popularly known as the "hernia of St. Mihiel," and it has existed for almost four years. In 1914 the German horde forced its way to this point, which has been held by the enemy ever since.

The salient has an area of some 150 square miles, almost the size of the former Chateau-Thierry salient, and among other things, it contains a very important railway junction. It is a grand and glorious feeling to know that it is the American army which will carry on this operation.

These fellows have so much confidence that they swear they will capture Metz if ordered to, or die in the attempt. I actually believe it is possible for us to deliver the knock-out punch to the enemy within three months, though, of course, that isn't probable.

Signal detail has been running new lines and repairing old ones today, and communications are in shipshape. The guards make every one wear gas masks at alert; can you beat that? I suppose the order was designed primarily to protect the green troops who are in battle for the first time, and who might forget in the confusion that they have gas masks.

I asked one of these birds if any one had been gassed on this front, and he said, "No," but added that a soldier had been hit by a shell yesterday. He seemed to think it a terrible calamity, and I told him the fellow might have been hit by a street car if he had stayed in the States.

11

Beaucoup ammunition has been placed at our gun positions and we are all set for the party. Unlike the Champagne front, we do not have any reserve positions picked out in case of retreat on this front. Evidently Pershing feels that there is no doubt but that this battle will go our way.

12

The zero hour was 1:05 A.M., the heavy artillery starting it off. The earth seemed to give way when the rest of our guns joined in the stupendous and fierce barrage. The roar was so loud that we could scarcely distinguish the deep intonation of our own howitzers from the reports of the 75s.

For four hours the deafening roar continued as our messengers of death were hurled into enemy territory. Then at 5:00 our infantry preceded by tanks went over the top, making a picture of dash and activity.

Not content with ordinary progress the boys of our division leaped ahead of the clumsy tanks and pressed forward in irresistible waves to the German trenches.

The enemy artillery reply was feeble, though the infantry machine-gun and rifle fire was more menacing.

Our artillery fire in the first place demoralized enemy resistance, and the Boche are surrendering in droves. Surely they must regret giving up these luxurious dugouts and trenches which they have lived in for four years. Many of them even have electric lights and good furniture "requisitioned" from nearby French villages.

We must have slipped up on the enemy because they left a great deal of equipment, ammunition and food. Before we left the battery on detail work, two or three hundred prisoners passed our position. Up here in the advance we pass prisoners in droves of from ten to a hundred with a doughboy in the rear prodding the laggards with a bayonet whenever necessary.

A good many of the Germans are being utilized to carry back wounded. A sedate-looking officer wearing white gloves had to bow his back in the work just as his men did. It seemed to do these enemy enlisted men good to see their officers thus reduced to their own plane. Most of them became quite cheerful after they found that they weren't going to be scalped as they had been led to believe these aboriginal Americans were wont to do.

The condition of the roads is very bad and No Man's Land is a mess of shellholes and mud. A good many enemy dead are lying about and a few of our own men are lying where they were struck down by enemy fire this morning.

The doughboys are still advancing swiftly. In the air we are supreme. We are not in the position of the rat in the cage, as we were at Chateau-Thierry when enemy planes swooped down upon us and threw streams of machine-gun bullets into our ranks. This time the tables are turned. We see our aviators flying over the retreating enemy, dropping bombs and creating havoc.

13

No rest for the weary last night. We were on the go, or rather on the march, but the battery did not make much headway because of the bad condition under foot and the congestion of what roads are left since our bombardment of yesterday.

By inches we progressed to Seicheprey, the town which saw such terrific fighting between the 26th division and the Germans late last winter.

At daybreak we pulled into a wood and made camp for a short rest.

Everything is going along swimmingly, as all objectives were taken yesterday and things are moving along even better today, so reports say.

One thing is sure, our bull (prison) pens are becoming glutted with captured Boches. Some of them have lived in the United States and want to fraternize, but our fellows aren't much in the mood. These Germans are under real Yankee authority now. Some of them are used in constructing roads and others in carrying litters.

Several majors and colonels, one general, a couple of counts, and a prince were among the captives.

It seems as if America is coming across with what it takes to win the war. The Allies could not have done it without us. Of course, the war isn't over, by any means, but this battle is a darn good omen of ultimate victory for the Allies. . . .

An Unknown Aviator

June 22 [1918]

I was some distance back of the patrol and saw a Hun two-seater about three miles across the lines so went for him. I expected about thirty seconds at close quarters under his tail and then to watch him go down in flames. It looked like cold meat.

I started my final dive about one thousand feet above him and opened fire at one hundred yards.

Then I got a surprise. I picked the wrong Hun. Just as I opened fire, he turned sharply to the left and I was doing about two hundred so couldn't turn but had to overshoot and half-roll back. As I half-rolled on top of him, he half-rolled too and when I did an Immelman, he turned to the right and forced me on the outside arc and gave his observer a good shot at me as I turned back the other way to cut him off from the other side.

I fired a burst from my turn but my shots went wild so pulled up and half-rolled on top of him again and opened fire from immediately above and behind. He stalled before I could get a burst in and side-slipped away from me but gave me a no-deflection shot at him when he straightened out.

I didn't have to make any allowance for his speed or direction and his observer was shooting at me. The observer dropped down in his cockpit so I suppose I killed him. But I couldn't get the pilot.

He put the plane in a tight spiral and I couldn't seem to get in position properly. Cal and Tiny Dixon came in about that time and everybody was shooting at him from all angles. I know he didn't have any motor because he came down very slowly and didn't attempt to maneuver.

We were firing from every conceivable angle but we couldn't seem to hit the tank or the pilot and every now and then he'd take a crack at me with his front gun when I'd try him head on.

He was a stout fellow. A good fighter and I hope he is still alive. If his observer had been any good I wouldn't be writing this now. He hit one of my front spars and that was all. I left him at one hundred feet as my engine was overheating and sputtering.

June 24

My motor got to acting funny and the water began to boil. It cut out a few times and I just did get back. I am going to ask for a new one. These Hispano Vipers are fine when they are all right but the slightest trouble bawls them all up.

June 25

Springs and I flew up to Dunkirk to get some champagne yesterday.

There was a brand new American major up there in a new Cadillac named Fowler. We turned our nose up at him but he insisted on being nice. He was so new the tags were still on his gold leaves and he didn't know how to salute—saluted like an Englishman.

When he heard why we'd come up he insisted on driving us into Dunkirk in his Cadillac. We got the champagne and he insisted on taking us into the Chapeau Rouge for a drink. We shot down a couple bottles of champagne, and he was all right, we thought, even for a new Kiwi.

He kept on asking such simple questions. He wanted to know all about how our patrols were led and if we led any ourselves, and how we got along with the British. He acted awfully simple, just like an ordinary U.S. major, and we did the best we could to enlighten him as to the proper method of picking cold meat and bringing most of our men back.

His ideas were all wrong and we concluded that he must have been reading some of the books by the boys at home. We got a snoutful and he brought us back to the field and we invited him down to dinner at 85 and then he left.

We asked Sam what Fowler had done to get a gold leaf and he told us that Fowler had been out with the British since 1914 and had the Military Cross and had done about five hundred hours of flying over the lines. The joke is certainly on us. But he ought to know better than to fill a pilot full of champagne and then ask him how good he is. To tell the truth I think we were very modest.

ROD MC KUEN: *LISTEN TO THE WARM*

Times Gone By

Remember how we spent the nighttime counting out the stars.
Too late for the beach, too early for the bars.
All of us together would raise our glasses high
and drink a toast to times gone by.

The times, oh we had some times
when the world was the color of neon signs.
Each of us and all of us killed our dreams with rye
and tried to crowd a lifetime into times gone by.

Remember how the Sunday morning bells were always ringing
and out along the waterfront we'd hear the big men singing.
In some long-forgotten time, some August or July.
Even then we'd talk about the times gone by.

The times, oh we had some times
when love cost only nickels and dimes.
Always when our secret needs were hard to satisfy
we'd talk of going back again to times gone by.

Remember how we talked and laughed and cried into the dawning
and the terrible taste of kisses in the morning.
Crowded rooms and lonesome tunes and very little sky.
Even then the better times were times gone by.

The times, you know we had some times
with gentle women and vintage wines.
But that was when we didn't know our youth was passing by.
Now all we have to think about are times gone by.

I'll Say Good-bye

Now that the summer's come and gone I'll say good-bye.
Now that the winter's comin' on I'll say good-bye.
I'm not the first man or the last
who had a thirst to leave the past.
So while the autumn rain is falling I'll say good-bye.

For every star that falls to earth a new one glows.
For every dream that fades away a new one grows.
When things are not what they would seem
you must keep following your dream.
So while my heart is still believing I'll say good-bye.

Love is a sweet thing caught a moment
and held in a golden eye.
You can borrow but never own it
after a while it says good-bye.

Heavy's the heart that has to turn and say good-bye.
But as we love so do we learn, I'll say good-bye.
Cage a bird he will not sing
I can't be caged in by a ring.
So while the chilly wind is blowing I'll say good-bye.

So as the winter says hello I'll say good-bye.
I never ever did like snow I'll say good-bye.
I'm just a man and nothing more
in the face of love I'll close the door.
Because another road is calling I'll say good-bye.

Tongue-twisters, puns, and other outrages on the language have always formed a part of popular culture. (From *The Liberty Years, 1924–1950*, ed. Allen Churchill, 1951.)

TONGUE-TWISTERS

Arthur's Adam's apple attracts Alice's assiduous attention.
—*Miss K. Ryan, Clayton, Mo.*

Salvation Sally served several shell-shocked soldiers sandwiches.
—*Mary McFall, Philadelphia, Pa.*

When will Winnie Winkle wed, we wonder?
—*Billy Fitzgerald, Chicago.*

Sociable Sally Sachs spends Sundays swimming.
—*Mrs. R. E. Hadley, Chicago.*

Sandy Sammy Samson saw Sally Sanders sew socks.
—*Samuel L. Hane, Wheeling, W. Va.*

Betsy Brown bakes bigger biscuits by buying better butter.
—*George Plankenhorn, Erindale, Ont.*

Sue Shedd saw Simon Seths' shed.—*Robert O'Neill, Stamford, Conn.*

Cousin Clarence censored coquette Constance's costly costume.
—*Lona Machler, Chicago.*

Shy Susie sat singing sea songs sweetly.—*G. Mariner, Chicago.*

Red ruffles raise ructions round royal Russian rosters.
—*I. Travers, Chicago.*

Sarah Shannon sold six silk shawls.—*M. Sullivan, Chicago.*

Hatty Hixom's husband's horse hurt his hoof.
—*Martin Bowes, West Philadelphia, Pa.*

Friendly, fleshy Flossie fed Farmer Fred's father flounder fish.
—*Marie Lawrence, Chicago.*

Faithful, forlorn Freddy followed fair, frivolous, flitting Freda.
—*Anna Gentry, Maywood, Ill.*

Gloomy Gussie's glazed glasses glittered glaringly.
—*Gertrude Anderson, Chicago.*

Pretty Patsy Pumpernickel preferred pickled pretzels picked
promptly.—*W. Carnelli, Chicago.*

Pretty Patty Parker practices prelude pieces patiently.
—*Helen Dupont, Fall River, Mass.*

Some silly saps save sloppy soap suds.—*Frances Kingsley, Chicago.*

Laughing lively, little Lillie lisps lots.—*Mrs. J. O'Brien, Chicago.*

Silly Sally Saucer sits sewing Sammy's stockings.
—*Josephine Wezeman, Chicago.*

Bertha's big brother Ben bowled big balls breathlessly.
—*Mrs. William Barry, Chicago.*

Dan dangled dazzling daggers dangerously.—*Jean Neill, Chicago.*

Terrence tried till twelve to teach Tommy typing.
—*Harris Persons, Marshall, Minn.*

Frantic Florence finished Flora's fussy frock Friday.
—*Agnes Moore, Los Angeles, Cal.*

Prudent Polly politely pardoned Peter's perky pun.
—*Louis Renschlein, Burlington, Wis.*

Peter pawned Polly Pepper's pretty pink pearls.
—*Hazel Unverzagt, New York City.*

Four ferocious foxes fought five furious ferrets.
—*Mary Pastoret, St. Paul, Minn.*

Sunday Simple Simon sat solving sums.
—*Josephine Costigan, Chicago.*

Surely Shirley shall see Saul's show.
—*George Blumenthal, Detroit, Mich.*

Peter purchased Pansy's priceless pup, Pal.
—*Patsy Finn, Austin, Ill.*

Silk socks soaked soapily sometimes save splitting seams.
—*Mrs. I. Cunningham, Chicago.*

Six sleek, slick shaven sheiks sent Shebas silk stockings.
—*Mrs. M. S. Ensrud, Rushford, Minn.*

Thousands thronged Tillie Tooley's theater Tuesday.
—*Patsy Finn, Austin, Ill.*

Many mathematicians make mathematical mistakes.
—*Ben Stolarz, Hammond, Ind.*

"Razor Rastus" raced rarin' running, ragged rascal.
—*Walter G. Horton, Chicago.*

Sweet Sylvia served several shrimp sandwiches Sunday.
—*Catherine McGuire, Chicago.*

Billy Brooks bought buxom Beatrice beautiful beads.
—*Mrs. M. Byron, Litchfield, Ill.*

Fair French fashion fascinates foreign females.
—*Mrs. L. Constant, Hartsdale, N.Y.*

War songs can take the high road or the low. "Lili Marleen" was an unusual song to achieve enormous wartime popularity; it came from the other side, and it was hardly music to march by. "Dirty Gertie" is more characteristic; apparently it had more verses and they were a lot dirtier than the W.W.I doughboys managed in making up lyrics about their Mad'moiselle from Armentières. (From *G. I. Songs,* ed. Edgar A. Palmer, 1944.)

LILI MARLEEN

In front of the barracks, right near the heavy gate,
Stood once a street-lamp, and if it stands to date,
Then we shall meet there once again,
Beneath the street-lamp, shine or rain,
As once, Lili Marleen,
As once Lili Marleen.

The street-lamp knows your footsteps, so lovely and so free,
For you it keeps on burning—it has forgotten me.
And if I don't return again,
Who'll be beside you in the rain?
Who will, Lili Marleen,
Who will, Lili Marleen?

DIRTY GERTIE FROM BIZERTE

Dirty Gertie from Bizerte
Hid a mousetrap 'neath her skirtie,
Strapped it to her knee-cap purty,
Baited it with Fleur de Flirte,
Made her boyfriends' fingers hurty,
Made her boyfriends most alerte!
She was voted in Bizerte
Miss Latrine for 1930.

Dirty Gertie from Bizerte
Saw the Captain, made ze flirty
Captain zink she verra purty,
Lose his watch and lose his shirty,
Call ze general alerte.
The gendarmes look for Dirty Gertie
From Casablanc' to Gulf of Sirte:
Haz any one seen Dirty Gertie?

Dirty Gertie from Bizerte
Roll zee eyes and make ze flirty,

Wears no chemise and wears no skirty,
Wears wan veil and wan night-shirtie.
All ze soldats in Bizerte
Vant to meet wiz zis here Gertie,
Drink ze toast to Dirty Gertie.
Vas wan cute keed when she's zirty!

MISCELLANY

Memorable Headlines from the National Enquirer

MY MILK KILLED MY NINE BABIES

MY IN-LAWS DROVE FOUR NAILS INTO MY SKULL

I AM A MEMBER OF THE FIFTH SEX

THEY LEFT ME OUTSIDE FOR 17 YEARS

I CUT OUT HER HEART AND STOMPED ON IT!

Chain Letter

Dear Friend:

As you know, chain letters have been barred by the Post Office Dept.

This chain letter, however, is not illegal because it does not involve money.

In this chain you send your wife, because the purpose of the chain is not wealth but happiness.

Here is how it works: Send your wife to the man at the head of the list printed below, along with the names of five other husbands willing to participate in the chain. The man you select in turn sends his wife to the top name on your list.

If the chain is not broken, you will eventually receive 3,246 wives, which should be enough for a normal lifetime, especially if you don't go broke.

DO NOT BREAK THE CHAIN.

The man who broke the first chain in this series GOT HIS OWN WIFE BACK.

A Religious Tract

I Wish My Mummy Didn't Smoke: As Confided to Roy L. Smith in the Christian Advocate

I know my Mummy loves me. She dresses me up in nice clothes. She feeds me on the things that are good for me. She buys me lots of things. She reads books about how to take care of me. She sits up with me when I don't feel good. She will do 'most anything for me. But I wish she didn't smoke!

I've never had a clean kiss in all my life. Sometimes her breath is awful bad; and when she kisses me just after she has been smoking, it almost makes me sick. All the time there's something funny tasting about it. Once it did make me sick and I cried, and she said it was something I had eaten.

She was fixing my oatmeal the other morning and smoking, and she got ashes in it. 'Course she didn't see it, but I had to eat it.

I get so tired of living in smoke all the time. It hurts my eyes and I rub them hard and she doesn't know what is the matter. The worst thing is when she lays a cigarette down and the blue smoke gets into my eyes and nose and stings and stings. She doesn't know why I fuss so much, and sometimes she shakes me for being bad.

Sometimes my lungs hurt from so much smoke, and I cry and Mummy gets cross, and I don't know how to tell her, and then we both get fussy and Mummy tells my Daddy that I have been just awful all day.

And I don't like the way some men look at my Mummy when we are eating in a restaurant and she is smoking.

Maybe I'll get used to it, but it's awful hard on a little fellow like me. I like fresh air and clean things. I feel so good when I go outdoors and away from my Mummy's smoke.

Sometimes Mummy has company in the afternoon and when all the "girls" begin to smoke and there aren't any windows open, it gets terrible and I get cross and Mummy says, "I don't know what's wrong with that child today. Why can't he be good when there's company in the house?"

Once, when she was holding me and smoking, I got some ashes in my eye and it hurt awful and I screamed and screamed, and that night she told Daddy I had a temper tantrum. I don't know what a temper tantrum is, but it sure hurts.

It's awful hard growing up with grown-ups. And now, Grandma's started smoking too!

I don't know what people want to smoke for. I wish my Mummy didn't.

Shocked—we would be shocked beyond human endurance, if we could see the frown on the face of Almighty God, as He looks down upon us as we go about making TOBACCO FURNACES out of our bodies— "bodies which He made after His own likeness" (Gen. 1:26). And who admonishes us: "Know ye not that ye are the temple of God, and the Spirit of God dwelleth in you? And if any man defile the temple of God, him shall God destroy: for the temple of God is holy, which temple ye are" (I Cor. 3:16-17). Oh, my friend, if we could see the seriousness of the cigarette habit, as God sees it, we would tremble with fear, each and every time we looked upon another smoking a cigarette—especially young motherhood, upon whose shoulders rests the responsibility of perpetuating the population of the nations. What a tragedy, America's MOTHER-HOOD has become the prey of COMMERCIALIZED VICE, drinking, gambling and SMOKING! "Smoking down the wrath of almighty God upon the children of disobedience" (Eph. 5:1-6). Listen to the verdict: "If thou do that which is evil, BE AFRAID; for he beareth not the sword in vain; for he is the minister of God, a revenger to execute wrath upon him that doeth evil" (Romans 13:14).

A Cure that Is Sure!

Some twelve years ago, the writer came face to face with the seriousness of the cigarette habit—at which time he in child-like faith, asked pardon for the sin, and deliverance from the HABIT. Then and there, God very graciously performed a miracle, and from that day to this, the DESIRE to smoke a cigarette has NEVER RETURNED! Praise His Holy Name! Say, reader of mine, it was as easy as that, (ASK PARDON FOR THE SIN), and believe YOU me, God is no respecter of persons. Therefore, right NOW: "If thou wilt confess with thy mouth the Lord Jesus, and shalt believe in thine heart that God has raised Him from the dead, thou SHALT BE SAVED." (Rom. 10:9). SAVED from HABIT—from HELL—for HEAVEN.

Let's get this one into every factory—home and office—and quickly. —Jan. 17, 1946. Thos. B. Hart, PILGRIM TRACT SOCIETY, Inc., Randleman, N.C. Tracts free, as the Lord supplies the means. Send postage for over 100 samples. This work supported by voluntary offerings of its readers.

vaudeville

Vaudeville comedy acts dealt heavily in ethnic and racial stereotypes. The Polish jokes of the present are but a pale reflection of the endless visions of stupidity that audiences entertained about the groups they felt free to poke fun at. (From *Vaudeville Varieties*.)

VAUDEVILLE VARIETIES

Chloe Gets a Job

(Talking Act for Two Ladies)

CHARACTERS

MRS. WHITE..in need of a maid
CHLOE JOHNSON...............................the maid she wants

Mrs. White is a wealthy, well-dressed lady. Chloe is a typical colored mammy. *(They meet at Center.)*

MRS. WHITE.   Well, Chloe Johnson!

CHLOE.   Howdy, Mrs. White. You sho' lookin' unsurmountable dis mornin'.

MRS. WHITE.   *(Laughs.)* Still using big words, aren't you, Chloe?

CHLOE.   I does a lot o' browsicatin' through de dictionary.

MRS. WHITE.   The dictionary?

CHLOE.   Yes, ma'am. It sho' got a heap o' fancy words in it, but I don't think much of de story.

MRS. WHITE.   Where do you think you're going this wonderful mornin', Chloe?

CHLOE.   Oh, ma'am, I's been where I's goin'. I's on mah way back from dere.

MRS. WHITE.   Anyway, you are just the person I've been wanting to see. We haven't had a good maid since you left us to get married.

CHLOE.   An' I isn't had no money since I left you to git married.

MRS. WHITE.   Haven't you worked any place since you were married?

189

CHLOE.   Jes' a li'l work off an' on, now an' den, here an' dere, sort of. One place was foh dat wealthy Mrs. Topnotch. She craves foh a maid what am high class like what I is, so I works foh her. Mah, mah! Dat woman got more guestses den a graveyard is got ghostses.

MRS. WHITE.   Then you did some serving.

CHLOE.   Mostes' when I wallops dat Rosebud Jackson foh flirtin' wif mah ol' man. I served ten days foh dat.

MRS. WHITE.   I mean you served the guests of Mrs. Topnotch.

CHLOE.   Oh, yes,'m, both ways.

MRS. WHITE.   What do you mean, you served the guests both ways?

CHLOE.   So dey'd come again, or stay away. But I's sort o' skeered workin' foh dat woman account I has to stay 'way from mah home so much, an', Mrs. White, I don't trust mah man enough to leave him alone.

MRS. WHITE.   Is he liable to do something rash when you're not around?

CHLOE.   Dat man done need a bodyguard an' I's de body what can do de guardin'. Now jes' last night he say to me, "Honey, you know what?" I say, "Does I know what what?" And he say, "Honey, I reckons I put on mah bestes' clothes an' ramble ovah to dat show what is got all dem purty dancin' gals in it."

MRS. WHITE.   And you didn't exactly agree with the suggestion?

CHLOE.   I say to him, "Man, you listen to me. You isn't gwine put on nothin' to go no place no time to see nobody do nothin', nevah nohow an' not at all!"

MRS. WHITE.   But, Chloe, could you come and work for me again?

CHLOE.   Well, not prezactly right now, Mrs. White. I's got a disappointment wif de dentist foh a distraction of a cuspidor. An' I's a li'l bit worried.

MRS. WHITE.   Why be worried about that? Dentists aren't so bad. I always go to the dentist with a smile on my face. If you smile, Chloe, you'll forget all the awful things you've heard about dentists. Of course, if you think it will be a painful ordeal you can take gas.

CHLOE.   You mean dat laughin' gas?

MRS. WHITE.   I think some people refer to it as laughing gas.

CHLOE.   Tell me somethin'. How many smiles to a gallon of laughin' gas?

MRS. WHITE (*Much amused.*)   What kind of work are you going to have done at the dentist's?

CHLOE.   Invasion.

MRS. WHITE.   Invasion?

CHLOE.   Uh-huh. De yanks are comin'. Uh-huh. Tooth distracted, yanked out. Pulled. Sort of a chicken deal. You know—pullet. Can you tell me, does I go to de drawin' room foh to git a tooth pulled?

MRS. WHITE. That would be a logical place. Of course, if you need some drilling . . .

CHLOE. I marches out on de drill grounds. Br-r-r! I don't like dem dentists. Long time ago I done went to de dentist an' right 'way he told me to open mah mouth an' shut up. He makes me open mah mouth so wide he sticks his fist in it, an' den he says, "How's yoh fam'ly?" Den he staht lookin' at all mah teeth. I say to him, "Man, you don't have to look at mah teeth to see how old I is. I isn't a horse." Fin'ly he says, "Mrs. Johnson, is you ever had dat tooth filled?" I say, "No, sah, I isn't nevah had dat tooth filled." So he stahts drillin' an drillin' and drillin'. If I'd been in Texas he'd o' struck oil. Den he stops an' looks at his drill, an' says to me, "Woman, you is lyin' to me. Dey's metal on mah drill." Dat makes me mad, an I says to him, "Man, you didn't git dat metal out'n mah tooth. You drill so deep you struck mah belt buckle."

MRS. WHITE. Now to get back to business, Chloe. Will you come and work for me?

CHLOE. How much you-all pays me, Mrs. White?

MRS. WHITE. I'll pay you whatever you are worth.

CHLOE. I's pow'ful sorry, Mrs. White, but I couldn't live on such a li'l amount.

MRS. WHITE. Perhaps, Chloe, you do not practice economy.

CHLOE. I don't even have time to practice de piano.

MRS. WHITE. I mean, you should be—well, let's say, just a wee bit stingy to get along in life.

CHLOE. Golly, Mrs. White, I git dem spells evah once in a while. Know what I do last week? I done found a whole box o' cough drops. I didn't have no use foh dem cough drops. Know what I do?

MRS. WHITE. You threw them away?

CHLOE. No, ma'am. I showed a wee bit o' stingy. I make mah ol' man sleep out in de cold so he'd ketch cold. I don't waste nothin'. Mah pappy was de stingy one. Mah goo'ness! When he'd take a nickel out'n his pocketbook de buffalo would blink at de light.

MRS. WHITE. Your husband should save, at least, one-third of his wages.

CHLOE. He don't earn dat much. Yes'm, mah pappy was de stingies' man what evah lived. Know what he do to me?

MRS. WHITE. What did your father do to you?

CHLOE. He done gib me a nickel if I wouldn't eat no suppah. Den in de night he swipe dat nickel back.

MRS. WHITE. Really?

CHLOE. Yes, ma'am! Den he wouldn't gib me any breakfast account I'd lost de nickel.

MRS. WHITE.   I still maintain that you should put something away for a rainy day.

CHLOE.   I done do dat. I sho' got somethin' put away foh a rainy day.

MRS. WHITE.   You have?

CHLOE.   Yes'm. A umbrella.

MRS. WHITE.   Speaking of your father being so stingy—did he never take your mother out?

CHLOE.   Dat man nevah took anythin' out 'cept his teeth.

MRS. WHITE.   As I understand it, your husband is anything but stingy.

CHLOE.   Oh, dat man a reg'lar spenderthrift.

MRS. WHITE.   I thought as much.

CHLOE.   He don't care how he spend his money a-tall. Why, I's seed dat man buy a all-day sucker at seven o'clock at night. Now you know what he want to do?

MRS. WHITE.   I'm a poor guesser, Chloe.

CHLOE.   He want me to work an' git 'nough money so he can go in de chicken business.

MRS. WHITE.   Does he know anything about raising chickens?

CHLOE.   He nevah raise any 'cept at night. Most always he git ketched at it, too. But now he think he's got a won'erful idea. He done figure if he put a mirror 'longside each hen, den dem hens lays a egg, an' when dey look in de mirror dey think it am anothah hen what am layin' de egg, an' dey git jealous an' lay anothah egg.

MRS. WHITE.   I'm not very familiar with the ways of the hen, but there is a great difference in chickens, isn't there?

CHLOE.   Oh, yes'm, quite some tremendicate dif'rence.

MRS. WHITE.   For instance, what hens lay the longest?

CHLOE.   Dead ones. I know. I's been in de chicken business.

MRS. WHITE.   When you take your chickens to the market do you dress them?

CHLOE.   Lawsy, no. I don't dress 'em. When dey goes to de market dey wears dere old clothes. I done bought a chicken last night.

MRS. WHITE.   Pullet?

CHLOE.   No, ma'am, I carried it.

MRS. WHITE.   I believe you told me one time that you used to live on a farm.

CHLOE.   Oh, sho' 'nough, Mrs. White, I used to live on a fo' acre farm.

MRS. WHITE.   Four acre farm? That isn't a very large farm, is it?

CHLOE.   But dese was mighty big acres.

MRS. WHITE.   Just what is the hardest thing to learn about farming?

CHLOE. Gittin' up at fo' 'clock in de mornin'.

MRS. WHITE. You got up with the chickens?

CHLOE. Co'se not. We didn't go to bed wif 'em. Yes'm, Mrs. White, our farm was so big we had two windmills.

MRS. WHITE. Very few farms have *two* windmills.

CHLOE. But we had to take one of dem windmills down.

MRS. WHITE. Why did you have to take one of the windmills down?

CHLOE. Dey wasn't enough wind foh two.

MRS. WHITE. I'd love to live on a farm and listen to the cowbells.

CHLOE. Glory-be, Mrs. White, cows don't have bells. Dey got horns. Mah pappy had fo' cows on dat farm an' he'd make dem sleep on dere backs at night.

MRS. WHITE. My land! Why did he make them sleep on their backs?

CHLOE. So all de cream would be on top in de mornin'. When I was on de farm I had to drink fo' quarts o' milk evah day.

MRS. WHITE. Why did you have to drink so much milk?

CHLOE. To keep it from turnin' sour.

MRS. WHITE. Perhaps I may sound very ignorant about farming, Chrole, but what kind of cows give evaporated milk?

CHLOE. Dry cows.

MRS. WHITE. How much milk did your father's cows give?

CHLOE. Dem fo' cows give twenty gallons.

MRS. WHITE. And how much did he sell?

CHLOE. Thirty gallons. Mah pappy was a milkman of de first water.

MRS. WHITE. Was there very much cream on the milk he sold, then?

CHLOE. Dey wasn't no cream a-tall. He filled dem bottles so full dey wasn't no room foh cream.

MRS. WHITE. Why is it, that you are no longer on the farm?

CHLOE. Pappy done hab a ax'dent an' move off'n de farm.

MRS. WHITE. What happened, Chloe?

CHLOE. Well, Mrs. White, it was like dis: pappy done buy a new 'lectric milkin' machine.

MRS. WHITE. Yes?

CHLOE. An' one night he turn on de 'lectricity an' go in de house an' forgot all 'bout dem cows.

MRS. WHITE. And left that electric milking machine running? Then what happened?

CHLOE. When he went out in de mornin' all dem cows was turned inside out.

MRS. WHITE. I'm going to ask you again, Chloe. Are you going to work for me?

CHLOE.   If'n I work foh you does I git a day off evah week to take mah singin' lessons?

MRS. WHITE.   Don't tell me you're taking singing lessons.

CHLOE.   I is tellin' you just dat.

MRS. WHITE.   Have you ever sung in public?

CHLOE.   Yes, ma'am. I sing in de choir till dey find out what is de matter wid it. When I sing people clap dere hands—ovah dere ears.

MRS. WHITE.   Where did you learn to sing?

CHLOE.   Cor'spondence school, but I sho' lose a lot o' mail.

MRS. WHITE.   I'd love to hear you sing something, Chloe.

CHLOE.   Now?

MRS. WHITE.   Why not?

CHLOE.   Den you go ovah dere an' sit on de curb an' I'll sing sumpin'. (MRS. WHITE *exits and* CHLOE *sings an appropriate number, making her exit on the final notes of the song.*)

CURTAIN

Back and Forth

(The following gags and comebacks are very appropriate for a dance team doing tap or soft toe.)

Did you marry the girl of your dreams?
I hope not. I have terrible dreams.

He's familiar with many tongues.
Linguist?
No. Doctor.

Why did you park in front of the fire plug?
It said "Fine for Parking."

What is the outstanding contribution that chemistry has given to the world?
Blondes.

Why are you limping? Do your shoes hurt?
No, but my feet do.

Do you know Art?
Art who?
Artesian.
Yes, I know Artesian well.

Do you know what they do with holes in stale doughnuts?
Sure. They whittle 'em down and put 'em in spaghetti.

When you sleep do you lie on the left or right side?
I'm a lawyer. I lie on both sides.

I'm going home.
Why?
I live there.

The death of movie stars is always of some public interest, but the death of the great silent movie lover, Rudolph Valentino, resulted in uniquely dramatic displays of mourning and despair. Only in the last few years have the annual stories of the "heavily veiled woman" placing a rose on his grave disappeared from the news. (Selection from Stanley Walker, *Mrs. Astor's Horse*, 1935.)

VALENTINO'S DEATH

On August 26, 1926, millions of women wept over the death of a slim, slick-haired Italian they had never known—Rudolph Valentino, the great lover of the films, who was christened Rodolpho Alfonzo Rafaelo Pierre Filibert Guglielmi di Valentina d'Antonguolla. When the news went out of his passing in Polyclinic Hospital, New York, women all over the world went on a grieving jag the like of which was never seen before. To these mourners Valentino was a conquering Casanova and an infinitely tender, wistful boy. He was the symbol of romance; his death meant that love itself was dead.

Hundreds of women and girls gathered at a cathedral in Rio de Janeiro at a solemn high mass for the actor. In London Peggy Scott, a dancer, swallowed poison and left dying instructions to her girl friend to "look after Rudolph's picture." In a tenement in Cherry Street, New York, Mrs. Angelina Celestina, a 20-year-old mother with two children, drank iodine, fired two shots into her body, and fell on a heap of pictures of Valentino. She finally recovered. In Chicago 2,000 members of the Valentino Memorial Association crowded into the Trianon ballroom to pay homage to his black-draped portrait, place flowers at the base of a statuette of him, and to hear him lauded as "the beloved impersonation of the spirit of romance." Nine-tenths of the crowd were women.

Even as late as 1933 a theater on the north side of Chicago made a profit with Valentino Days on which his old pictures were shown. Dowagers would come, sit in the theater and have a good cry. The Valentino Memorial Association of London commemorates the anniversary of their idol's death with a mass in Westminster Cathedral, and later they play a gramophone record of his voice and attend a showing of one of his pictures. Valentino's funeral was an orgy of bespangled insanity. Women adored him, and men hated him in a baffled, helpless fashion.

To many, Valentino was not particularly handsome. He was of less than medium height, but managed to convey the impression of height by his easy carriage and the way he poised his head. His nose was prominent and slightly flaring at the nostrils. This nose so impressed Jack Dempsey that when the fighter came to have his own bashed nose reshaped he stipulated that it should be made over on the lines of Valentino's. The great lover's features were extremely mobile. He could look sad, wistful, sly, hard or enraged. His eyes were dark, brilliant, and with a certain softness. His hair, black and polished, remained in place even under trying circumstances, no matter whether he was riding through a sandstorm, teasing bulls or romping with dogs.

The man was careful about his clothing, and discarded a garment as soon as he thought it was the least bit out of fashion. In 1925 he came back from Europe with 40 new pairs of shoes, 32 new suits, and many shirts and neckties. However, rich, fantastic costumes suited him best, and in his last years, when he could afford it, he gratified his taste for exotic luxuries.

Valentino was one of three children. He was born May 6, 1895, near the Italian village of Castellaneta. His father died when Rudy was 11 years old, and the family finances soon became meager. The boy applied for admission to the Royal Naval Academy, but was turned down for deficient chest expansion. From that time he observed a training schedule. He at least developed an excellent body. In Italy he learned the rudiments of horseback riding, which became his favorite sport in Hollywood and one of his greatest assets in the pictures. After attending the Royal Academy of Agriculture at Genoa he set off, at the age of 18, to see Paris. There he went in for so much hell-raising that his mother sent word that, as he undoubtedly would come to a bad end, he might as well go to the United States.

The young man arrived in New York unable to speak a word of English, and with little money. He reasoned, however, that he could make a living, as he regarded himself as both a scientific farmer and a gentleman who knew the Argentine tango. He became a landscape gardener in Central Park, quit after a row, and then went to work on the Long Island estate of Cornelius Bliss, Jr., living in a room over the Bliss garage.

During his time off he attired himself in his Parisian evening clothes and visited the better supper places of New York. It was in this period, according to the records of the New York Police Department, that he became known as a petty thief and a blackmailer, although this fact never became widely known, and would not have been believed by millions in later years. He got a job dancing the tango at $50 a week at the Winter Garden. He danced in supper clubs, sometimes with Joan Sawyer and other pre-war favorites. But he wanted to be an actor. He got a part in 'The Masked Model," a musical comedy which was finally stranded in San Francisco.

Now he changed his name from Guglielmi to the more romantic Rudolph Valentino and went to Los Angeles as the guest of Norman Kerry, a young actor with money. He stayed with Kerry in a bungalow for years. He had a slow, hard time. Although really a great egotist, he had an air of bewilderment and diffidence. Sometimes he danced at night clubs, and he often appeared in ballets and prologues at the famous Hollywood palace of the cinema, Grauman's Chinese Theater. By 1919 he was playing regular parts. He was the villain who pursued Dorothy Gish in "Out of Luck." He was a sinister Italian count in "The Married Virgin." In this period he managed to get about socially. He met a small girl with black bobbed hair named Jean Acker at a party given by Pauline Frederick. He proposed to her in the afternoon and they were married before midnight.

Two years later he was seeking a divorce. He received an interlocutory decree from Miss Acker in March, 1922, paying her $12,000 alimony. Meanwhile he had been doing better in pictures. He had been picked by June Mathis, scenario writer, to play the part of Julio in "The Four Horsemen of the Apocalypse." It was a natural part for him, since as a youth he had known pre-war Paris, and he could dance the tango. When this picture was finished he was recognized as a star, but although the picture grossed more than $2,000,000, Valentino received only $350 a week, and when he asked for a raise he was told he did not merit it. In 1921 and 1922 he worked hard. His greatest triumph was "The Sheik," in which he, as a strong young Arab, galloped across the burning sands on a stallion with a beautiful blonde flung across his saddle. Flappers loved it when he held her down with one hand and said, "Stop struggling, you little fool!" Another great scene was the one in the tent, where he refused to rape his captive, preferring to rely on his powers of persuasion. For this he got $700 a week. Fan letters began coming in by the hundreds of thousands.

Soon he was getting $1,000 a week. He met Natacha Rambova, a strange, slithery creature whose real name was Winifred Hudnut. She was the daughter of a New York perfumer. Rudy fell in love with her and persuaded her to go with him to Mexico, where, at Mexicali, they were married on May 13, 1922. Under the terms of his interlocutory decree of divorce from Jean Acker, he was not free to remarry until March, 1923. Thus he laid himself open to prosecution for bigamy and violation of the Mann Act.

He was arrested on the bigamy charge and held in $10,000 bail. He insisted he had not known he was violating the law. Natacha Rambova fled California and hurried to New York. Finally the case against Valentino was dropped, much to the relief of every one. Missing Natacha and feeling abused, Valentino quarreled with his employers; he abrogated his contract and went East to join Natacha. His employers sued for $30,000 damages and got an injunction restraining him from appearing before the camera for any other firm.

Broke, he went to dancing again. For seventeen weeks, at $7,000 a week, he and Natacha toured the United States in a private railroad car, making personal appearances under the direction of a manufacturer of beauty clay. S. George Ullman, who later became Valentino's manager, represented the manufacturer on this trip. During this period Valentino wrote "How You Can Keep Fit" and "Day Dreams," a book of poems. A sample of his poetry, dealing with lust:

"I am a slave
In the rat-trap of disgust
Sold into bondage
By the lurid kiss of lust."

On March 12, 1923, Valentino became a free man. He and Natacha were dancing in a Chicago cabaret. On the 15th they motored to Crown Point, Indiana, accompanied by her aunt, and were married by a justice of the peace.

Natacha not only inspired her husband to write poetry, but she also interested him in spiritualism. She initiated him into the mysteries of automatic writing. One of their chief spirit contacts was an old Egyptian who called himself Meselope and instructed them in natural science. After Valentino's death Natacha said that she had been receiving messages from him which disclosed that he was playing in heavenly theatricals with Bernhardt, Caruso and Wallace Reid. She said, moreover, that he had seen his own funeral, and was both saddened and pleased by the commotion.

Soon Valentino, with the aid of the astute Ullman, patched up his difficulties with the film producers. He made "The Young Rajah" and "Blood and Sand," the latter a great success not only with the women but with young men who began growing sideburns and otherwise imitating the toreador Valentino. His next picture was called "Cobra." He liked the part so well that he adopted the representation of a coiled cobra as his personal crest. Another eccentricity was his slave bracelet. He also had a cigarette case, match container and holder made of platinum with a diamond cobra mounted on an onyx inset. Shortly before his death he designed a special body for a new roadster. It was blue-gray with aluminum motor cowling and fenders, and resembled a great scaly snakeskin. He died before the machine was delivered, and it was finally sold to Peggy Hopkins Joyce.

By 1925 Valentino was in a position to dictate his terms. He got $200,000 a picture and 50 per cent of the profits. His income in 1925 was $1,000,000. He had worked first for Famous Players, but he made two pictures for United Artists, "The Eagle," a Cossack story, and "The Son of the Sheik." The desert picture netted his estate almost $1,000,000 after his death.

In the Valentino stables were four fine horses. One was Firefly, the black Arabian stallion he rode in "The Son of the Sheik." Firefly brought $1,225 at auction after the star's death. The other horses, two Irish jumpers and an Arabian gelding, were sold for more than $2,000. The Valentino garage housed five automobiles: a Ford truck, a Chevrolet for the servants, an Isotta-Franchini town car with a specially constructed body, a Franklin coupe, and an Avion-Voison phaeton with a torpedo body.

Valentino in 1925 bought a new place in Beverly Hills. His old place on Whiteley Heights, with bizarre furnishings, had been the talk of the colony, but, after all, it was merely a bungalow. The new house was called Falcon's Lair. When the unfortunate sheik died it was sold at auction for $145,000. It was built of blue stucco. It had a terrace, a pointed white tile roof, and was heavily masked with shrubbery and young trees. Into this castle went $100,000 worth of art works. Valentino's favorite pieces were two full-length portraits of himself by Beltran-Masses, painter for former King Alfonso of Spain. One of them, showing him in Argentine costume, was supposed to have cost $5,000. There were statuettes of ivory, jade and silver. One golden cashmere shawl was sold for $2,965 at the auction.

A weapon collection was mounted on cerise velvet and used as wall decorations at Falcon's Lair. In this group was a flintlock pistol with a diamond and emerald studded handle. The library was valuable from the point of view of a collector. More than half of the books in it dealt with customs of the Middle Ages, and many were written in Latin and Greek, languages with which Valentino was unfamiliar.

Many of these books, as might have been expected, were the selections of Natacha Rambova. With her, Valentino, the great lover, was not altogether a success. He was not unfaithful, but his ideas of love and marriage were patriarchal. He wanted to raise a family. In his heart the sheik was a farmer. He once said:

"Love only means one thing to a man, possession. All a man asks is to have and to hold, and all a woman seems to want is to be taken and to be held. In my country men are the masters, and I believe women are happier so. It is the way it should be."

In his Hollywood days Valentino, for all his ostentation, was known as highly moral. Women pursued him, but he was bright enough to steer clear of all of them except Pola Negri. This fiery Pola, whose greatest picture bore the simple title, "Passion," was a female Valentino. In the fall of 1925 Valentino started going about with the actress. Six weeks after Natacha Rambova had divorced Rudy, Miss Negri announced their engagement, although Valentino never confirmed the announcement.

In July, 1926, Valentino, having completed "The Son of the Sheik," started East for a vacation. As he was passing through Chicago the *Tribune* printed an editorial headed "Pink Powder Puffs," which said:

"A new public ballroom was opened on the north side a few days ago, a truly handsome place and apparently well run. This pleasant impression lasts until one steps into the men's washroom and finds hung on the wall a contraption of glass tubes and levers and a slot for the insertion of a coin. The glass tubes contain a fluffy pink solid, and beneath them one reads an amazing legend which runs something like this: 'Insert coin. Hold personal puff beneath the tube, then pull the lever.' A powder vending machine! In a man's washroom! Homo Americanus! Why didn't some one quietly drown Rudolpho Guglielmi, alias Valentino, years ago?" Then followed more derision of masculine cosmetics, sheiks, floppy pants and slave bracelets. All this angered Valentino. He wrote a naïve letter challenging the editor to a fist fight, and concluding with this paragraph:

"I will resent with every muscle of my body attacks upon my manhood and my ancestry. Hoping I will have an opportunity to demonstrate to you that the wrist under the slave bracelet may snap a real fist into your sagging jaw, and that I may teach you respect of a man even though he happens to prefer to keep his face clean, I remain with utter contempt, Rudolph Valentino."

There was no battle. Valentino arrived in New York in an extremely touchy state of mind. He realized that he had not handled the situation with finesse. He wanted solace and advice. He sought out H. L. Mencken, and the sage and the sheik had a long session. Valentino rather charmed Mencken, who found that there was an "obvious fineness" to him, and that he was, for want of a better word, a "gentleman." The Baltimore psychiatrist found that it was not that "trifling Chicago episode" which bothered the actor, but "the whole grotesque futility of his life." It was a pleasant meeting, this conference between the understanding man's man, Mencken, and the idol of womankind, the baffled sheik. But it was too late to help the actor.

Valentino passed three weeks in New York loafing. One of his last purchases was a $100 shaving brush at the chemist shop at the Ritz-Carlton. A short time before noon on August 15, 1926, Valentino gasped, clutched at his side, and fainted. He was taken to Polyclinic Hospital in a private ambulance. Four grave members of the medical profession decided to operate for appendicitis and gastric ulcers. When he came out from under the anesthetic he asked: "Doctor, did I act like a pink puff?" As soon as reports of his illness appeared in the newspapers, many notables, including Jimmy Walker and Peaches Browning, telephoned. More than 1,000 telegrams arrived. From the West Coast came calls from Pola Negri, Marion Davies and Charlie Chaplin. An information booth was set up in the hospital lobby. By August 17 peritonitis had set in. By every conceivable ruse visitors sought to reach Valentino's eighth-floor suite. A girl brought some verses, and wept when she was barred. A private detective was hired to eject gate crashers.

On the 18th the great sheik showed signs of improvement. Rumors started—that he wasn't ill at all, that he had been poisoned by bootleg booze, and that he had been stabbed. By August 20 it was touch and go. Airplanes brought serum and goofy nostrums from far-off admirers. The crowds hung on. Jean Acker sent a white counterpane with lace ruffles. On August 22 the watchers got a shock. Pleurisy had developed in Valentino's left chest and his temperature was 104. Major Bowes on the radio asked his audience to "hold an encouraging thought" for the stricken actor.

The newspapers held their presses. A priest was summoned. Finally, at 10 minutes after noon on August 23, the misunderstood lover turned his face to the wall, muttered a word in Italian which no one could understand, and died. When word of his death reached the street, traffic was blocked. Only a few saw the wicker basket that was removed from the Fifty-first Street entrance and placed in a hearse belonging to Frank E. Campbell, The Funeral Church, Inc., the master morticians.

On the afternoon of August 24 the body of Valentino, clad in full evening dress, was laid out on a gold-draped catafalque in Campbell's excellent Gold Room. Campbell believed in making death as beautiful, expensive and pleasant as possible. But when he saw the crowd he hastily put away a number of valuable objects of art which ordinarily decorated the room. Even a bronze statue of Father Time, which weighed more than a ton, was moved back from the door. Campbell's press agent, the resourceful Harry Klemfuss, knew he had a good show, but he never expected anything like what happened.

There was hysteria and trouble. The crowd became so dangerous that the body was placed in the silver-bronze coffin. The crowd wanted to snatch buttons and even to touch the face of the dead man. More than 30,000 tried to get in. The police summoned reënforcements, and Commissioner George V. McLaughlin himself appeared to help unscramble the jam. One of Campbell's large plate glass windows was broken. Ten persons were cut by falling glass. The mounted police rode their horses in the mob. After one charge by the centaurs 28 separate pairs of shoes were picked up. In this crowd were men, women, and children, ranging from flappers to derelicts. Among those present were Mrs. Alfred E. Smith, Jr., and Mrs. Richard Reese Whittemore, widow of the robber and murderer who had recently been put to death in Baltimore.

Ingenious fellows rubbed cakes of soap on the sidewalks to make the police horses slip and fall. It was bedlam; no New York policeman ever had seen anything like it. Inside, the Fascist guard at the bier was jittery over the possibility of a raid by anti-Fascists. Flower filchers were busy. The undertaking staff took the body to an upstairs room. In single line 150 persons a minute passed the coffin, but they were hurried along by strong-arm men. At midnight on August 25 this macabre pageant was stopped by Ullman, Valentino's manager. It was a great show for the newspapers. On the first day the reporters drank $273 worth of Campbell's bootleg booze. Campbell thought this was a shade high, and thereafter he served them cheaper booze. But after it was all over Campbell gave each reporter covering the story a personal coffin plate, inscribed with the recipient's name, birth date, and a blank space for another date. The gifts carried with them a certificate promising a fancy funeral "on the house." Up to 1935 only one of these notes on Charon had been cashed.

The actual funeral was postponed until August 30 to give some important mourners a chance to get to New York. Pola Negri came in on the 29th. She hurried to Campbell's. The coffin was opened. For five minutes she stood rigid. She knelt, said the "Litany of the Dead," and then threw her arms above her head and collapsed. Later, at the Ambassador, she had pulled herself together enough to answer the questions of reporters. She said:

"My love for Valentino was the greatest love of my life. I shall never forget him. I loved him, not as one artist loves another, but as a woman loves a man."

The funeral was held in the little green and gold actors' chapel in the Roman Catholic Church of St. Malachy in West Forty-ninth Street. Five hundred friends were admitted; 100,000 were in the crowd outside. Mary Pickford, Pola Negri and Texas Guinan were sobbing. Jean Acker, the sheik's first wife, collapsed and was revived by "Dr. Weyman," a notorious celebrity hunter who had established a first-aid station outside. It was a shambles.

On September 2, Pola Negri, Mr. and Mrs. Ullman, Rudolph's

brother, Alberto, and a few newspapermen, accompanied the body of the actor on the train trip back to Hollywood. There were demonstrations in Chicago and other cities. Campbell, thoughtful mortician, had equipped the compartment car with whisky. Two cases of champagne were taken aboard at El Paso.

Even in Hollywood, a young girl was found hiding in the undertaker's chapel; she confessed that she had been there all night and most of the day, hoping to see "her Rudy." The poor fellow was never destined for a decent burial. His body was placed in a borrowed crypt, lent for the occasion by his discoverer, June Mathis. A year later Miss Mathis dropped dead in a New York theater. The Valentino body remained in the crypt, and it was not until 1933 that the sheik's brother, Alberto, who inherited one-third of the million-dollar estate, reimbursed the Mathis family.

In the summer of 1935 Alberto Valentino, his wife, and his 19-year-old son, were living in Rudolph's old place in Hollywood. The plaster was falling off the walls. There was a "ouija-board typewriter" which interpreted daily messages from Rudolph, riding his fiery stallion over the heavenly sands. In a dark room was a picture of Rudy. He had a turban on his head. A fresh rose was stuck each day through the canvas at the mouth.

"Vodvil" was the great American stage entertainment during the first thirty years of the twentieth century. Any city or town large enough to maintain a theater could be booked by the many entertainers who followed the chains of theaters throughout the nation. Vaudevillians, with their nomadic family lives somehow became romantic heroes to many Americans and dispelled much of the aura of demimondaine vice that had surrounded theatrical people earlier. Fred Allen, who spent many years on the circuits before he became one of the most famous radio performers, describes the way vaudeville entertainers lived and explains the meaning of "variety" in the phrase "variety acts." Much radio and televison comedy takes its origins from this earlier entertainment. (Selection from Fred Allen, *Much Ado About Me*, © 1956 by Portland Hoffa Allen. Reprinted by permission of William Morris Agency, Inc. on behalf of the author.)

FRED ALLEN: "VODVIL"

This chapter is an autobiographical parenthesis. It is more about vaudeville than me. . . .

Vaudeville is dead. The acrobats, the animal acts, the dancers, the singers, and the old-time comedians have taken their final bows and disappeared into the wings of obscurity. For fifty years—from 1875 to 1925—vaudeville was the popular entertainment of the masses. Nomadic tribes of nondescript players roamed the land. The vaudeville actor was part gypsy and part suitcase. With his brash manner, flashy clothes, capes and cane, and accompanied by his gaudy womenfolk, the vaudevillian brought happiness and excitement to the communities he visited. He spent his money freely and made friends easily. In the early days, the exact degree of prosperity the smalltimer was enjoying could be determined by taking inventory of the diamonds that adorned his person. If he was doing well, the smalltimer wore a large diamond horseshoe in his tie and two or three solitaires or clusters on his fingers; his wife, dripping with necklaces, rings, earrings, and bracelets, looked as though she had been pelted with ice cubes that had somehow stuck where they landed. The smalltimer's diamonds didn't have to be good. They just had to be big. What difference if the eight-karat ring was the color of a menthol cough drop as long as the stone sparkled in the spotlight during the act? To the smalltimer, a diamond represented security. It impressed the booker, the manager, and the audience, but, more important, the diamond was collateral. Confronted with a financial crisis in a strange community, the smalltimer didn't have to embarrass himself by attempting to convince a tradesman or a hotel manager that his credentials were valid. To obtain emergency funds, he merely stepped into the nearest pawnshop, slipped the ring from his finger, and consummated a legitimate routine business transaction. When his diamonds were temporarily on location, the smalltimer avoided his friends and his usual haunts, knowing that the absence of his Kimberley gravel was an admission that the panic was on. The instant his luck changed, the diamonds were redeemed and returned to their customary places. Back in the spotlight, with the horseshoe pin and the rings sparkling, the smalltimer's necktie and his ring fingers resumed strutting their stuff.

The herd instinct was a dominant impulse in the vaudeville actor's behavior pattern. When the season closed, the smalltimers congregated at vacation resorts to revel in each other's company. The smalltimer lived in another world. He thought and talked only about his act and about show business. Nothing else interested him. If you said to him, "Do you remember the Johnstown flood?" he would probably reply, "Remember the Johnstown flood? Are you kidding? I and the wife were playing Pittsburgh that week. Eva Tanguay was the star. Walter Kelly was next to closing. After the first show the manager comes rushing back and says, 'You kids is the hit of the bill!' He moves us down to next to closing for the rest of the week. Kelly is blowing his top. All week long I and the wife murder them!" Everybody in Johnstown could have been swept out of town: the smalltimer wouldn't know or care. He had nothing in common with anybody who was not in his profession.

The two vaudeville centers of the country were New York and Chicago. During the summer layoff season—theaters had no air conditioning then, and many closed during the hotter months—vaudeville colonies were formed. The Chicago acts rented or bought cottages near the lakes in Wisconsin or Michigan; the New York vaudevillians huddled together in Connecticut and down on Long Island. The most famous of the actors' colonies was founded at Freeport, Long Island. The stars first established summer homes at Freeport, and then the smalltimers precipitated a real-estate boom fighting to buy property and houses to make their home in Freeport to let the stars see how the other half lived.

The Long Island Good Hearted Thespians Society was formed. This was a social club whose members reduced the name to the Lights. The first president was Victor Moore. One of the traditional Lights Club functions was the celebration of Christmas on the Fourth of July. In December, most of the vaudeville actors were on the road, away from their homes, their families, and their friends. They spent their Christmas Days on trains, in dingy dressing rooms, or in drab hotels. Members of the Lights ignored the conventional Yule season and saved their Christmas greetings and presents until the return to Freeport. On July Fourth, though the temperature be in the nineties, the Lights' Christmas tree was decorated and lighted, Santa Claus was dressed in his heavy suit with the ermine trimmings, presents were placed under the tree, and the members and their children arrived in their furs, mittens, and earlaps, some even clattering into the club on snowshoes.

A vaudeville actor could relax and enjoy himself only in the company of another vaudeville actor. You could sit a vaudeville actor in front of a mirror and he would stay there contentedly for days on end. In cities on the road, the vaudeville performers congregated at the same boarding-houses or cheaper hotels. There was a time when the actor was *persona non grata* at the better inns, and this was especially true of vaudevillians, who were presumed to be irresponsible from the very fact that their profession was uncertain and their living precarious. It was generally understood that vaudeville performers went in for wild parties in their homes and that their domestic habits were rarely awarded the Good Housekeeping Seal of Approval. Accordingly it was deemed best for hotel clerks to smile blandly when they were asked for rooms and inform the vaudevillian that the hotel was "full up." Stage folk, except for those who had attained stellar rank, were pretty much pariahs around the decent hotels.

Duke Pohl, the manager of the Breevort Hotel in St. Louis, once told me that he was traveling in a special train to attend an annual convention of the Greeters of America, the official organization of the hotel men. Each man was asked to name his hotel and tell something about it. Duke later told me that when he announced that his Breevort catered to stage folks, "I could almost hear the gasp that went around the circle. I told them I considered stage people the most maligned persons on earth. I said that my experience with vaudevillians had been uniformly pleasant, that they paid their bills, were quiet in their rooms, were sober, sedate, and serious people trying to make a living."

Duke defended the profession at a time when many hotel and rooming-house owners were complaining that some vaudeville people were stealing towels. This practice was so common that jokes were being told about it. One joke was about the vaudeville actor who died and left an estate of eight hundred hotel and Pullman towels. Then there was the charge that actors checked into their hotels with heavy suitcases, stayed a week or two, then disappeared without paying their bills. Credit had been extended because the manager had seen the heavy suitcases; when, later, these were pried open, they were found to contain nothing but a collection of bricks and old telephone books. Indigent vaudeville actors were known to lower their suitcases out the window in the back of the hotel, then walk through the lobby empty handed, reclaim their cases, and leave town. An actor who had a trunk in his room received an extension of credit. When the bill mounted, the actor, anticipating that the manager would tip the trunk to ascertain its contents and to try to find out if clothing had been pawned, took the precaution of nailing the trunk to the floor. Ted Healy, a comedian, once owed a sizable bill at the Lincoln Hotel in New York. Ted brought the three stooges he used in his act up to his room and ordered each stooge to don two or three sets of his underwear, two complete suits of clothes, and an overcoat. Healy followed the stooges out of the Lincoln lobby wearing three suits and one topcoat, and carrying a raincoat with every pocket bulging. Healy left the Lincoln Hotel with two mementos of his stay: an empty room and an empty trunk. Things of this kind took place occasionally, and hotel owners were suspicious, but Duke Pohl believed in befriending actors, and they showed their appreciation. As Duke used to say, "I've never lost anything by it. They all paid me eventually."

Vaudeville could not vouch for the honesty, the integrity, or the mentality of the individuals who collectively made up the horde the medium embraced. All the human race demands of its members is that they be born. That is all vaudeville demanded. You just had to be born. You could be ignorant and be a star. You could be a moron and be wealthy. The elements that went to make up vaudeville were combed from the jungles, the four corners of the world, the intelligentsia and the subnormal. An endless, incongruous swarm crawled over the countryside dragging performing lions, bears, tigers, leopards, boxing kangaroos, horses, ponies, mules, dogs, cats, rats, seals, and monkeys in their wake. Others rode bicycles, did acrobatic and contortion tricks, walked wires, exhibited sharpshooting skills, played violins, trombones, cornets, pianos, concertinas, xylophones, harmonicas, and any other known instrument. There were hypnotists, iron-jawed ladies, one-legged dancers, one-armed cornetists, mind readers, female impersonators, male impersonators, Irish comedians, Jewish comedians, blackface, German, Swedish, Italian, and rube comedians, dramatic actors, Hindu conjurors, ventriloquists, bag punchers, singers and dancers of every description, clay modelers, and educated geese: all traveling from hamlet to town to city, presenting their shows. Vaudeville asked only that you own an animal or an instrument, or have a minimum of talent or a maximum of nerve. With these dubious assets vaudeville offered fame and riches. It was up to you.

radio

"Amos 'n' Andy," the show about a comic collection of stereotype blacks, was the brainchild of two white men, Charles J. Correll and Freeman Gosden. Probably the greatest success in the history of radio, the comic series continued on in movies and television until changing concepts of human dignity drove it off the airways. (Selection from Charles Correll, *All About "Amos 'n' Andy" and Their Creators Correll and Gosden,* 1929.)

"AMOS 'N' ANDY"

The battle is on. Again we find the boys in court, while the breach of promise suit is going on. Today Mrs. Parker testified on the witness stand, much to the embarrassment of Andy. She told how he came into her life, how he led her on and then threw her down. She wept and cried, and at the end of her testimony she was carried from the witness stand after fainting. The Judge called a short recess in order to allow Mrs. Parker time to revive. As we find the situation now, Amos and Andy are seated with their attorney. Directly across from them Mrs. Parker's attorney is holding smelling salts under his client's nose. The Judge has not returned to the bench. Here they are:

AMOS. Andy, it ain't no use to worry now. Jus' do de best you kin, dat's all.

ANDY. Dat gal git up on de witness stand dere an' tell all dat stuff. It's enough to make me worry.

POLICEMAN (fading in and out). Say, cut out that smokin'. Where do you think you are?

ANDY. 'Scuse me, Misteh.

AMOS. Mr. Spielman, how you think ev'vything is comin' out?

SPIELMAN (discouraged attitude). Well, boys, it looks very bad. This woman has made a great impression on the Court with that sob stuff, and I'm afraid the Court is in sympathy with her side of the case.

ANDY (more discouraged). Looks bad, don't it?

AMOS (helpful attitude). Andy, don't fo'git to do whut Mr. Spielman tell yo' to do now, when yo' git on de witness stand.

SPIELMAN (to his consulting attorney). Possibly you can get those details finished by tomorrow, but we will need the statistics at that time.

CONSULTING ATTORNEY. I'm going back to the office and get a few papers. I will possibly return before recess is over. (Fading out.)

SPIELMAN (to Andy). Brown, if you can just remember everything I've told you, it will help us a lot.

ANDY. You bettah 'splain dat to me again now.

SPIELMAN. Now I think you'll be the next one on the stand to be cross examined by Mrs. Parker's attorney. When you get there, sit down very quietly, and, whatever you do, don't show any signs of nervousness.

AMOS. Git dat in yo' head now.

ANDY (to Amos). Shut up!

AMOS. 'Scuse me. I was jus' trying to he'p yo'.

SPIELMAN (confidentially to Andy). And Brown, when you get on the witness stand, admit nothing.

ANDY. Do whut to nuthin'?

SPIELMAN. I say, when you get on the witness stand, admit nothing.

ANDY. Admit nuthin' where?

SPIELMAN. On the witness stand.

ANDY. Oh, in otheh words, don't let nuthin' git on de witness stand.

AMOS. Why don't you listen, Andy?

ANDY (resentful of Amos). Is you gonna shut up, or is I gotta kick you out de cou't room? De mo' you talk, de worse off I is.

SPIELMAN. Now, Brown, you can occasionally use the expression "I don't remember." Don't make it noticeable, but occasionally say, "I don't remember." Now, don't forget that. Now, what are you going to say?

ANDY. "Now, don't fo'git dat."

SPIELMAN. No, no; "You don't remember."

ANDY. Oh, dat's right; "You don't remembeh."

SPIELMAN. No, no; "*I* don't remember."

ANDY (mixed up). You don't remembeh whut?

AMOS. No, no, Andy. Listen, "*You* don't remembeh."

ANDY. Oh, oh! Who is my lawyeh?

SPIELMAN. Now, Brown, just say, "I don't remember."

ANDY. Ain't it some way dat I kin keep off o' dat chair again up dere? All dese people in the cou't room looks at me when I git up dere. I feels rebarrassed.

SPIELMAN. No, no, you *must* get up there, but remember, "I don't remember."

ANDY. "Remembeh I don't remembeh." I got-cha.

AMOS. Stop shakin' now, Andy. Don't let 'em know dat you is nervous. You act like you is scared to death.

ANDY (disgusted with Amos). Dey is gonna be tryin' me fo' bustin' yo' head open in a minute if you don't shut up.

SPIELMAN. Here comes the Judge now. Don't overdo it, but remember to say "I don't remember," and don't say anything that will incriminate you.

ANDY. Dey ain't goin' to *cremate* me, is dey?

AMOS. De Judge is gittin' ready to staht-look at him.

JUDGE (in distance, rapping twice). Order in the court room.

SPECIAL POLICE (in distance, talking to spectators). Quiet, or you'll go out.

JUDGE. We will proceed with the case—Parker versus Brown. Andy Brown to the witness stand for cross examination by attorney for the plaintiff.

ANDY. (in low tone to himself). Oh, oh! I gotta git up dere again.

SPIELMAN. All right, Brown; get on the witness stand.

ANDY (to bailiff, who is waiting to administer the oath). I'se comin', Misteh, I'se comin'.

BAILIFF (in quick, jerky tone). Raise your right hand.

ANDY (shaking head as if making a positive reply). I don't remembeh.

BAILIFF. Raise your right hand!

ANDY. Yessah, yessah.

BAILIFF (rattling off the oath in quick, inaudible tone). Do you solemnly swear that the evidence you are about to give in this case is the truth, the whole truth, and nothing but the truth, so help you God?

ANDY. I don't remembeh.

BAILIFF. Say "I do."

ANDY. I do.

JUDGE (in distance). Attorney for the plaintiff will proceed with the cross examination.

ATTORNEY RADA (fading in to cross examine Andy). Your name is Andrew Brown?

ANDY. I don't remembeh.

JUDGE (raps twice). The witness will answer the attorney for the plaintiff. Proceed with the cross examination.

RADA. Your name is Andrew Brown. Is that correct?

ANDY. Yessah, dat's right.

RADA. You are president of the Fresh-Air Taxicab Company?

ANDY (boastfully). Yessah—yessah.

RADA. Do you know Mrs. Parker?

ANDY. I *did* know her, but I ain't speakin' to her now.

RADA. Brown, how long have you been in Chicago?

ANDY. Well-a, we left Atlanta, Georgia, last March, an' I been up heah evah since.

RADA. Brown, when did you first meet Mrs. Parker?

ANDY. I met Mrs. Parker over at Ruby Taylor's house one night.

COURT CLERK. What was that last statement?

ANDY. I met Mrs. Parker oveh at Ruby Taylor's house one night, but I'se sorry I eveh went oveh dere.

RADA. That's neither here nor there.

ANDY. Yes, 'tis. It's oveh dere.

RADA (impatiently, to Andy). Just a minute!

ANDY (settling in seat). I don't remembeh.

RADA. Brown, did you ever write Mrs. Parker a letter?

ANDY. Yessah.

RADA. Is this your handwriting?

ANDY. Dat kind-a look famil'ar to me—I don't make no "a" like dat, though. Maybe I *did* make it, though. Yessah, I guess dat's it. Is it got my name on it heah—Yeh?—Well, dat's mine all right.

RADA (turning to Judge and jury). I am going to read this letter to the Court which I shall refer to as Exhibit A.

ANDY (to himself). Oh, oh! Dere goes one o' dem 'zibits.

RADA. A letter from Andrew Brown addressed to Mrs. Parker, the plaintiff. (Turning to Andy.) And, Mr. Brown, I want you to verify this for the Court as I read it.

ANDY. Du whut to it?

RADA. Let the Court know if this is correct. (Addressing Court.) This letter starts out in the following manner. (Takes on affectionate tone of voice.) My darling, baby-face Snookems (direct to the Judge). My darling, baby-face Snookems, your honor.

JUDGE. You are cross examining the witness—not me. (Raps.) Proceed.

RADA. Brown, take a look at that. Do you remember writing those words, "My darling, baby-face Snookems"?

ANDY (excited). It seem like I is, an' den it seems like I aint. I b'lieve I *is*, though. I know one thing, I was crazy to write it.

RADA. But, nevertheless, you wrote this letter?

ANDY. Yessah.

RADA (to Court). The next line of this letter—"How can I live without you, my darling? We must fly away together, my little Snookems." (To Brown, with high pressure.) Brown, did you really love this woman?

ANDY. I don't remembeh.

RADA. Didn't you plead with her to be your wife? Didn't you beg her, on your bended knees, not to love anyone else?

ANDY (quick, mixed-up reply). Yessah—I mean, nosah—I mean, I don't remembeh.

RADA. You are trying to evade the question.

ANDY. Tryin' to do whut?

RADA. Brown, did you kiss Mrs. Parker, and tell her that her lips were like honey from the bee?

SPIELMAN (in distance). I object.

JUDGE. Objection overruled.

ANDY (looking from Judge to Spielman). Whut happened?

RADA (to Court). I next call the attention of the Court to another letter which I shall refer to as Exhibit B. A letter written to the plaintiff by the defendant in which is incorporated a poem from Popsy-boy to Snookems. (To Andy.) Is this your handwriting?

ANDY. Dat *do* look kind-a famil'ar. I dont make no "s" like dat, though-yes, I do too, I guess.

RADA (to Court). I would like to read the Court the last two lines of the poem written by Andrew Brown. "Come fly with me and we will hide—Just Popsy-boy and his little bride." (Repeating in flowery manner, with much affection in voice.) "Come fly with me and we will hide—Just Popsy-boy and his little bride." (To Andy.) Brown, do you know what the word bride means?

ANDY. I don't remembeh.

RADA (shaking finger in Andy's face). Is it true that you went to the Easy Buying Furniture Company and signed a note for the balance which Mrs. Parker owed on her furniture?

ANDY. Yessah, an' dat man done called me up 'bout dat.

RADA. In other words, that was just a shield.

ANDY. Nosah, it wasn't no shield. She owed fo' chairs an' a table an' a lot o' otheh stuff.

RADA (more high pressure). Is it true that you have called up Mrs. Parker as often as ten times in one day?

ANDY. I guess I is.

RADA (pounding fist on palm of hand in front of Andy). Then you admit that you led this little girl within a few feet of the altar, leading her to believe that she was to be Mrs. Andrew Brown? Before answering that question I want you to look at Mrs. Parker, seated there crying.

SPIELMAN (in distance). I object.

JUDGE. Objection overruled.

SPECIAL DEPUTY (in distance, to crowd). Order in the court room.

RADA. Andrew Brown (slow and deliberate), I want to ask you one question.

ANDY. I don't remembeh.

RADA (to Judge, pleading for assistance as if impatient). Your honor, how can I cross examine this witness (start fading out) when he evades the question before I even ask him (and other similar wording until fadeout is completed).

✿   ✿   ✿

Amos and Andy figuring up the day's receipts:

AMOS. Six an' five is—'leven.

ANDY. Wait a minute heah! Whut is you doin'? Is you mulsiflyin' or revidin'?

AMOS. I ain't doin' neitheh one—I'se stackin' 'em up.

ANDY. Well, I gits half o' dis money, yo' know.

AMOS. You goin' git half of it soon as I figgeh.

ANDY. I b'lieve you is deduckin', Amos.

AMOS. If I is, de pencil's doin' it widout me knowin' it.

ANDY. Wait a minute.

AMOS. Whut's de matteh?

ANDY. Hand *me* dat papeh an' pencil.

AMOS. Whut you goin' do?

ANDY. I'm goin' *times* it. Now listen, Amos—all I need is a few dollahs.

AMOS. I can't lend yo' no money.

ANDY. You know dat Snookems' mama an' papa is comin' to town.

AMOS. I ain't goin' lend you no money. Don't ast me no mo'.

ANDY. I is done promised Snookems dat I would git a chicken an' bring it oveh to her house 'cause she wants to have a chicken dinneh de day her mama an' papa gits heah from de country.

AMOS. How come *you* gotta buy de chicken?

ANDY. I furnish de chicken an' her mama an' papa is goin' bring up some preserves.

AMOS. *You* gits de chicken an' *dey* gits de preserves.

ANDY. Dat's right, dat's right.

AMOS. You betteh have dat switched around.

ANDY. Don't gimme no back talk, now. Do whut I tell yo' to do. I is de president o' dis comp'ny.

AMOS. Wait a minute now, wait a minute—don't rush me.

ANDY. Yo' see, Amos, no matteh whut bizness you is in, de business is *gotta* have a head man to tell 'em whut to do and when to do it. So dat's de way 'tis wid us. I strains my brain an' figgehs out whut *you* gotta do. Yo' see de brain work is de most reportant thing. Amos, take dis letter on de typewriteh. I'll detate it.

AMOS. All right; I'll do de bes' I kin.

ANDY. Staht out de letteh—Mr. John Smith—

AMOS. Wait a minute now, wait a minute! Take it slow.

ANDY. All right. Mr. John Smith—

AMOS. Where is he at?

ANDY. Mr. John Smith—at Boston, Massachusetts.

AMOS. B-o-s-t-u-n—Boston. Wait a minute heah. How yo' spell Massachusetts?

ANDY.   Dat's easy. M-a-s—wait a minute now—M-a-s—M-a-s—I tell yo' whut yo' do. Change dat to Ohio—O-h-i-o.

Orson Welles's Mercury Theater of the Air made what is doubtless the most famous single broadcast in the history of radio: the dramatization of H. G. Wells's science fiction novel, *The War of the Worlds*. Broadcast on October 30, 1938, just one month after the Munich Agreement (also widely covered by radio in the United States) had brought Europe back from the brink of war, this account of Martians landing in New Jersey stirred panic among thousands of people all over the country. In the 1920s people had learned that the nation could, all together, enjoy events such as Lindbergh's flight or the Dempsey-Tunney heavyweight prize fight. Now they were seeing that they could be collectively scared out of their wits by the same device. (Selection from Hadley Cantril, *The Invasion from Mars*, Copyright 1940, © 1968 by Princeton University Press, pp. 85-101. Reprinted by permission of Princeton University Press.)

ORSON WELLES: *WAR OF THE WORLDS*

Columbia Broadcasting System
Orson Welles and Mercury Theatre
on the Air
Sunday, October 30, 1938
8:00 to 9:00 p.m.

CUE.   (Columbia Broadcasting System) (. . . 30 seconds . . .)
ANNOUNCER.   The Columbia Broadcasting System and its affiliated stations present Orson Welles and the Mercury Theatre of the Air in *War of the Worlds* by H. G. Wells.

Theme

ANNOUNCER.   Ladies and gentlemen: the director of the Mercury Theatre and star of these broadcasts, Orson Welles. . . .

ORSON WELLES.   We know now that in the early years of the twentieth century this world was being watched closely by intelligences greater than man's and yet as mortal as his own. We know now that as human beings busied themselves about their various concerns they were scrutinized and studied, perhaps almost as narrowly as a man with a microscope might scrutinize the transient creatures that swarm and multiply in a drop of water. With infinite complacence people went to and fro over the earth about their little affairs, serene in the assurance of their dominion over this small spinning fragment of solar driftwood which by chance or design man has inherited out of the dark mystery of Time and Space. Yet across an immense ethereal gulf, minds that are to our minds, as ours are to the beasts in the jungle, intellects vast, cool and unsympathetic regarded this earth with envious eyes and slowly and surely drew their plans against us. In the thirty-ninth year of the twentieth century came the great disillusionment.

It was near the end of October. Business was better. The war scare was over. More men were back at work. Sales were picking up. On this particular evening, October 30, the Crossley service estimated that thirty-two million people were listening in on radios.

ANNOUNCER CUE. . . . for the next twenty-four hours not much change in temperature. A slight atmospheric disturbance of undetermined origin is reported over Nova Scotia, causing a low pressure area to move down rather rapidly over the northeastern states, bringing a forecast of rain, accompanied by winds of light gale force. Maximum temperature 66; minimum 48. This weather report comes to you from the Government Weather Bureau.

. . . We now take you to the Meridian Room in the Hotel Park Plaza in downtown New York, where you will be entertained by the music of Ramon Raquello and his orchestra. (SPANISH THEME SONG . . . FADES)

ANNOUNCER THREE. Good evening, ladies and gentlemen. From the Meridian Room in the Park Plaza in New York City, we bring you the music of Ramon Raquello and his orchestra. With a touch of the Spanish, Ramon Raquello leads off with "La Cumparsita." (PIECE STARTS PLAYING)

ANNOUNCER TWO. Ladies and gentlemen, we interrupt our program of dance music to bring you a special bulletin from the Intercontinental Radio News. At twenty minutes before eight, central time, Professor Farrell of the Mount Jennings Observatory, Chicago, Illinois, reports observing several explosions of incandescent gas, occurring at regular intervals on the planet Mars.

The spectroscope indicates the gas to be hydrogen and moving towards the earth with enormous velocity. Professor Pierson of the observatory at Princeton confirms Farrell's observation, and describes the phenomenon as (QUOTE) like a jet of blue flame shot from a gun. (UNQUOTE.) We now return you to the music of Ramon Raquello, playing for you in the Meridian Room of the Park Plaza Hotel, situated in downtown New York. (MUSIC PLAYS FOR A FEW MOMENTS UNTIL PIECE ENDS. . . . SOUND OF APPLAUSE)

Now a tune that never loses favor, the ever-popular "Star Dust." Ramon Raquello and his orchestra. . . . (MUSIC)

ANNOUNCER TWO. Ladies and gentlemen, following on the news

given in our bulletin a moment ago, the Government Meteorological Bureau has requested the large observatories of the country to keep an astronomical watch on any further disturbances occurring on the planet Mars. Due to the unusual nature of this occurrence, we have arranged an interview with the noted astronomer, Professor Pierson, who will give us his views on this event. In a few moments we will take you to the Princeton Observatory at Princeton, New Jersey. We return you until then to the music of Ramon Raquello and his orchestra. (MUSIC . . .)

ANNOUNCER TWO.   We are ready now to take you to the Princeton Observatory at Princeton where Carl Phillips, our commentator, will interview Professor Richard Pierson, famous astronomer. We take you now to Princeton, New Jersey. (ECHO CHAMBER)

PHILLIPS.   Good evening, ladies and gentlemen. This is Carl Phillips, speaking to you from the observatory at Princeton. I am standing in a large semicircular room, pitch black except for an oblong split in the ceiling. Through this opening I can see a sprinkling of stars that cast a kind of frosty glow over the intricate mechanism of the huge telescope. The ticking sound you hear is the vibration of the clockwork. Professor Pierson stands directly above me on a small platform, peering through the giant lens. I ask you to be patient, ladies and gentlemen, during any delay that may arise during our interview. Besides his ceaseless watch of the heavens, Professor Pierson may be interrupted by telephone or other communications. During this period he is in constant touch with the astronomical centers of the world. . . . Professor, may I begin our questions?

PIERSON.   At any time, Mr. Phillips.

*   *   *

PHILLIPS.   Thank you, Professor. Ladies and gentlemen, for the past ten minutes we've been speaking to you from the observatory at Princeton, bringing you a special interview with Professor Pierson, noted astronomer. This is Carl Phillips speaking. We now return you to our New York studio. (FADE IN PIANO PLAYING)

ANNOUNCER TWO.   Ladies and gentlemen, here is the latest bulletin from the Intercontinental Radio News. Toronto, Canada: Professor Morse of Macmillan University reports observing a total of three explosions on the planet Mars, between the hours of 7:45 p.m. and 9:20 p.m., eastern standard time. This confirms earlier reports received from American observatories. Now, nearer home, comes a special announcement from Trenton, New Jersey. It is reported that at 8:50 p.m. a huge, flaming object, believed to be a meteorite, fell on a farm in the neighborhood of Grovers Mill, New Jersey, twenty-two miles from Trenton. The flash in the sky was visible within a radius of several hundred miles and the noise of the impact was heard as far north as Elizabeth.

We have dispatched a special mobile unit to the scene, and will have our commentator, Mr. Phillips, give you a word description as soon as he can reach there from Princeton. In the meantime, we take you to the Hotel Martinet in Brooklyn, where Bobby Millette and his orchestra are offering a program of dance music. (SWING BAND FOR 20 SECONDS . . . THEN CUT)

ANNOUNCER TWO. We take you now to Grovers Mill, New Jersey. (CROWD NOISES . . . POLICE SIRENS)

PHILLIPS. Ladies and gentlemen, this is Carl Phillips again, at the Wilmuth farm, Grovers Mill, New Jersey. Professor Pierson and myself made the eleven miles from Princeton in ten minutes. Well, I . . . I hardly know where to begin, to paint for you a word picture of the strange scene before my eyes, like something out of a modern Arabian Nights. Well, I just got here. I haven't had a chance to look around yet. I guess that's *it*. Yes, I guess that's the . . . *thing*, directly in front of me, half buried in a vast pit. Must have struck with terrific force. The ground is covered with splinters of a tree it must have struck on its way down. What I can see of the . . . object itself doesn't look very much like a meteor, at least not the meteors I've seen. It looks more like a huge cylinder. It has a diameter of . . . what would you say, Professor Pierson?

PIERSON *(off)*. About thirty yards.

PHILLIPS. About thirty yards. . . . The metal on the sheath is . . . well, I've never seen anything like it. The color is sort of yellowish-white. Curious spectators now are pressing close to the object in spite of the efforts of the police to keep them back. They're getting in front of my line of vision. Would you mind standing on one side, please?

POLICEMAN. One side, there, one side.

PHILLIPS. While the policemen are pushing the crowd back, here's Mr. Wilmuth, owner of the farm here. He may have some interesting facts to add. . . . Mr. Wilmuth, would you please tell the radio audience as much as you remember of this rather unusual visitor that dropped in your backyard? Step closer, please. Ladies and gentlemen, this is Mr. Wilmuth.

WILMUTH. I was listenin' to the radio.

PHILLIPS. Closer and louder, please.

WILMUTH. Pardon me!

PHILLIPS. Louder, please, and closer.

WILMUTH. Yes, sir—while I was listening to the radio and kinda drowsin', that Professor fellow was talkin' about Mars, so I was half dozin' and half . . .

PHILLIPS. Yes, Mr. Wilmuth. Then what happened?

WILMUTH. As I was sayin', I was listenin' to the radio kinda half-ways . . .

PHILLIPS.   Yes, Mr. Wilmuth, and then you saw something?

WILMUTH.   Not first off. I heard something.

PHILLIPS.   And what did you hear?

WILMUTH.   A hissing sound. Like this: sssssssss . . . kinda like a fourt' of July rocket.

PHILLIPS.   Then what?

WILMUTH.   Turned my head out the window and would have swore I was to sleep and dreamin'.

PHILLIPS.   Yes?

WILMUTH.   I seen a kinda greenish streak and then zingo! Somethin' smacked the ground. Knocked me clear out of my chair!

PHILLIPS.   Well, were you frightened, Mr. Wilmuth?

WILMUTH.   Well, I—I ain't quite sure. I reckon I—I was kinda riled.

PHILLIPS.   Thank you, Mr. Wilmuth. Thank you.

WILMUTH.   Want me to tell you some more?

PHILLIPS.   No. . . . That's quite all right, that's plenty.

PHILLIPS.   Ladies and gentlemen, you've just heard Mr. Wilmuth, owner of the farm where this thing has fallen. I wish I could convey the atmosphere . . . the background of this . . . fantastic scene. Hundreds of cars are parked in a field in back of us. Police are trying to rope off the roadway leading into the farm. But it's no use. They're breaking right through. Their headlights throw an enormous spot on the pit where the object's half-buried. Some of the more daring souls are venturing near the edge. Their silhouettes stand out against the metal sheen. (FAINT HUMMING SOUND)

One man wants to touch the thing . . . he's having an argument with a policeman. The policeman wins. . . . Now, ladies and gentleman, there's something I haven't mentioned in all this excitement, but it's becoming more distinct. Perhaps you've caught it already on your radio. Listen: (LONG PAUSE) . . . Do you hear it? It's a curious humming sound that seems to come from inside the object. I'll move the microphone nearer. Here. (PAUSE) Now we're not more than twenty-five feet away. Can you hear it now? Oh, Professior Pierson!

PIERSON.   Yes, Mr. Phillips?

PHILLIPS.   Can you tell us the meaning of that scraping noise inside the thing?

PIERSON.   Possibly the unequal cooling of its surface.

PHILLIPS.   Do you still think think it's a meteor, Professor?

PIERSON.   I don't know what to think. The metal casing is definitely extra-terrestrial . . . not found on this earth. Friction with the earth's atmosphere usually tears holes in a meteorite. This thing is smooth and, as you can see, of cylindrical shape.

PHILLIPS.   Just a minute! Something's happening! Ladies and gentlemen, this is terrific! This end of the thing is beginning to flake off! The top is beginning to rotate like a screw! The thing must be hollow!

VOICES.

She's a movin'!

Look, the darn thing's unscrewing!

Keep back, there! Keep back, I tell you.

Maybe there's men in it trying to escape!

It's red hot, they'll burn to a cinder!

Keep back there! Keep those idiots back!

(SUDDENLY THE CLANKING SOUND OF A HUGE PIECE OF FALLING METAL)

Voices.

She's off! The top's loose!

Look out there! Stand back!

Ladies and gentlemen, this is the most terrifying thing I have ever witnessed. . . . Wait a minute! Someone's *crawling out of the hollow top*. Some one or . . . something. I can see peering out of that black hole two luminous disks . . are they eyes? It might be a face. It might be. . . . (SHOUT OF AWE FROM THE CROWD)

Good heavens, something's wriggling out of the shadow like a grey snake. Now it's another one, and another. They look like tentacles to me. There, I can see the thing's body. It's large as a bear and it glistens like wet leather. But that face. It . . . it's indescribable. I can hardly force myself to keep looking at it. The eyes are black and gleam like a serpent. The mouth is V-shaped with saliva dripping from its rimless lips that seem to quiver and pulsate. The monster or whatever it is can hardly move. It seems weighed down by . . . possibly gravity or something. The thing's raising up. The crowd falls back. They've seen enough. This is the most extraordinary experience. I can't find words. . . . I'm pulling this microphone with me as I talk. I'll have to stop the description until I've taken a new position. Hold on, will you please, I'll be back in a minute. (FADE INTO PIANO)

ANNOUNCER TWO. We are bringing you an eyewitness account of what's happening on the Wilmuth farm, Grovers Mill, New Jersey. (MORE PIANO)

We now return you to Carl Phillips at Grovers Mill.

PHILLIPS. Ladies and gentlemen (Am I on?). Ladies and gentlemen, here I am, back of a stone wall that adjoins Mr. Wilmuth's garden. From here I get a sweep of the whole scene. I'll give you every detail as long as I can talk. As long as I can see. More state police have arrived. They're drawing up a cordon in front of the pit, about thirty of them. No need to push the crowd back now. They're willing to keep their distance. The captain is conferring with someone. We can't quite see who. Oh yes, I believe it's Professor Pierson. Yes, it is. Now they've parted.

The professor moves around one side, studying the object, while the captain and two policemen advance with something in their hands. I can see it now. It's a white handkerchief tied to a pole . . . a flag of truce. If those creatures know what that means . . . what anything means! . . . *Wait!* Something's happening! (Hissing sound followed by a humming that increases in intensity)

A humped shape is rising out of the pit. I can make out a small beam of light against a mirror. What's that? There's a jet of flame springing from that mirror, and it leaps right at the advancing men. It strikes them head on! Good Lord, they're turning into flame! (Screams and unearthly shrieks)

Now the whole field's caught fire. (Explosion) The woods . . . the barns . . . the gas tanks of automobiles . . . it's spreading everywhere. It's coming this way. About twenty yards to my right. . . . (Crash of microphone . . . then dead silence . . .)

Announcer Two.   Ladies and gentlemen, due to circumstances beyond our control, we are unable to continue the broadcast from Grovers Mill. Evidently there's some difficulty with our field transmission. However, we will return to that point at the earliest opportunity. In the meantime, we have a late bulletin from San Diego, California. Professor Indellkoffer, speaking at a dinner of the California Astronomical Society, expressed the opinion that the explosions on Mars are undoubtedly nothing more than severe volcanic disturbances on the surface of the planet. We continue now with our piano interlude. (Piano . . . then cut) . . .

* * *

Pierson.   After parting with the artilleryman, I came at last to the Holland Tunnel. I entered that silent tube anxious to know the fate of the great city on the other side of the Hudson. Cautiously I came out of the tunnel and made my way up Canal Street.

I reached Fourteenth Street, and there again were black powder and several bodies, and an evil ominous smell from the gratings of the cellars of some of the houses. I wandered up through the thirties and forties; I stood alone on Times Square. I caught sight of a lean dog running down Seventh Avenue with a piece of dark brown meat in his jaws, and a pack of starving mongrels at his heels. He made a wide circle around me, as though he feared I might prove a fresh competitor. I walked up Broadway in the direction of that strange powder—past silent shop windows, displaying their mute wares to empty sidewalks— past the Capital Theatre, silent, dark—past a shooting gallery, where a row of empty guns faced an arrested line of wooden ducks. Near Columbus Circle I noticed models of 1939 motor cars in the show rooms facing empty streets. From over the top of the General Motors Building, I watched a flock of black birds circling in the sky. I hurried on. Suddenly I caught sight of the hood of a Martian machine, standing somewhere in

Central Park, gleaming in the late afternoon sun. An insane idea! I rushed recklessly across Columbus Circle and into the Park. I climbed a small hill above the pond at Sixtieth Street. From there I could see, standing in a silent row along the Mall, nineteen of those great metal Titans, their cowls empty, their steel arms hanging listlessly by their sides. I looked in vain for the monsters that inhabit those machines.

Suddenly, my eyes were attracted to the immense flock of black birds that hovered directly below me. They circled to the ground, and there before my eyes, stark and silent, lay the Martians, with the hungry birds pecking and tearing brown shreds of flesh from their dead bodies. Later when their bodies were examined in laboratories, it was found that they were killed by the putrefactive and disease bacteria against which their systems were unprepared . . . slain after all man's defenses had failed, by the humblest thing that God in His wisdom put upon this earth.

Before the cylinder fell there was a general persuasion that through all the deep of space no life existed beyond the petty surface of our minute sphere. Now we see further. Dim and wonderful is the vision I have conjured up in my mind of life spreading slowly from this little seed-bed of the solar system throughout the inanimate vastness of sidereal space. But that is a remote dream. It may be, that the destruction of the Martians is only a reprieve. To them, and not to us, is the future ordained perhaps.

Strange it now seems to sit in my peaceful study at Princeton writing down this last chapter of the record begun at a deserted farm in Grovers Mill. Strange to see from my window the university spires dim and blue through an April haze. Strange to watch children playing in the streets. Strange to see young people strolling on the green, where the new spring grass heals the last black scars of a bruised earth. Strange to watch the sightseers enter the museum where the dissembled parts of a Martian machine are kept on public view. Strange when I recall the time when I first saw it, bright and clean-cut, hard and silent, under the dawn of that last great day. (MUSIC)

This is Orson Welles, ladies and gentlemen, out of character to assure you that the *War of the Worlds* has no further significance than as the holiday offering it was intended to be. The Mercury Theatre's own radio version of dressing up in a sheet and jumping out of a bush and saying Boo! Starting now, we couldn't soap all your windows and steal all your garden gates, by tomorrow night . . . so we did the next best thing. We annihilated the world before your very ears, and utterly destroyed the Columbia Broadcasting System. You will be relieved, I hope, to learn that we didn't mean it, and that both institutions are still open for business. So good-bye everybody, and remember, please, for the next day or so, the terrible lesson you learned tonight. That grinning, glowing, globular invader of your living-room is an inhabitant of the pumpkin patch, and if your doorbell rings and nobody's there, that was no Martian . . . it's Hallowe'en. (Music)

ANNOUNCER. Tonight the Columbia Broadcasting System, and its affiliated stations coast-to-coast, has brought you *War of the Worlds* by H. G. Wells . . . the seventeenth in its weekly series of dramatic broadcasts featuring Orson Welles and the Mercury Theatre of the Air. *Theme*

ANNOUNCER. Next week we present a dramatization of three famous short stories. This is the COLUMBIA . . . BROADCASTING SYSTEM.

(FADE THEME 20 SECONDS). 9:00 P.M. B-U-L-O-V-A Bulova Watch Time, WABC—New York.

Editorial, New York *World Telegram*, November 1, 1938.

"Frighted with False Fire."

It is strange and disturbing that thousands of Americans, secure in their homes on a quiet Sunday evening, could be scared out of their wits by a radio dramatization of H. G. Wells' fantastic old story, "The War of the Worlds."

We're sure the 23-year-old actor, Orson Welles, didn't realize the panic he was spreading from coast to coast among people who believed that monsters from Mars actually had invaded New Jersey.

Yet young Mr. Welles, a student of Shakespeare, might have remembered Hamlet and, remembering, might have foreseen the effect of too much dramatic realism on an audience already strung to high nervous tension.

Hamlet it was who staged a play to "catch the conscience" of the King of Denmark, his uncle, who had murdered Hamlet's father, seized the throne and married the widowed queen. This play within a play also concerned the murder of a king. And, as Hamlet had intended, his uncle and his mother were driven to such hysterical terror that they refused to watch it to the end.

"What, frighted with false fire!" exclaimed Hamlet with bitter scorn, certain now of his uncle's guilt.

Unlike Hamlet, young Mr. Welles did not plan deliberately to demoralize his audience. And no guilty consciences, but nerves made jittery by actual, though almost incredible, threats of war and disaster, had prepared a good many American radio listeners to believe the completely incredible "news" that Martian hordes were here.

Of course it should never happen again. But we don't agree with those who are arguing that the Sunday night scare shows a need for strict government censorship of radio programs.

On the contrary, we think it is evidence of how dangerous political control of radio might become. If so many people could be misled unintentionally, when the purpose was merely to entertain, what could designing politicians not do through control of broadcasting stations.

The dictators in Europe use radio to make their people believe falsehoods. We want nothing like that here. Better have American radio remain free to make occasional blunders than start on a course that might, in time, deprive it of freedom to broadcast uncensored truth.

And it should be easy for radio to avoid repeating this particular blunder. The Columbia system, as a result of its unhappy experience Sunday night, has already pointed the way. Let all chains, all stations, avoid use of the news broadcasting technique in dramatizations when there is any possiiblity of any listener mistaking fiction for fact.

Radio sportscasters were something special: they had to talk so fast to report all the action that they inevitably fell behind and made mistakes. They also made some sports, notably baseball and boxing, seem ten times as fast as they really were. Radio sports in the 1930s and 1940s was a big and fiercely competitive business and the great announcers were household names.   (From *The Taste of Ashes* by Bill Stern with Oscar Fraley. Copyright © 1959 by Oscar Fraley and Bill Stern. Reprinted by permission of Holt, Rinehart, and Winston, Inc.)

A RADIO RIVALRY: WHO'S GOT THE BALL?

. . . My greatest rivalry throughout these days was with Ted Husing, the ace sports announcer for the Columbia Broadcasting System and a man with a crisp, authoritative voice. It is only natural, I suppose, that he should have resented me, particularly after I regularly began to displace him at the top of various polls.

We were thrown together a great deal, because as I took over the major sports events for NBC Ted was covering them for CBS. He left no doubt that he considered me an imitator, although I honestly didn't feel that I was. After one Notre Dame football game, while we were both standing in the South Bend station waiting for the train to take us back to New York, I admired a sports jacket he was wearing.

"That's a beautiful jacket," I told him, asking idly, "where did you get it, Ted?"

Husing, always impeccable and capable of adopting a scathing tone, drew himself up haughtily, gave me a scornful look, and said sarcastically, "My God, Stern, now are you going to start copying my clothes, too?"

Each of us did everything we could to plague the other. There was one occasion when I almost ruined myself trying to pull a fast one on him.

We were both at an Illinois-Army game in Champaign, Illinois, and the NBC and CBS booths were side-by-side on the top of the triple-deck stadium. Our cable lines ran along a narrow concrete ledge in front of the booths, and on a moment's impulse I slipped a pair of cutting pliers from our engineer's bag, edged my way precariously out on the narrow ledge, and proceeded to snip what I thought were Husing's lines. It never entered my head that one slip of my foot would plunge me to my death. Crawling back inside of my own booth, I sat there with satanic delight waiting for my cue to take the air at 1:45 P.M., fifteen minutes before game time.

But I was filled with consternation as, at the appointed moment, there was no cue for us to start on NBC. Through the thin panel separating us from Husing I dimly could hear Ted opening right on the dot for CBS. Frantically my engineer scrambled out on the ledge and returned shortly with a disgusted look on his face.

"You're a real genius," he growled.

"What was the matter?" I demanded.

"You," he replied with scorn, "cut our lines by mistake."

Both of us were in difficulty on another occasion when we broadcast the Vanderbilt-Alabama football game from Nashville. Our booths, as usual, were perched high atop the rim of the stadium, and when we arrived we discovered that early that same morning some wag had freshly painted both booths, inside and out, with gray paint, which by the end of the afternoon had all of us daubed like Indians. But the perpetrator hadn't let it go at that. On the door to Husing's booth there was painted, in large letters, a sign which said "Ladies." On the door to my booth had been painted "Men." We spent the entire afternoon trying to stay out of fresh paint and directing urgent and persistent ladies and gentlement in other directions.

Another time NBC had bought exclusive rights to the U.S. Amateur Athletic Association's annual national track and field championships. These were to be broadcast from the Marquette University stadium in Milwaukee, and when I began checking over the arrangements everything was fine except for one item.

Overlooking the stadium was a towering church spire and on top of it a platform had been erected, complete right down to a huge beach umbrella. It was obvious to me that Husing intended to bootleg the track meet from outside the stadium with the use of high-powered binoculars as well as by monitoring my broadcast. My suspicions were confirmed shortly when Husing appeared on the platform.

Irritated, I sought out the pastor of the church and explained that NBC had bought exclusive rights to the meet. The minister, a mild, smiling man, replied gently that there was nothing he could do.

"We couldn't possibly ask Mr. Husing to get off the steeple," he said. "Mr. Husing is a God-fearing man and besides he made a substantial cash contribution to the church."

Hastening to the telephone company I ordered them to install two poles directly in line of Husing's vision. Between these we strung huge sheets of cheesecloth. That Husing was ingenious. He simply bought some firecrackers and threw them into the cheesecloth. It vanished in a puff of smoke.

Refusing to be beaten I searched around and hired two mammoth klieg lights to shine up into his eyes. But they were no sooner set up than they had to be discarded on orders of our legal department, which ruled that Husing could sue us on grounds of having done permanent damage to his eyes. We knew, however, that he couldn't see enough of the meet to do it properly without monitoring my broadcast. New York instructed me to make a few intentional mistakes, such as having certain runners fall down when they hadn't. By monitoring his broadcast, NBC found that, within moments, Husing had the same runner falling.

Throughout the rest of the afternoon I made just enough intentional mistakes to hang him. NBC officials summoned CBS officials the following Monday and played back recordings of both broadcasts to show that he had imitated everything I had done, proved, of course, by the intentional mistakes.

As a result of this incident, the networks got together and decided there would be no more piracy. But it didn't last long. Competition was keen and soon we both were back at it.

I did my share, too. Shortly thereafter it was CBS which came up with an exclusive, this time on the Poughkeepsie Regatta. Our legal department decided, cautiously, that while Husing had exclusive rights to broadcast from the observation train which followed the race along the riverbank, nobody had a legal option on the Hudson River.

Thereupon NBC put me atop a house overlooking the Hudson at Poughkeepsie, from which I had a fine view of the water but little else. The four-mile course was impossible to see so I simply listened to Husing broadcast from the observation train, dressed up his report, and repeated his information.

There was just one difficulty.

The usually accurate Husing called the wrong winner.

So did Bill Stern.

Husing's mistake naturally became mine, too. But it wasn't my first, or my last. I have, over the years, taken a great deal of ribbing for my facility in coming out of these situations right side up. Sometimes you just don't have time to make corrections such as the occasion when I had Doc Blanchard of Army running "all by himself" for a touchdown, "down to the thirty, the twenty, the ten. . . ."

Then, to my consternation, I saw that it was Glenn Davis.

Without dropping a syllable I snapped, "And he laterals off to Glenn Davis, who goes over for the touchdown."

Sure, it was a boner and, certainly, I covered it up quickly. Was anybody really hurt in the process? I don't believe so. The vast radio audience had enjoyed a smooth description of a football game. Had I called attention to my error, many listeners might have felt I was balling up the whole game with corrections or would have begun wondering how many other mistakes I was making.

Sometime later, when I went to the Kentucky Derby, I asked Clem McCarthy how he thought I might do with a horse race.

"Okay," Clem said, "but remember, you can't lateral a horse."

(Bill Stern was absent from the airwaves for a time due to illness, but after making a complete recovery he was able to resume his career successfully.)

Radio put great stress on accuracy of presentation and good diction. Mispronunciations and outright errors—called "bloopers"—became instantly famous collectors' items. There was also a famous joke about the stutterer who claimed he had not been hired as a radio announcer "because I'm J-J-J-J-Jewish." (From *The Taste of Ashes* by Bill Stern with Oscar Fraley. Copyright © 1959 by Oscar Fraley and Bill Stern. Reprinted by permission of Holt, Rinehart, and Winston, Inc.)

BILL STERN: RADIO BLOOPERS

Sure, we make mistakes . . . don't you? Radio is a business where mistakes are costly, sometimes funny. Announcers don't always mean what they say. For instance, on the "Martha Jane" show recently, the local lad let go with, "Martha Jane will be back on the air tomorrow with the new babies that have arrived courtesy of Ramsey's Department Store" . . . . And the blurb Jack Frasier, NBC announcer, let fly in a late Army recruiting plug, "Don't forget, men, put your name on a penny post card before you forget it". . . . Or maybe you like this one voiced by Sam Hayes, announcing for pancake and waffle flour, "Every time you have company they stick to the waffle iron". . . . Bob Elson is one of America's top sports announcers yet Bob let fly with "It's printed in clear tripe easy to read". . . . Or the time Ken Carpenter turned red, when he heard himself saying "J. P. Watertown, horse dealer, will stand behind every horse he sells". . . . Don Wilson likes to forget the time he stated "Now ladies I will climb up on the fire escape to get a better view. I will hold on with one hand and talk with the other". . . . And we mustn't forget the one Graham McNamee once used on the O'Sullivan Heel program, "O'Sullivan has been the outstanding heel for years". . . . We could go on and on. Want more?

It was Andre Baruch who, on the "American Album of Familiar Music" stated, "When you have a headache ask for it by its full name" . . . . Or Fletcher Wiley's "Franco-American spaghetti contains a rich, creamy sauce that few people can eat". . . . Or Ben Grauer's immortal crack, "Go to the Plaza Theater where the feature is 'The Vanishing Virgin'—er—I mean 'Virginian'". . . . Or Everett Mitchell announcing on the "Farm and Home Hour" when he said "Fertilizer has twice as much organic matter in it—now there's something to sink your teeth into". . . . Or Milton Cross in his never to be forgotten "A & P Gypsy Show" stating "You will now listen to the music of the A & P Pipsies". . . . And we mustn't forget Harry Von Zell who introduced the then President of the United States by saying "Now I present the President of the United States —Heever Herbert, I mean Hoobert Heever, aw nuts, Herbert Hoover!"

But announcers aren't the only ones who make mistakes in radio . . . For instance, the time "Amos and Andy" got twisted in a commercial being done by Bill Hay, who said, "The rich tomato sauce, the pork and beans, are all half-baked—how about your family?" . . . Or the day when the late Lou Gehrig was guesting on a beer show and closed by saying "Fill up your glass with Bupperts reer." . . . But then guest stars have made more than one bull. . . . Max Baer in the middle of a heavyweight championship fight leaned over the ropes and yelled down at Clem McCarthy who was broadcasting the fight: "Hey Clem, take it easy, I can't keep up with you." . . . Or, for that matter, the night Sam Taub in describing another fight excitedly yelled into the mike: "He hit him in a neutral corner where it don't hurt". . . . Or maybe you like the one Harriet Hilliard pulled last season on the Red Skelton show: "This is the best bed George Slepington washed in". . . .

News commentators have had their troubles, too. . . . H. V. Kaltenborn gets credit for this one: "I'll be back on Monday with the same sad news". . . . Or perhaps you'd care for the one Fulton Lewis, Jr., let fly. Said Mr. Lewis: "Remember Bar Harbor!" . . . Or the day Raymond Gram Swing announced, "The bill was sent by airplane to President Roosevelt who was fishing in Florida waters for his signature". . . . Or the night George Putnam wound up his evening news show with the soap suds commercial "It burps into snuds."

Sure we make mistakes but as I said before don't you? And lest you think yours truly is immune to the error department let me briefly call back to your mind one I pulled which caused me no end of embarrassment. I was describing the Army-Notre Dame football game when for no reason at all I said "Bertelli of Notre Dame is forced out of bounds by a whole group of Army ticklers."

Once a television show embodies a successful formula or embraces an attractive personality, it is bound to be with us for a long time. Such was the case with "What's My Line?" Its gentle, lighthearted format entertained millions until, somehow, it fell victim to the changing tastes of the 1960s.

WHAT'S MY LINE?

ANNOUNCER. Time now for everybody's favorite guessing game *What's My Line?* Yes, time now for *What's My Line?* Now let us hear our award winning *What's My Line* panel. First, the popular columnist whose "Voice of Broadway" appears in the Journal American and papers coast to coast, Miss Dorothy Kilgallen.

DOROTHY KILGALLEN. And on my left, the brilliant young humorist who conducts his own very funny television show nightly Monday through Friday, on another network, Mr. Steve Allen.

STEVE ALLEN. Thanks very much. I now want you to meet one of the loveliest ladies of radio and television who has her own show on another network. We are all working at a great pace these days. Arlene Francis.

ARLENE FRANCIS. And on my left substituting for Bennett Cerf tonight, a vastly entertaining gentleman who is packing them in at his own one-man show at the Golden Theater in New York, Mr. Victor Borge.

VICTOR BORGE. On my left, that well known news commentator and moderator, Mr. John Daly.

JOHN DALY. Good evening ladies and gentlemen and welcome to *What's My Line?* Once again tonight we have some friends in from around and about the country who brought with them some very interesting occupations and the panel will have to tussle with the occupations— Victor Borge, getting his baptism of fire. We hope that they will have a lot of trouble so that our guests will carry home some prizes although the more important thing is that they have some fun. We will also have a famous guest challenger a bit later on. But right now it's time for our experts to meet the first challenger whose job has to be spotted. Will you sign in please, Sir.

(*Guest signs J. L. May on blackboard*)

JOHN DALY.   Come over here with me. Well Mr. May don't stand so far away. What does J. L. stand for?

MAY.   Julius L. May.

DALY.   Where from, Sir?

MAY.   New York City.

DALY.   New York City, well I don't think there are any strangers over there as far as you're concerned, but you may be a stranger to them. Will you go over and say, "Hello" to them, please.

(*May walks to panel to shake hands*)

KILGALLEN.   Good evening.

DALY.   All right Mr. May, will you come over here now please and sit down next to me. I think perhaps you know at this point the panel gets one free guess as to what your line may be. We always begin the free guessing with Miss Kilgallen.

KILGALLEN.   I think he is in the tailoring business.

DALY.   Mr. Allen.

ALLEN.   I think he is in charge of bird seed at the old flow plant here in town.

ARLENE FRANCIS.   I think he is a tea bag tester.

VICTOR BORGE.   I think he is a floor walker.

DALY.   No, I am afraid not. Now we'll let our viewers at home have a further look at Mr. Julius May and at the same time we will tell them what his line is.

(*Card saying: Printer of Parking Tickets*)

Mr. May or Mr. Julius May, if I may—I think perhaps you know the rules here. Everytime I flip a card you have given the panel a "no" answer. When you have given the panel 10 "no" answers you have got it all in the bag. All set?

MAY.   All right.

DALY.   Mr. May is salaried. With that, let us begin the general questioning with Steve Allen.

ALLEN.   Pardon me, Mr. Julius LaRosa May. (*Arlene Francis laughs*) Thank you, Arlene. Is there a product connected with what you are doing?

MAY.   Yes.

ALLEN.   The sort of thing that I might come into contact with?

DALY.   Is it the sort of thing *you* might come into contact with? Yes, yes indeed.

ALLEN.   I can never tell why, every time I ask that question, it always seems amusing. However, trying to figure it out I might say, if you were to wear this on Fifth Avenue would people laugh?

DALY.   If you were to wear this on Fifth Avenue would the people laugh? If *you* were to wear it, I think they would.

ALLEN.   Could this be anything that might be associated with a woman?

DALY.   Yes, this could be associated with a woman.

ALLEN.   Is it something a man might give to a woman?

DALY.   Yes.

ALLEN.   Are they or is this as the case may be fairly expensive?

DALY.   Could it be fairly expensive? Well, I would say this. I think it is only fair, and I think Mr. May would agree with me, it could be expensive. Yes, don't you think?

(*Looking at May*)

MAY.   Absolutely.

ALLEN.   Is this something a woman might pick up on Fifth Avenue around Tiffany's or Cartier's neighborhood?

DALY.   Is this something a woman might pick up on Fifth Avenue around Tiffany's or Cartier's neighborhood?—Yes.

ALLEN.   If a man gave a woman one of these could she wear it around her neck?

DALY.   Mr. May makes the point that she could wear it around her neck. Yes.

ALLEN.   Let me come right out and straighten the whole thing out. Is this anything in the jewelry line at all?

DALY.   No, that's one down and nine to go. Miss Francis.

FRANCIS.   Is it possible that Mr. May may deal with something other than human beings?

MAY.   How do you mean that?

FRANCIS.   You know what is other than a human being, John. Could he have anything to do with animals?

DALY.   No. Two down and eight to go. Mr. Borge.

BORGE.   Is it something Steve Allen can get in contact with? Something I can get in contact with also?

DALY.   Yes.

BORGE.   As well as Steve?

DALY.   Yes. Steve.

ALLEN. I'll split it with you, Victor.

BORGE. Is it something a lady can wear around the neck?

DALY. Yes, it was answered already. Preferably, she would not.

BORGE. Would it be below the, uh, below the lower neck?

DALY. Well, Victor, I think I will have to give you a "no" on that. It cannot be worn below the lower neck. Three down, seven to go.

KILGALLEN. All right, I want to know if Arlene and I can come in contact with it, then we'll get the whole panel going with this thing.

DALY. Yes.

KILGALLEN. Would I enjoy coming in contact with it?

DALY. I am afraid not. Four down, six to go. Mr. Allen.

ALLEN. Would I also not enjoy it?

DALY. Would he also not enjoy coming in contact?

MAY. I think not.

DALY. Yes, you would not enjoy coming in contact with this thing.

ALLEN. Now let us keep it off our necks. It is unpleasant in some way?

DALY. He thinks it might be unpleasant.

MAY. In most cases, yes.

DALY. As a matter of fact he is having a hard time thinking of a case where it would not be unpleasant.

ALLEN. Is the idea of punishment associated with this product?

DALY. I think we would better say yes.

ALLEN. Something you wear around your neck? That's a noose. Do you find this associated with prisoners, they're in jail?

DALY. No, I don't think so. That's five down and five to go. I am going to give you another minute to try and guess it. Miss Francis.

FRANCIS. Do you say, Mr. May that all of us could come in contact with it, but we would not be likely to come in contact with it?

MAY. I cannot say a single soul on that panel would not be likely to come in contact with it.

DALY. That's six down four to go. Mr. Borge.

BORGE. Is it something that is worn?

DALY. No, seven down three to go and thirty seconds. Miss Kilgallen.

KILGALLEN. Is this something that in order to be used must be imposed by one person upon another?

DALY. I think that is correct.

KILGALLEN. Would anyone ever strike a person with it?

DALY. Would anyone ever strike a person with it?

KILGALLEN. Yes, or otherwise belabor.

DALY. That would be eight down two to go. I don't think you are even close to what this might be. Mr. May prints parking tickets. Mr. May you won the full prize.

MAY. I am giving my money to the March of Dimes.

DALY. Yes sir, the full prize is yours and will go to the March of Dimes. Well panel, a rather inauspicious beginning but a lot of fun. Let us see what you can do with the second challenger. Will you sign in, please, Ma'm?

(Guest signs in on blackboard)

DALY. Amy E. Shortie Hiller. You are not so short, you are not so short at all as a matter of fact. Is it Miss or Mrs.?

HILLER. Miss.

DALY. And where are you from?

HILLER. Houston, Texas.

DALY. Sounds very much like all of Texas has moved to New York this weekend. Well, we have got some folks here from New York. Would you like to say hello to them?

(Guest walks to panel)

I think perhaps you know that after the panel has had a chance to meet you, we give the panel one free guess as to what your line may be. We always begin with Dot.

KILGALLEN. I think she's a steer roper.

ALLEN. I think she's a rope steerer and we have heard these jokes before.

FRANCIS. I think she teaches ballet.

BORGE. I think she's awfully cute.

(Gorilla Hunter)

DALY. We'll let our viewers have another look at Miss Hiller of Houston, Texas. And now Miss Hiller the panel has got to take it from here and I will flip the card every time they give a no answer. Miss Hiller is self-employed. Let us begin the general questioning with Mr. Borge.

BORGE. Oh my goodness! Is there a product involved?

HILLER. Yes.

BORGE. Thank you. Is this a thing? Could it be found in the home?

HILLER. Yes, yes it can be but it is not normally found in the home.

BORGE. Can it be found outside the home?

Americans have a continuing passion for ranking the popularity of shows, books, people, birds, flowers, criminals, and so on. Television ratings are perhaps the most statistically sophisticated version of the interest, and many people follow the ratings of television programs as carefully as they do standings in the National or American League. (Selection from Dick Hobson, "Who Watches What?", *TV Guide,* July 27, 1968.)

"WHO WATCHES WHAT?"

Southerners watch Westerns.
Eggheads dig Gleason.
Literates prefer Don Adams.
Less-literates go for Jim Nabors.
Blue collar workers choose countrified situation comedies.
Affluents prefer movies to anything else.
Lawrence Welk is boss with the Geritol Tribe.
Sophisticates pick specials.
Everybody likes Tennessee Ernie Ford.

If it sounds like plain common sense, it is that and more. It all derives from highly sophisticated demographic surveys designed to show just who watches what. Gone are the days when it's enough to say that a program rates in the Top 10 or 20 or Top 40. Today's sponsors want to know the "demographies."

These elaborate sampling surveys would never have been undertaken were it not for the insistent demands of TV merchandising. Yet the facts themselves remain uncontaminated by commercialism. The findings are sound sociology. We can forget consumer products for the moment and focus on the Sociology of Viewing Preferences—who watches what.

The following "demographies," determined by the A.C. Nielsen Co. and excluding specials, reflect the tastes of America over a six-week period from October 23 to December 3, 1967.

First, consider the U.S. as a whole:

U.S. Top 10

1. Lucy Show
2. Andy Griffith
3. Bonanza
4. Red Skelton
5. Gunsmoke
6. Family Affair
7. Jackie Gleason
8. Gomer Pyle

9. Saturday Movies

10. $\begin{cases} \text{Beverly Hillbillies} \\ \text{Friday Movies} \end{cases}$

Here we see that there are three "countrified" comedies (*Griffith, Pyle* and *Hillbillies*), two Westerns (*Bonanza* and *Gunsmoke*), two variety shows (one "countrified"—*Skelton;* one "citified"—*Gleason*), two family comedies (*Lucy* and *Family Affair*), and two movie nights. This is just a start. Industry wants to know the viewer's age, sex, geographical location, income, education, occupation and a lot more.

Nielsen begins by breaking down viewing preferences by geographical region. For contrast, consider the Top 10 ranking shows for the South and the Northeast:

Top 10 in South	Top 10 in Northeast
1. Gunsmoke	1. Jackie Gleason
2. Bonanza	2. Smothers Bros.
3. Andy Griffith	3. Dean Martin
4. Lucy Show	4. Ed Sullivan
5. Gomer Pyle	5. Friday Movies
6. Red Skelton	6. Saturday Movies
7. Family Affair	7. Lucy Show
8. Virginian	8. Thursday Movies
9. Daniel Boone	9. Tuesday Movies
10. Beverly Hillbillies	10. My Three Sons

The South's Top 10 is similar to the U.S. as a whole, with eight shows in common. Conspicuously absent are movies, originally made for a more sophisticated theater audience. Also missing is *Gleason,* an urban taste. In their place are two more Westerns.

The Top 10 in the Northeast has only four shows in common with the U.S. nationally. Out are all the countrified situation comedies and Westerns. In are the citified variety shows which occupy the top four places. *Gleason* leads the pack. The Northeast has two more movie nights.

Comparing Northeast and South, the two regions have only one show in common: *Lucy*. For the rest, their tastes are dissimilar. In movies, it's 4 to 0. In variety shows it's 4 to 1.

So much for geography. Breakdowns by income give us a new look:

Top 10 for Incomes Under $5000	Top 10 for Incomes $10,000 & Over
1. Lucy Show	1. Saturday Movies
2. Gunsmoke	2. Dean Martin

3. Andy Griffith	3. Friday Movies
4. Red Skelton	4. Andy Griffith
5. Lawrence Welk	5. Thursday Movies
6. Bonanza	6. Smothers Bros.
7. Gomer Pyle	7. Family Affair
8. Family Affair	8. Jackie Gleason
9. {Ed Sullivan / Virginian}	9. Tuesday Movies
	10. FBI

Tastes of the lower income group are similar to the U.S. as a whole except that movies are out, *Gleason* is out, and *Welk* and *Sullivan* are in.

The most conspicuous feature of the upper income group is the prominence of movies—four of the Top 10, including the No. 1 show. The upper income groups have three citified variety shows and the first dramatic show to appear in these ratings, *The F.B.I.*

In comparing the two income groups, the uppers prefer movies and drama, the lowers prefer Westerns and situation comedies. In the variety field, the uppers prefer *Gleason, Martin* and *Smothers,* the lowers prefer *Skelton, Welk* and *Sullivan.* Education changes the picture again:

Top 10: Grade School Education

1. Lucy Show
2. Andy Griffith
3. Gunsmoke
4. Red Skelton
5. Bonanza
6. Gomer Pyle
7. Family Affair
8. Lawrence Welk
9. Virginian
10. Jackie Gleason

Top 10: 1 + Years of College

1. Saturday Movies
2. Mission: Impossible
3. Smothers Bros.
4. Dean Martin
5. Jackie Gleason
6. Tuesday Movies
7. Bewitched
8. NFL Football
9. Thursday Movies
10. Get Smart

The Top 10 for the grade school educated mostly follows the national rankings except for the exclusion of movies and the addition of *Lawrence Welk* and a Western.

The Top 10 for the college educated, however, is dissimilar. *Gleason* and movies are all they have in common with the U.S. as a whole. Next to *Saturday Movies,* the highest rated show is a drama, *Mission: Impossible.* Their two situation comedies, *Bewitched* and *Get Smart,* are considered more sophisticated than *Lucy* or *Pyle.*

Classifying TV households by education of the head of the household, the Nielsen Company estimates there are 15.3 million homes in the grade school category and 12.7 million in the one-plus years of college. Grade school types prefer Andy Griffith and Jim Nabors; college types

prefer Elizabeth Montgomery and Don Adams. The grade school educated go for *Skelton* and *Welk;* collegers like the *Smothers Brothers* and
Dean Martin.

The blue collar Top 10 generally goes along with the U.S. as a
whole, but the white collar Top 10 has more movies, citified variety
shows, and a drama, *Mission: Impossible.* Blue collars comprise 48 percent of all TV households; white collars 36 percent.

Top 10: Blue Collar	Top 10: White Collar
1. Andy Griffith	1. Saturday Movies
2. Lucy Show	2. Dean Martin
3. Bonanza	3. Andy Griffith
4. Red Skelton	4. Smothers Bros.
5. Beverly Hillbillies	5. Mission: Impossible
6. Gunsmoke	6. Jackie Gleason
7. Gomer Pyle	7. Tuesday Movies
8. Bewitched	8. Family Affair
9. Green Acres	9. Thursday Movies
10. {Family Affair / Saturday Movies}	10. {Friday Movies / Lucy Show}

The blues have two Westerns in their Top 10 to the whites' none,
four country comedies to the whites' one. Both like *Lucy* and *Andy Griffith.*

There is strikingly little overlap between the Top 10's of the South
and of the Northeast (one show) between those of the Under $5000 and
the Over $10,000 (two shows), between the Grade School Only and the
One-Plus Years of College (one show), and between the Blue Collar and
the White Collar (four shows). The next time one hears the phrase "Top
10," it is fair to ask which Top 10.

On the other hand, there is a great deal of overlap in the Top 10's
of the South, the Under-$5000 income group, the Grade School educated,
and the Blue Collar workers, which we shall consider together under the
heading "Just Plain Folks." Almost as much overlap is found among the
Northeast, Over-$10,000 income group, One-Plus Years of College, and
White Collar workers, an aggregation which some advertisers call "Sophisticates."

A goodly number of "specials" were aired during the six-week period under study. They were excluded. Were these taken into account,
the Top 10's of the Sophisticates would include between five and eight
specials; the Top 10's of Just Plain Folks would include only one or two.
The Tennessee Ernie Ford special is the only one that consistently scored
as well with both.

Further demographic breakdowns are regularly conducted by the

Home Testing Institute of Manhasset, Long Island, and expressed as numerical "TvQ" scores. Whereas the *Nielsen* ratings are based on a sample of [1200] homes and show merely whether the household TV set is switched on and, if so, which channel the set is tuned to, TvQ scores are based on a survey of 2000 individuals in 750 families and go further to measure attentiveness and degree of enthusiasm for programs.

The shows in TvQ's Top 10's are generally more sophisticated than those in Nielsen's because they are programs the viewers are interested in rather than possibly just the best of a bad lot—the least bad at the time period. Significantly, Nielsen's two big rating leaders, *Andy Griffith* and *Lucy*, are entirely absent from TvQ's Top 10's. In fact, *The Lucy Show* fails to appear on a single TvQ Top 20 breakdown.

The following demographics, supplied by HTI, reflect the tastes of selected age and sex categories in November 1967, during the period under discussion:

Top 10 Among Children 6-11

1. Flying Nun
2. Second Hundred Years
3. Family Affair
4. Monkees
5. Gomer Pyle
6. Bewitched
7. Beverly Hillbillies
8. Gentle Ben
9. Off to See the Wizard
10. Walt Disney

Top 10 Among Teenagers 12-17

1. Guns of Will Sonnett
2. Second Hundred Years
3. Monkees
4. Star Trek
5. Smothers Brothers
6. Flying Nun
7. Saturday Movies
8. I Spy
9. Dragnet
10. Family Affair

Top 10 for Adults 18-34

1. Saturday Movies
2. Friday Movies
3. Thursday Movies
4. Wed. Movies
5. Mission: Impossible
6. Tuesday Movies
7. Dean Martin
8. I Spy
9. Sunday Movies
10. High Chapparral

Top 10 for Adults Over 50

1. Lawrence Welk
2. CBS News
3. Bonanza
4. Walt Disney
5. Virginian
6. Family Affair
7. Gunsmoke
8. Dean Martin
9. Gomer Pyle
10. Daniel Boone

From these Top 10's as well as from other HTI Top 10's that fill out the total age and sex picture, some new sociological perspectives emerge:

Family Affair appeals to children, teen-agers, women, and middle-aged and old people—everybody, in fact, but young adults.

Westerns are most liked by men of all ages and old people. There are no Westerns in the Top 10's of children or women [except for women over 50].

Movies are the Top 10 choice of young adults but not of children (it's bedtime) or the elderly.

The Flying Nun is No. 1 with children and No. 6 with teen-agers, and appears on no Top 10 for older folks.

It should be no surprise that the No. 1 show for the age group 50 and older is *Lawrence Welk*. Other shows in the Top 10 of the Over 50's —and for no younger age group—are *The Virginian, Gunsmoke* and *Daniel Boone*.

Shows that are Top 10 choices of husbands but not of housewives are Westerns and action-adventure series. Housewives prefer movies.

Gentle Ben, of course, is strictly a kiddy passion, and *The Smothers Brothers* a prime teen taste, but *Gomer Pyle* is something of an anomaly, appearing only on the two Top 10's at either end of the age spectrum: children and adults over 50. Certainly something to ponder.

Does violent entertainment lead its viewers to crime? The question arises in every generation: attacks on the first movies were couched in the same terms. A number of psychological and sociological studies have found no connection between viewing and the perpetuating of violence. But perhaps there are other ills forthcoming. (J. Edgar Hoover, "To All Law Enforcement Officials," May 1, 1958).

TV VIOLENCE: J. EDGAR HOOVER SPEAKS OUT

As a law enforcement officer and as an American citizen, I feel duty-bound to speak out against a dangerous trend which is manifesting itself in the field of film and television entertainment. In the face of the Nation's terrifying juvenile crime wave, we are threatened with a flood of movies and television presentations which flaunt indecency and applaud lawlessness. Not since the days when thousands filed past the bier of the infamous John Dillinger and made his home a virtual shrine have we witnessed such a brazen affront to our national conscience.

As an illustration, two brothers, aged 10 and 12, who a few weeks ago terrorized a town in Oklahoma in a shooting spree that left one man dead and two others wounded, told the police they got the idea from watching television and movie crime stories.

There are, of course, many responsible leaders in the motion picture and television industries who dedicate their efforts to producing wholesome entertainment and to upholding the worthwhile principles of established production codes of ethics. Again and again, they serve the best interests of law enforcement and the public welfare by genuine portrayals of criminals in their true light—wretched, unglamorous leeches who bring nothing but degradation to themselves and human suffering to their fellow men.

Regrettably, however, there are some unscrupulous individuals who value money above morals, and whose actions should be exposed in the searching klieg light of public opinion. In their lust for bigger and bigger profits, they glorify violence, glamorize corruption, and picture criminals as heroes for youth to idolize.

One movie code official recently declared that the number of murders in a film is not particularly important—only the reason why the criminal committed a murder is of concern. He said he would not permit a wanton killing to be depicted but indicated that the killer first had to be "wronged." What kind of double moral stand is this? This same official, in describing a film, said there were *only* twelve murders—not an excessive number according to his interpretation of the production code. What kind of rationalization is this?

I deplore censorship—and certainly law enforcement officials have no right to dictate what should or should not be shown on the rectangular screens. They do have, however, the obligation to insist on the observance of the moral law which binds men in all matters. They also have the right to speak out when law enforcement is held up to ridicule and the criminal is elevated to heroic proportions.

No standard of decency or code of operations can justify portraying vile gangsters as modern-day Robin Hoods. Film trash mills, which persist in exalting violence and immorality, spew out celluloid poison which is destroying the impressionable minds of youth. In commenting on a current blood-drenched screenplay, one reviewer wrote, "If you enjoy turning over rocks to see what crawls out, you'll have a gay time. . . ."

Parental supervision over the entertainment fare of children, discretion on the part of movie and television viewers, fulfillment of community responsibility by film exhibitors and television station executives, and citizen protests to producers of offensive shows can solve this problem.

Unless the leaders in the television and motion picture industries take the initiative to correct this ominous trend of crime glorification, they may be assured it can be accomplished by the strong pressure of public opinion. Time after time, the voice of the citizen has brought action, and it can be done again.

Perhaps no other form of popular entertainment has established as close a rapport with its audience as did the movies in their golden age from early in the century until the rise of television in the late 1940s. Fan magazines rapidly followed in the wake of identification with the actors and actresses. Mary Pickford was one of the first of "America's sweethearts." (Selection from *Photoplay*, August 1913.)

THE CHARM OF WISTFULNESS

An Interview with "Little Mary" Pickford,
"The Good Little Devil" by Estelle Kegler

A captious critic once offered a reward of a thousand dollars for any one of his ilk who had written about the art of Mary Pickford without using the word "wistful."

Up to now no one has come to claim the reward. The critic knew he was safe.

The morning New York awoke to place the laurel wreath of a new fame on the childish brow of its "good little devil," you might have read of Mary's wistful eyes, her wistful smile, her wistful voice. That solemn group of folks who sit in aisle seats and sharpen their pencils over the trembling forms of terrified authors, behaved quite as if they had discovered Mary.

As a matter of fact, Mary had been "discovered" long before these reviewers of plays, who never speak of the "movies" without a shudder, ever suspected anything artistic could come from pictures. Out in Manhattan, Kansas, or Moose Jaw, they knew all about little Mary long before Mr. Belasco, dealer in high-brow drama, ever considered offering her a prominent place in a Broadway production. And she burst upon the "Big Way" with the acclaim of more than a million picture fans trailing her right up to the stage door. The acclaim has now turned to clamor—clamor for the return of Mary to the world of photoplays.

"When I think of that great big generous world out there really wanting me to come out on the screen and play with its fancy, it makes me so homesick I could weep," is the confession of Miss Pickford.

It was in Shanleys, after one of the best performances the lady,

late of the silent drama, had ever given in "The Good Little Devil."
Around in front of the Republic theatre playgoers lingering for their
carriages, were still discussing the appeal of the blind "Juliet." The
newest star in Mr. Belasco's constellation looked as weary as the bouquet
of violets drooping in her nervous fingers.

"Of course I love the spoken drama, too," she hastened to add,
brightening at the contemplation of her established success. "When I
left the motion picture field it was not necessarily a final farewell. I believed people in my profession should know how to do a great many
things and do them well.

"When the pictures are peopled with actors and actresses who have
the solid foundation of experience beneath them they will be infinitely
better than they have been under the regime of amateurs whose only
claim to being cast is that they photograph well. There must be something more than mere photography. There must be technique, ease,
versatility, and seriousness of intent."

It seemed so incongruous to have this child creature sit there and
deliver judgments on subjects so serious as the future of a national
amusement. One must constantly revert to the kingdom of careers where
it is written that Mary began wielding the grease paint and hare's foot
when she was a mere baby, and that she has been building up fame
and a bank account ever since.

"It is a long way from the glamour of face to face applause to the
heaps of admiration and approval that come to the picture favorite
through the mails." said Mary. "For the one there are invitations to sip
tea, to dine, to sup, to go here and there and everywhere, to meet this
celebrity and that man and the other woman.

"For the other there is the peace, the security, the privacy of the
woman whose circle of admirers is limited to her family and her friends.
The actress finds it difficult to draw a definite line between her professional and her home lives. The picture actress slips off her screen identity
with her screen wardrobe, and the minute she leaves the studio she is just
like any other private citizeness. It is all a matter of preference. Oh yes,
and of dollars."

Mary didn't tell me, but I happen to know she is a bit of a home-
body herself. In a cozy little, rosy little apartment not very far from the
Hudson river, she is the daintiest chatelaine that ever presided over the
destiny of a happy home and an adoring, awfully good looking husband.

Yes, Lovey Mary has fallen victim to the wiles of Danny, the boy
with the bow and arrow. If you should call at the apartment and inquire
for Mrs. Owen Moore, who do you think, would be the answer? Why
none other than the girl with the sunny curls, the blue violet eyes, the
pouting lips of the "good little devil."

Perhaps the curls would be twisted up into a grown-up knot as becomes one who deals with the servant problem and other items of housewifely lore, but the wistful smile would be there to greet you.

Will little Mary return to delight the hearts of her nickle-a-half-a-dime public? Perhaps so. You know she promised "maybe."

The 1930s were the peak years for Hollywood, if for no other industry. Eighty million admissions a week made motion pictures a leading industry, and the effect of movies on the American imagination was probably at its height. The talkies introduced a whole new dimension, opening careers for some and closing them for others. (Jack Gilbert, lover of the silent stage, was through.) The letters from fans are particularly suggestive of the degree to which the lives of the stars figured in the dream life of the great audience. (Selections from *Photoplay* magazine, Katherine Albert, "Is Jack Gilbert Through?" February 1930; "Letters," March, 1935.)

IS JACK GILBERT THROUGH?

When beautiful Ida Adair, second-rate actress in a traveling theatrical troupe, bore an unwanted, unloved man child in Logan, Utah, she didn't know that some day he would hold the fate of two enormous studios in the hollow of his hand.

She didn't know that the little boy, cradled in the top of a trunk, lulled to sleep by the clicking of wheels over rails, would grow up to be one of the most glamorous contemporary figures.

Lovely Ida, as profligate as a Winter wind, as vivid as a sunset, called her son John. It was a plain name for a plain little boy—a sullen child who resented life before he could talk and who looked upon the world into which he had been unfortunate enough to be born with a growing distaste.

Jack Gilbert, erstwhile soldier of fortune, erstwhile rubber salesman, extra boy, director, writer, itinerant actor, has become one of the most exciting personalities that ever flashed across a screen.

He holds one of the most unusual contracts ever given a star. And it's an iron-bound contract, without options!

In two years he will be paid, as salary, one million dollars! His studio bungalow is more elaborate than most of the homes in Hollywood.

His fame has spread around the world. Thousands of women who have never seen him are in love with him.

And now Hollywood says that the great Gilbert, the amazing lover of the screen, is through—has failed at the very height of his career.

It says that his enemies (and he has plenty) are glad. But that the studio officials who must pay him a million dollars in two years, whether his pictures play to vacant seats or not, are turning white-haired over night.

Is Jack Gilbert finished? Is his art but dust and ashes? Let us consider the facts in this amazing case.

The signing of the name John Gilbert to a little piece of paper was of utmost importance to a fifty million dollar deal. Jack was more or less of a pawn. He didn't realize how vital he was to the financial gods.

He had been discontented, miserable—as he usually is, except when he is radiant, enthusiastic—with his lot at the Metro-Goldwyn-Mayer studios. He had argued with the producers about stories and characterizations. United Artists had made him an offer. He decided to accept.

But forces of which he knew nothing were working around him. The West Coast officials had heard only rumors of the Fox-M-G-M merger, or rather, the sale of the controlling interest of Loew's Inc. to the Fox organization.

But the New York powers knew of the deal and they also knew that if Gilbert, one of the most important stars, slipped through their fingers, the deal might not go through. Fox wanted M-G-M, but it needed all their stars.

Greta Garbo was safely bound under a long-term contract. Lon Chaney, Marion Davies, Billy Haines, Ramon Novarro, Joan Crawford were all secure. Only Gilbert showed signs of leaving.

Gilbert and his manager went to New York and the executives there told him that he must remain with M-G-M. Gilbert refused. At last he was asked, "But what will make you stay?"

His manager answered. He outlined a contract so absurd, so preposterous that he expected only loud guffaws. But the executive didn't laugh. He knew that if Gilbert didn't sign, the tremendous deal might fall through.

"You will stay on those terms?" asked the executive. "Very well, I will draw up such a contract."

And such a contract! It is for two years, two pictures a year at $250,000 a picture or about $10,000 a week. Gilbert has the right to O.K. or N.G. all stories. He was given an enormous dressing room bungalow, second to none on the lot. His manager was included with a nice job and the right to handle Gilbert's affairs as well. An iron-bound document, without options!

But as the great financial powers of the studios battled for Gilbert's signature, another force was working.

Warner Brothers had used a trick device whereby the shadows of the screen stepped up and spoke words.

The device was crude and the wise guys shook their heads and said, "Oh, it can't last. It's just a novelty. There will always be silent pictures."

Gilbert returned to Hollywood with his contract in his pocket. He watched his bungalow grow on the lot. He was anxious to rid himself of the old agreement and start on the new. He was happier than he had been for some time.

Fox bought the controlling interest in M-G-M. All was saved. But the little talking device had been perfected.

The films had learned to speak and all the stars must speak, too. Gilbert's voice!

What about Gilbert's voice?

What about the voice of the man who is virile as a steel mill, lusty as Walt Whitman, romantic as a June moon?

Gilbert's voice! You heard it in "His Glorious Night." It is high-pitched, tense, almost piping at times.

His friends have known for years that it was completely unsuited to the strength and fire of the man.

Jack's great art is pantomime. Remember those remarkable close-ups of intense eyes? Gilert is always keyed up to the highest pitch of excitement.

It is the thing that made him the great actor he is. It was tremendous on the silent screen. He spoke through his eyes.

But any singer will tell you that the voice is right only when the body is relaxed. The voice, to be convincing, must flow calmly.

Gilbert was caught unprepared for the talkies.

While other stars were trotting to elocution teachers and voice specialists, Gilbert was flying to an obscure town in Nevada and getting married to Ina Claire.

He had one more picture to make under the old contract, and he threw in another for good measure because he was happy and because he was a boy with a new wife, a new contract and the anticipation of a honeymoon in Europe.

"Redemption" was his first talking picture. It was a great mistake. He tried too hard. He was nervous in the new medium. He had been so sure of himself in the old.

All during this time, sitting across from Jack at the breakfast table, was a woman who could have taught him every *nuance* of line delivery. Ina Claire could have taught him to speak.

If you have ever tried to learn anything from your wife, anything that she knows better than you, you will understand.

"Redemption" was a sorry affair. It was temporarily shelved. But in the meantime Gilbert had to make a talking début. He promised to do a picture before he went to Europe if it could be rushed through in four weeks. It was rushed. The result was "His Glorious Night." It was released while he was in Europe.

Almost before he stepped off the boat, upon his return, he asked: "How's my picture? What do the critics think of my picture?" For Gilbert's career has dominated his life.

His friends had to tell him that his first talkie was not good. He could see the criticisms for himself.

He suffered anger, then shame, and then anger again.

What went on in his mind was masked by a forced gaiety.

And the studio officials, bound to him irrevocably under the contract which had cinched a financial deal, heard bitterly the echoes that Gilbert's picture inspired. Gilbert's voice had failed in his first talking release. The fans were shocked when he spoke.

He rides into the driveway of his studio bungalow in the morning. The studio is bound to him under a contract that cannot be broken. He gives every outward appearance of a successful man, but his voice has failed, he has lost heavily on the stock market and he is separated from his wife.

They call it a temporary separation, but I cannot help but believe that it is the beginning of the end.

Gilbert has no talent for domesticity and Ina is a positive woman.

His career has gotten on his nerves and Gilbert must fight his battles alone. Garrulous as he is, he remains at heart a lonely soul, as all creative artists are.

Well, what is there left for him to do? No matter what happens he will earn a million dollars in the next two years. But it isn't money that counts with him. Gilbert could not retire. His art means more to him than wealth and fame. He would go insane if he were idle.

What then? He *must* learn to talk. But how?

If he could go away and have six months in a small stock company it would make him over. But John Gilbert could not do this for professional as well as personal reasons. Well, then, a teacher.

The actor, himself, takes first one side and then the other. One minute he is angry and considers himself the victim of a huge plot, the next minute he is sad for what he considers a failure, but dominating it all is this spirit:

> "Damn it! I'll show 'em. I'll show 'em I can talk. I'll get a human story. I'll play a real rôle and not that of a puppet. I'll make a comeback. I'll show 'em. They can't down me. They can't ruin me with one bad talking picture!"

He was caught unprepared. Hollywood said that Corinne Griffith couldn't talk, but she learned. Hollywood said that Gloria Swanson was through, but she isn't. Some folks in Hollywood persist that Gilbert is finished. You hear it from his enemies, of course, not from his friends.

Personally, I don't believe it. Or maybe it's because I won't. But I cannot believe that a man who has battled life single-handed, who has taken all the hard knocks right on the chin, will let a little thing like a talkie device down him.

I believe that Gilbert will come back strong, that he will wake up, start in earnest, make some vital gesture, hurl some new defiance and really equip himself for the microphone, the terror of Hollywood.

Gilbert is not through!

He'll learn. He'll equip himself. He'll show 'em. And more power to him!

LETTERS

Censors Cuffed

I am free, white, and able to vote, and I see no reason why my right to life, liberty and the pursuit of a good picture should be denied me. I, of course, will not allow my children to attend a picture that would leave a morally bad impression on them, and for both them and me there is the guide in Photoplay. So, why should some sour-faced censor tell me what to see?

—R. F. Farmer, San Pedro, Cal.

No Shame?

I just wonder why all actresses wear so little. Don't they have shame? They go so near naked there is nothing left to the imagination. I don't object to love scenes, but let the ladies keep their bodies covered.

—Mrs. B. I. H., Cheyenne, Wyo.

Thank You!

Would it help a bit to know that your magazine is doing more real good now than ever before? Well, it is. Sez me, and I know. I see weary eyes light up at the sight of it, as I take it about with me. You see, I am a visiting nurse.

—Mrs. Lee Zachary, R.N., Omaha, Neb.

Films Tremendous Power

If the film industry but realized its tremendous power in moulding fashions, manners and even morals, I believe it would give more thought to the great responsibility and influence within its hands, and take more seriously the effects it creates—giving its vast public films which are even better and more worthy of imitation. For we human beings are imitative, especially the young.

—Mary Mean, Evanston, Ill.

Two Body Blows

We think that Dolores Del Rio is terrible as Madame DuBarry. She is too much of an Indian-Mexican type to be a European vampiress. Her bony cheeks, her big mouth, her yellow-green color, etc., is not for the splendorous type of the mistresses of the French king Louis. Besides, why show her feet so much? They are not pretty. They are too big. All the other DuBarrys, with the exception of Pola Negri, are much better.

And, we don't want films in Spanish. They are awful. The stories are all right, but the actors and actresses, in general, are vulgarly cheap.

—Adoradora de la Pantalla, Buenos Aires, S. A.

Variety Demanded

Too much of anything becomes trite and wearisome. Too much Dick Powell and Ruby Keeler, John Boles and his inevitable "shady life" backstreets. Too much Jimmy Cagney and his socking feminine cheeks. Patrons crave something new and different, something unexpected, not typed. We want variety. Right?

—Annete Victorine, Grand Rapids, Mich.

More Brunettes!

It isn't any wonder that the public tires of going to the movies. All we ever see is a bunch of washed up, faded out blondes for leading ladies. They all look alike, and it gets monotonous and tiresome. Let's have some shiny dark hair and sparkling brown eyes.

—Mrs. W. Dieckmann, Cincinnati, Ohio.

Gruesome and Censors

Shortly after the death and capture of Dillinger, I saw a newsreel showing his bullet-punctured body in a morgue, with flies crawling over it. It left an impression on me that the perfectly good feature picture did not remove. Isn't it a bit foolish to permit a gruesome sight of that sort and then censor our other movies?

—Thelma Miller, Burlingame, Cal.

More Happy Endings

Critics have made no end of fun of the "happy ending" Hollywood invariably tacks on a movie whether it was in the original story. It's time somebody came to the support of "They lived happily ever after," and I'm willing to start the ball rolling. I may be a low-brow, but I don't like "artistic" pictures because they usually try to prove how futile it is for ordinary mortals like myself to attempt to overcome our obstacles.

—Ellyn Alcorn, Hatboro, Penn.

Violets for Old Books

Violets to the producers of many of the most familiar books of my girlhood. I anticipated the arrival of the films, and my expectations were most certainly fulfilled. Can't we have more of these old books brought to the screen?

—Laura M. Lardner, North Syracuse, N. Y.

Life Full of Sex

Why all this hue and cry about sex pictures? One does not need to go to a movie to get it, our everyday life is full of it, newspapers, schools, trolleys, busses, parks, autos—it's everywhere. It's life. Far worse is the cocktail drinking and smoking of our female players in the picture. Disgusting.

—J. M. Bibbins, Bridgeport, Conn.

Color Ruins Eyes?

In a few years the black and white pictures we now see will be ghosts of the past. But instead of taking color straight from the paint box, it would be better to experiment still further until softer tones have been found. Why ruin or injure people's eyesight for the cause of a noble experiment?

—Raymond Carney, Los Angeles, Cal.

Attention, Students

I used to feel tired and blue whenever I had a test facing me the next day at college, until I finally went to a movie the night before one. The next day, I made the highest mark I have ever made. No more do I dread test days.

—Naomi Holland, Rome, Georgia.

Who Is Right?

One point which everyone seems to disagree on is the relationship between Mr. Barrett and his daughter. I believe it was a strong fatherly love, but people who have read the book insist that it was not. Who is right?

—Ethel Stein, Paterson, New Jersey.

Right to Privacy

Overhearing someone criticising Gloria Swanson, deploring her "shocking" succession of off-screen romances set me to thinking— What audacity to criticize a star's private life—the circumstances of which we know nothing, when in their professional capacity they give us so much.

—Daisy Chapman, Los Angeles, Cal.

The movie business fell on hard times in the 1950s. With television succeeding it as the mass culture medium, the movies were in process of making a painful transition to a medium for young people and various coteries that began to see film as an art. But Hollywood did its best, mixing the tradition of glamor and ostentatious display with a bend toward the newer taste of the public. For a while, instead of being sinners, movie stars could come on as pious. Some have kept the image down to the present. ("Religion in Hollywood," by Don Allen, from *Photoplay*, January 1957.)

RELIGION IN HOLLYWOOD

The off-beat religions, like the off-beat people, make headlines, but what of the others?

"In their daily work," said Bishop Gerald Kennedy of Hollywood's Methodist Church, "movie people are constantly dealing with strong emotional and dramatic values. And perhaps for this reason, they seem to be more fully aware than the average person of a deep-felt need for divine guidance and spiritual understanding."

In past years, writers and critics have held Hollywood up as an example of much, if not all, that is weak, sinful or carnal in human nature. Hollywood is usually depicted as a land of tinsel and cardboard, built by pagan gold, and peopled by shallow "characters" whose only motivation is a desire for the fast buck. But today the exact opposite is true. Today the citizens of Hollywood are just as serious, hardworking, virtuous, civic-minded and God-fearing as people in any other town or city across the land.

"Hollywood people are human beings," says Rabbi Edgar F. Magnin of the Wilshire Boulevard Jewish Temple. "They have virtues in common with all mankind. They work hard, raise their families, build homes and churches, and worship God. And, just like others, they have their faults, too."

Unfortunately, it is for their non-conformity rather than for their conformity that these golden and glamorous creatures are known. For, as another church leader has pointed out, "Movie people exist in a perpetual spotlight. They live with their shades up. Most other people live with the shades down."

Undoubtedly there have been times when Hollywood has suffered from the wrong kind of publicity, sometimes deserved, sometimes not. In a community where more than 400 correspondents and 50 photographers constantly elbow each other in their efforts to gather "hot" movie news, this is perhaps understandable. Nevertheless, it is true that most Hollywood people are quite normal in their desires for a home, children, and a reasonable amount of emotional as well as financial security, which means spiritual peace of mind. And while national church membership recently reached a new record high of 60.9% of the total population, the Hollywood figures are slightly higher, showing 61.3% to be affiliated with some church organization.

Hollywood has never been a nightclub town. This is a fact that many visitors discover, to their surprise. In the yellow pages of the telephone book, for example, a total of 58 night clubs are listed. But the same book gives listings for 1,087 churches. A few of these are representative of such lesser known faiths as the Vedanta Society, The Sky Pilot Revival Center, I Am Accredited Sanctuary, and the Self-Realization Church. But a very large percentage are churches of the major denominations which have many affiliations across the country and throughout the world.

A great number of Hollywood's churches are imposing in appearance and modern in design. The First Presbyterian Church of Hollywood has the largest congregation of that denomination in the United States. The Wilshire Boulevard Jewish Temple is justifiably proud of a history in Los Angeles that dates back more than 100 years. And the new Mormon Temple, a massive Mayan-style building standing on twenty-five acres, is the largest and most magnificent of the ten Mormon Temples in the world.

But despite these encouraging figures, the question of divorce and other unconventional behavior in Hollywood is bound to be raised. "How can they be so religious," comes the concerted cry from a thousand Main Streets, "when they're always divorcing people to marry other people?"

Divorce, however, is not peculiar to Hollywood. The percentage of divorces in Hollywood is no larger than in New York. The difference is that in Hollywood the people suing for divorce have names that make news, and so it is that every day's headlines seem to carry some fresh report of one star or another going to Reno, Las Vegas or Mexico.

The really amazing thing that is revealed by a study of religion in Hollywood is the fact that people who are generally so temperamental and so emotionally unstable, people who have usually come up the hard way and taken enough knocks to drive the love of humanity out of one's heart forever, are actually more deeply emotional than people whose lives are not subjected to these fantastic strains and stresses. It would seem to indicate that the more worldly we become, the more we realize the existence of Someone greater than ourselves. The more powerful we become, the more humble we become because we understand more than ever how fleeting are material rewards.

Jeff Chandler is a good example of this. Over at the Wilshire Boulevard Temple they will tell you that Jeff is unstinting in his religious and charity work. "His services are always available," they say. "Whether it be a fund-raising campaign, a charity bazaar, or any other worthy cause." But, although he does go to Temple on Jewish High Holidays, Jeff is not a regular church member.

"I believe that a man's religion is in the way he lives," says Jeff, "and has nothing to do with the four walls in which we pray. I believe in the sincerity of all forms of worship. I have respect for the other man's religion, and for his right to worship God as he sees fit. My wife, Marge, is a Protestant, and this has never at any time been an issue between us. As for my religious views, they can be summed up in the words that are part of Christ's sermon on the mount: 'Whatsoever ye would that men should do to you, do ye even so to them.' This, of course, is the Golden Rule. I try to live by it."

Richard Widmark is a man who has worshiped in many churches, but he says that he is not an official member of any congregation or faith. In a devotional mood, it has been his custom to drop in at any church whether it be Presbyterian, Catholic or Mohammedan mosque. Says he, "I think God hears you wherever you care to tarry to think about Him."

Kim Novak's attitude toward her religion is a combination of blind faith and intelligent curiosity. "I was always asking 'Why, why, why?' " she says. "And I still do. In a religious sense I still have much to learn. Much to understand."

Kim was born of a Catholic mother and father, and she grew up in close association with her church. But she says that she didn't gain any real religious appreciation until she was in her teens. "I think I was fascinated by the beauty of the church, and perhaps a little awed by the pageantry of it all. But I didn't really understand it.

"I particularly remember my first communion. It was so beautiful. My dear grandmother had made my dress for me, all of embroidery and white lace, and it made me feel akin to the angels. But it wasn't until after my confirmation, when I was sixteen, that I really became aware of the glories that can be found in a nearness to God.

"At that age I used to take my questions and my problems to Father Connors of the Church of the Blessed Sacrament in Chicago. My mother and father were unfailingly patient and understanding with me, but somehow Father Connors could always provide the answers I sought. He combined a fatherly wisdom with a true religious spirit."

Nick Adams, who worked with Kim in "Picnic," tells this revealing story: "While we were shooting the picture in Kansas we used to pray together every night. We found a little church near by, and after the day's work we'd slip away from the others. Kim would put a scarf over her hair, or sometimes she'd borrow my baseball cap. And there in the dim-lit sanctity of that quiet country church we'd pray for help and strength and guidance. Once as we knelt there side by side, I was tempted to glance at her lovely profile, at her lips as they moved softly with silent words of devotion to God. I remembered the words Kim had once said to me, 'Nick, everybody needs someone they can depend on.' And as I watched her quiet serenity, I knew that in God, Kim had found that Someone."

Are prayers answered? Without hesitation, Russ Tamblyn says a definite "Yes!" Russ is a Mormon, as are Terry Moore, Laraine Day and Rhonda Fleming. Russ's wife, Venetia, is an Episcopalian, and consequently they were married outside the Mormon Church. But Russ says they both live according to the precepts of the Mormon religion.

"Venetia and I say a prayer together every night," says Russ. "I have done this for many years now; my whole family prays together. And most certainly our prayers were answered last February when my younger brother accidentally shot himself in the eye with a B-B gun. The B-B lodged in his eyeball, and when we rushed him to the hospital the doctor shook his head. He said it was very serious, and my brother would probably lose the sight of his eye. We knew then it was all in the hands of our loving Father, and so we all prayed almost constantly after that. Two days later we had our answer, when our doctor told us my brother's sight would be saved. That was a moment of thanks and spiritual rejoicing for all of us."

Whether it's a Friday night service at the Chapel in the Hills, with its green walls and carpet, its piano, its Bible-reading . . . ; or whether it's a Solemn High Mass on Sunday morning at the church of St. Martin of Tours, a Saturday service at the Jewish Temple on Wilshire Boulevard, services in the Mormon Church at Pacific Palisades, or in the Presbyterian or Episcopal houses of worship, they all have one thing in common: on the day of the week that is set aside for their members to worship God, the pews are packed.

Hollywood will still make headlines because the people who live in Hollywood are people who make news. But behind the headlines, behind the tall hedges of the wealthy or the stucco plaster walls of the less luxurious apartment houses, on one day a week the citizens of Hollywood have one thing in common with the rest of the world. And on this Christmas as on any other Christmas, when the bells toll and the thoughts of mankind are on peace on earth, goodwill toward men, Hollywood, too, joins the pilgrimage to God that begins with the words of that lovely old hymn, "Oh, come all ye faithful, joyous and triumphant. . . ."

For it has always been true that, the more man gains of this world, the more he hungers for and needs the peace found only in the world of the spirit.

city slickers

HERBERT ASBURY: *THE GANGS OF NEW YORK*

The Old Gangs

While Big Jack Zelig was leading his gangsters in the wars against Chick Tricker and Jack Sirocco, and Owney Madden was welding a fraction of the old Gophers into a formidable organization, scores of other gangs were in process of formation throughout the city, for the sympathy with which the police and politicians regarded the activities of Zelig and his contemporary chieftains had vastly encouraged every ambitious young thug in New York. Early in 1911 Terrible John Torrio appeared along the East River water front, in the old Fourth Ward, and as chieftain of the James street gang terrorized a large area for almost five years, when he removed to the west and soon became a conspicuous figure in the underworld of Chicago. The gangs captained by Joe Baker and Joe Morello struggled fiercely for supremacy along the upper East Side; five men were killed in a great battle at 114th street and Third avenue on April 17, 1912, and eventually they simply shot each other to pieces. The Red Peppers and Duffy Hills continued their nightly brawling in East 102nd street in the vicinity of Third and Second avenues, while the Pearl Buttons, ancient enemies of the Hudson Dusters, moved uptown late in 1910 and became lords of the area around West 100th street from Broadway to Central Park. The Parlor Mob, hitherto a vassal organization of the Gophers, abandoned Hell's Kitchen when the special police of the New York Central Railroad went into action, and assumed control of the Central Park district around Sixty-sixth street, wherein were many low class tenements.

Late in 1911 the Car Barn Gang came into existence, and soon became one of the most feared collections of criminals and brawlers in the city. Its members were recruited principally from the young hoodlums who loafed around the East River docks, fighting, stealing, and rolling lushes. But as members of the gang they became gunmen and highwaymen, and the Car Barn area, roughly from Ninetieth to One Hundredth streets and from Third avenue to the East River, became as dangerous for respectable people as Hell's Kitchen. The first intimation that the police had that the thugs of this district had formally organized was when the following placard suddenly appeared on a lamp-post near the old car barns at Second avenue and Ninety-seventh street:

Notice

COPS KEEP OUT!

NO POLICEMAN WILL HEREAFTER BE ALLOWED IN THIS BLOCK.

By Order of

THE CAR BARN GANG.

The police soon found that the Car Barners were prepared and eager to enforce their proclamation. Half a dozen patrolmen who ventured into the forbidden area were stabbed or beaten with slung-shot and blackjack, and thereafter they patrolled the district in fours and fives. After Mayor Gaynor's Order No. 7 had been revoked the Strong Arm Squad made frequent excursions into the domain of the Car Barners and clubbed the gangsters unmercifully, but it was not until two of their principal captains had been sent to the electric chair that the gang was smashed. These martyrs were Big Bill Lingley and Freddie Muehfeldt, better known as The Kid. Lingley was reputed to have been one of the organizers of the Car Barn Gang; he was a widely known desperado and burglar, and habitually carried two revolvers, a blackjack and a slung shot, which he was very keen to use, either on the police or an inoffensive citizen. Freddie Muehfeldt came of a good family, and in his early boyhood was prominent in Sunday School work, so much so, indeed, that his good mother expressed the hope that he might in time become a clergyman. But in his late teens the boy acquired an aversion to work and took to loafing on the docks, where he conceived a tremendous admiration for Big Bill Lingley, whose swagger was imitated by the boys of the neighborhood. Big Bill saw possibilities in young Muehfeldt and took the lad under his wing, and together they set out to bring honor to the Car Barners and glory to their own names. Accompanied by half a dozen satellites, they began a series of raids upon saloons from Fourteenth street northward to the Bronx, meeting with much success and filling their pockets with gold. But at length a liquor dealer in the Bronx, just across the Harlem River, fought back in defense of his till, and Big Bill and Freddie Muehfeldt promptly killed him. Both paid the penalty for murder, and the career of The Kid was ended before he was twenty-one years old. . . .

Yoske Nigger, Charley the Cripple, and Johnny Levinsky specialized in stealing and poisoning horses; and by the end of 1913 the invariable satisfaction which their work afforded had given them practically a monopoly of the business. They thereupon shrewdly divided the field and worked in harmony for some two years, on occasion lending thugs to each other to help carry out a particularly ticklish assignment. Yoske Nigger catered exclusively to the produce markets, truckmen and livery stables, while Levinsky confined his activities to the ice cream trade, and Charley the Cripple handled such commissions as developed from the rivalry between the seltzer and soda water dealers and manufacturers. Their fees varied according to the magnitude and danger of the task, but usually were as high as the traffic would bear. A gangster who finally divulged their methods of operations to the police said that these were the average rates:

Shooting, fatal	$500
Shooting, not fatal	100
Poisoning a team	50
Poisoning one horse	35
Stealing a horse and rig	25

The shooting items, the gangster explained, referred to human beings. However, these prices were extremely high; the chieftains of many of the East Side gangs were prepared to commit murder for as low as twenty dollars, while lower New York fairly swarmed with thugs who guaranteed a neat and workmanlike job, with no entangling consequences, for from two to ten dollars, depending upon the prominence of the victim and the state of their own finances when they received the commission.

These groups formed a very small minority of the gangs which sprinkled Manhattan Island during the final years of the gangsters' rule. By the latter part of 1913, about a year after Big Jack Zelig had passed to his reward, it is likely that there were more gangs in New York than at any other period in the history of the metropolis; their number and the ramifications of their alliances were so bewildering that of hundreds there now exists no more than a trace; they flashed into the ken of the policeman and the reporter and flashed out again like comets, leaving a gaseous trail of blood and graft. But it is improbable that the total number of gangsters was any greater than during the reign of Monk Eastman, for the gangs were smaller; the time when a chieftain could muster from five hundred to a thousand men under his banner had passed with the dispersal of such groups as the Eastmans, the Gophers and the Five Pointers, and there were few gang leaders who could take the field with more than thirty or forty thugs. Consequently an area which in former years had been plundered exclusively by a single great gang became the haunt of innumerable small groups, which constantly fought each other, frequently strayed beyond their own domains, and robbed and murdered whenever the opportunity for gain presented itself. Moreover, their organization was more elastic; there no longer existed the undying loyalty to the captain which had been such a distinguishing characteristic of the old-time gangs, and it was not unusual for a gangster to owe allegiance to three or four leaders at the same time, performing a different sort of thuggery for each. Throughout the city there were also a far greater number of independent thugs who bound themselves to a chieftain only for a definite campaign or for a specific blackjacking, stabbing or shooting assignment. The number of gangsters of this type continued to increase as decency invaded politics, and as the police became more honest and efficient and waged clubbing campaigns against the organized gangs.

The gangs which flourished throughout the eastern part of Manhattan during the few years that followed the death of Big Jack Zelig performed any sort of criminal work which their clients required, but their opportunities for enrichment were far fewer than in the old days. The disclosures which followed the murder of Herman Rosenthal had resulted in the closing of most of the gambling houses, and had compelled the remainder to operate with a minimum of police protection; and the gangsters had become such a stench in the public nostril that the politicians dared not employ them to the extent of former years. Consequently it became necessary to develop new sources of revenue, and the gang chieftains found a rich harvest awaiting them in the constant industrial strife with which the East Side was afflicted, especially among the needle and allied trades. Late in 1911 the labor unions began the practice of hiring thugs to murder and blackjack strike breakers and intimidate workmen who refused to be organized, while the employers engaged other gangsters to slug union pickets and raid union meetings. The thugs seldom became strike breakers, for actual physical labor was repugnant to them, but they acted as guards to the workmen who were recruited from the hordes of casual labor which haunted the Bowery and Sixth avenue employment agencies. In time a distinct class of men arose who refused to perform any other sort of work, and went from city to city earning high wages as strike breakers. They were called finks, while the gunmen who protected them were known as nobles. For the most part they are now provided by private detective agencies.

Within a few months slugging, stabbing and shooting were accepted concomitants of industrial troubles throughout the East Side, and the bulk of the labor union business was carried on by the gangs captained by Dopey Benny, Joe the Greaser, Little Rhody, Pinchey Paul and Billy Lustig, while the employers were compelled to content themselves with the services of less efficient combinations. The chieftains of the important gangs were regularly on the payrolls of the local unions at from twenty-five to fifty dollars a week, and for each gangster assigned to blackjack strike breakers or frighten obstinate workmen they received ten dollars a day, of which they retained two and a half dollars. The remaining seven and a half dollars was the wages of the thug. The union officials also bound themselves to pay all fines, provide bail, engage lawyers and arrange for as much protection as possible through their political and police connections. Dopey Benny further safe-guarded himself by retaining a lawyer on an annual fee; and the legal luminary drew up contracts without too much mention of the character of the work involved, but specifying that the gang leader's salary was to continue if he went to prison. For several years Dopey Benny was constantly attended by a professional bondsman, who not only arranged bail for the chieftain when required, but for his henchmen as well.

Dopey Benny began his criminal career at the age of ten, when he prowled the streets of the East Side stealing packages from express wagons and delivery carts. From this lowly beginning he became a lush worker and a footpad, then a pickpocket of distinction, and at length the greatest, or at any rate the most successful, gang captain of his time, however unworthy he may have been to wear the mantle of Monk Eastman. Dopey Benny was not a drug addict, but adenoidal and nasal troubles from infancy gave him a sullen, sleepy appearance from which his nickname was derived. As a leader he was far superior to his contemporaries, and in time commanded the allegiance of half a dozen smaller gangs, among them the Little Doggies, the remnant of the Hudson Dusters, a few Gophers who had wandered into the East Side after the private police force of the New York Central had swept through Hell's Kitchen, and the groups led by Porkie Flaherty and Abie Fisher. Dopey Benny districted the lower half of Manhattan Island, and to each area assigned one of his vassal gangs, which wielded pistol, blackjack and slung-shot for the benefit of whichever side first spoke for its services, although in the main the thugs worked for labor unions. However, it was not uncommon for Dopey Benny to slug and stab for the unions in one district, and against them in another. For some three years there was scarcely a strike in New York in which these gangsters were not employed, and during this period Dopey Benny's annual income averaged between fifteen and twenty thousand dollars. So widely was he feared that a group of employers once offered him fifteen thousand dollars if he would remain neutral during a threatened strike. But Dopey Benny indignantly refused, saying that his heart was naturally with the working man, and that he would continue to hold himself and his gangsters at the disposal of the union officials. His methods were thus described in a confession which he made to the District Attorney after he had finally been brought to book:

"My first job was to go to a shop and beat up some workmen there. The men that employed me gave me ten dollars for every man that I had to use and one hundred dollars for myself. I picked out about fifteen men, and later met the man that employed me and told him that I couldn't do the job for the money that he wanted to pay—that it took more men than I had calculated on, and that I wouldn't touch it unless I was paid more money.

"Finally he agreed to pay me six hundred dollars for the job. I got my men together, divided them up into squads and saw that they were armed with pieces of gas pipe and with clubs, but this time not with pistols, and when the workmen came from work the men I had got set on them and beat them up. I wasn't right there when this was going on. I told the men what to do, and I was near by, but I didn't do any of it myself. After the job was over I saw the man I had made the agreement with and asked him how he liked the way the job was done. He said that it was fine and paid me the six hundred dollars in cash.

"From this time on one fellow would hear from another that I did these jobs, and would come to get me to do a job, and so I was kept busy all the time. Some of the jobs were just individual jobs. I would be told there was a certain fellow whom they wanted beaten up, and they would take me where I could get a look at him, and then when I got a chance I would follow him and beat him up, and afterwards get my pay.

"One time when we were doing a job in a place where there were some girls. who blew police whistles, and policemen came before we could get away. I was caught and got thirty days, and three of the other fellows got fifteen days apiece. All the time I was serving my thirty days my wages of fifteen dollars a day, which I was getting then for doing these jobs, kept on just the same, though some of it wasn't paid until later.

"After this I did a number of jobs for which I didn't get any special pay—just my regular payroll, which was then twenty-five dollars a week. At this time I was getting that regularly and wasn't charging any more for the jobs I did. Afterward I got to doing jobs again at so much a job. I got three hundred and fifty dollars for doing one job. That was in addition to the regular twenty-five dollars a week which I was getting. I had thirty men on this job, and a lot of the employes were hurt.

"In January, 1914, I was tried and convicted of assault, and sentenced to state prison for five years, but afterward the conviction was reversed and so I got out. All the time I was in the state prison I continued on the payroll and did several more jobs. Some of them were quiet work, without any weapons at all—just scaring people and threatening them—and some of them were violent work."

Attracted by almost constant opportunity to display their skill, some of the most ferocious of the independent thugs enlisted under Dopey Benny's banner, and his cohorts were further augmented by desertions from rival gang leaders. Even Joe the Greaser lost many of his best men, but that astute chieftain prevented his utter downfall by forming an alliance with Dopey Benny, and thereafter accepted the latter as generalissimo of all the gangs, although he continued to operate his own group as an independent unit. Through this alliance Dopey Benny and Joe the Greaser practically controlled the situation, and Little Rhody, Pinchey Paul and Billy Lustig, as well as a score of other minor captains, were ignored by the union officials who assigned the jobs. In desperation the smaller gangs combined, and late in 1913 declared war against Dopey Benny and Joe the Greaser, opening hostilities with a gun battle at Grand and Forsyth streets. But the gangsters were notoriously poor marksmen and no one was wounded, although the indiscriminate shooting smashed several store windows and caused a great scurrying in the crowded thoroughfares. One of the principal instigators of the war, and a constant schemer against the power of Dopey Benny and Joe the Greaser, was a man known as Jewbach, who finally became so obnoxious that Nigger Benny Snyder, a local henchman of Joe the Greaser, was dispatched to silence him. Nigger Benny attacked Jewbach with a knife at Rivington and Norfolk streets, but could only slash his enemy twice before he was arrested. Jewbach loudly proclaimed that he would prosecute Nigger Benny and send him to prison, whereupon Joe the Greaser called upon him with half a dozen of his thugs. While the gangsters held Jewbach down, Joe the Greaser cut a large piece out of his lower lip.

"Let that learn you," said Joe the Greaser, "not to talk so much."

Jewbach was unable to speak for several weeks, and had been so thoroughly cowed by Joe the Greaser that he failed to appear for the trial, and Nigger Benny was discharged. Subsequently, when Pinchey Paul was found dead, Nigger Benny was accused of the murder, and found himself in such a tight place that he promptly confessed to the District Attorney, shifting responsibility for the killing to the shoulders of Joe the Greaser, who he said gave him five dollars for the job. Nigger Benny was sent to prison for twenty years. Joe the Greaser pleaded guilty to manslaughter, and in December, 1915, was sentenced to ten years in Sing Sing.

In a city, informal neighborhood services often turned into formal commercial ventures; marriage brokers were a distinctly urban phenomenon growing out of the ethnic neighborhoods (From Junius Henri Browne, *The Great Metropolis,* 1868.)

MARRIAGES ARRANGED

MARRIAGE—Young ladies and gentlemen desirous of being wisely and happily married will consult their interest by applying to the undersigned, who gives all his attention to this branch of business, and who has already been very successful in bringing together persons adapted to each other by similarity of taste, temperament, and sympathy. Terms reasonable. All communications strictly confidential.

HENRY HYMEN, No. _____ Broadway

WEDDED HAPPINESS DESIRED—It is well known that nothing conduces so much to happiness in life as a proper marriage. To avoid all mistakes in selecting partners, persons of either sex, who contemplate matrimony, should call at once on

GEORGE JACOBS

Matrimonial Broker, No. _____ Bleecker Street

N.B.—Mr. Jacobs has the best of opportunities and the amplest facilities for accommodating his patrons. He has had large experience, and can say without vanity that he has made matches for which hundreds of ladies and gentlemen are eternally grateful to him. They have acknowledged their gratitude in autograph letters, which will be shown to his patrons if desired.

MATRIMONIAL BROKERS—John Johnson & Co., No. _____ Bowery, offer their services to ladies wishing agreeable and wealthy husbands, or to gentlemen desiring beautiful, rich, and accomplished wives. They arrange interviews or correspondence between parties, and leave nothing undone to insure a marriage that will result to the satisfaction of all. The success that has heretofore crowned their efforts induces them to believe they have a firm hold upon the public confidence. They respectfully solicit a continuance of patronage.

The "working girl" was a stock figure in the urban folklore of the period between the world wars. This story, on the theme of finding a "million dollar baby at the five-and-ten cent store" is, in its curious way, very much about the reality of class divisions in urban society. (O. Henry, "A Lickpenny Lover," from *The Voice of the City,* 1908.)

O. HENRY: A LICKPENNY LOVER

There were 3,000 girls in the Biggest Store. Masie was one of them. She was eighteen and a saleslady in the gents' gloves. Here she became versed in two varieties of human beings—the kind of gents who buy their gloves in department stores and the kind of women who buy gloves for unfortunate gents. Besides this wide knowledge of the human species, Masie had acquired other information. She had listened to the promulgated wisdom of the 2,999 other girls and had stored it in a brain that was as secretive and wary as that of a Maltese cat. Perhaps nature, foreseeing that she would lack wise counsellors, had mingled the saving ingredient of shrewdness along with her beauty, as she has endowed the silver fox of the priceless fur above the other animals with cunning.

For Masie was beautiful. She was a deep-tinted blonde, with the calm poise of a lady who cooks butter cakes in a window. She stood behind her counter in the Biggest Store; and as you closed your hand over the tape-line for your glove measure you thought of Hebe; and as you looked again you wondered how she had come by Minerva's eyes.

When the floorwalker was not looking Masie chewed tutti frutti; when he was looking she gazed up as if at the clouds and smiled wistfully.

That is the shopgirl smile, and I enjoin you to shun it unless you are well fortified with callosity of the heart, caramels, and a congeniality for the capers of Cupid. This smile belonged to Masie's recreation hours and not to the store; but the floorwalker must have his own. He is the Shylock of the stores. When he comes nosing around the bridge of his nose is a toll-bridge. It is goo-goo eyes or "git" when he looks toward a pretty girl. Of course not all floorwalkers are thus. Only a few days ago the papers printed news of one over eighty years of age.

One day Irving Carter, painter, millionaire, traveller, poet, automobilist, happened to enter the Biggest Store. It is due to him to add that his visit was not voluntary. Filial duty took him by the collar and dragged him inside, while his mother philandered among the bronze and terra-cotta statuettes.

. . . Carter strolled across to the glove counter in order to shoot a few minutes on the wing. His need for gloves was genuine; he had forgotten to bring a pair with him. But his action hardly calls for apology, because he had never heard of glove-counter flirtations.

As he neared the vicinity of his fate he hesitated, suddenly conscious of this unknown phase of Cupid's less worthy profession.

Three or four cheap fellows, sonorously garbed, were leaning over the counters, wrestling with the mediatorial hand-coverings, while giggling girls played vivacious seconds to their lead upon the strident string of coquetry. Carter would have retreated, but he had gone too far. Masie confronted him behind her counter with a questioning look in eyes as coldly, beautifully, warmly blue as the glint of summer sunshine on an iceberg drifting in Southern seas.

And then Irving Carter, painter, millionaire, etc., felt a warm flush rise to his aristocratically pale face. But not from diffidence. The blush was intellectual in origin. He knew in a moment that he stood in the ranks of the ready-made youths who wooed the giggling girls at other counters. Himself leaned against the oaken trysting place of a cockney Cupid with a desire in his heart for the favor of a glove salesgirl. He was no more than Bill and Jack and Mickey. And then he felt a sudden tolerance for them, and an elating, courageous contempt for the conventions upon which he had fed, and an unhesitating determination to have this perfect creature for his own.

When the gloves were paid for and wrapped Carter lingered for a moment. The dimples at the corners of Masie's damask mouth deepened. All gentlemen who bought gloves lingered in just that way. She curved an arm, showing like Psyche's through her shirt-waist sleeve, and rested an elbow upon the show-case edge.

Carter had never before encountered a situation of which he had not been perfect master. But now he stood far more awkward than Bill or Jack or Mickey. He had no chance of meeting this beautiful girl socially. His mind struggled to recall the nature and habits of shopgirls as he had read or heard of them. Somehow he had received the idea that they sometimes did not insist too strictly upon the regular channels of introduction. His heart beat loudly at the thought of proposing an unconventional meeting with this lovely and virginal being. But the tumult in his heart gave him courage.

After a few friendly and well-received remarks on general subjects, he laid his card by her hand on the counter.

"Will you please pardon me," he said, "if I seem too bold; but I earnestly hope you will allow me the pleasure of seeing you again. There is my name; I assure you that it is with the greatest respect that I ask the favor of becoming one of your fr—— acquaintances. May I not hope for the privilege?"

Masie knew men—especially men who buy gloves. Without hesitation she looked him frankly and similingly in the eyes, and said:

"Sure. I guess you're all right. I don't usually go out with strange gentlemen, though. It ain't quite ladylike. When should you want to see me again?"

"As soon as I may," said Carter. "If you would allow me to call at your home, I——"

Masie laughed musically. "Oh, gee, no!" she said, emphatically. "If you could see our flat once! There's five of us in three rooms. I'd just like to see ma's face if I was to bring a gentleman friend there!"

"Anywhere, then," said the enamored Carter, "that will be convenient to you."

"Say," suggested Masie, with a bright-idea look in her peach-blow face; "I guess Thursday night will about suit me. Suppose you come to the corner of Eighth Avenue and Forty-eighth Street at 7:30. I live right near the corner. But I've got to be back home by eleven. Ma never lets me stay out after eleven."

Carter promised gratefully to keep the tryst, and then hastened to his mother, who was looking about for him to ratify her purchase of a bronze Diana.

A salesgirl, with small eyes and an obtuse nose, strolled near Masie, with a friendly leer.

"Did you make a hit with his nobs, Masie?" she asked, familiarly.

"The gentleman asked permission to call," answered Masie, with the grand air, as she slipped Carter's card into the bosom of her waist.

"Permission to call!" echoed small eyes, with a snigger. "Did he say anything about dinner in the Waldorf and a spin in his auto afterward?"

"Oh, cheese it!" said Masie, wearily. "You've been used to swell things, I don't think. You've had a swelled head ever since that hose-cart driver took you out to a chop suey joint. No, he never mentioned the Waldorf; but there's a Fifth Avenue address on his card, and if he buys the supper you can bet your life there won't be no pigtail on the waiter what takes the order."

As Carter glided away from the Biggest Store with his mother in his electric runabout, he bit his lip with a dull pain at his heart. He knew that love had come to him for the first time in all the twenty-nine years of his life. And that the object of it should make so readily an appointment with him at a street corner, though it was a step toward his desires, tortured him with misgivings.

Carter did not know the shopgirl. He did not know that her home is often either a scarcely habitable tiny room or a domicile filled to overflowing with kith and kin. The street corner is her parlor, the park is her drawing room; the avenue is her garden walk; yet for the most part she is as inviolate mistress of herself in them as is my lady inside her tapestried chamber.

One evening at dusk, two weeks after their first meeting, Carter and Masie strolled arm-in-arm into a little, dimly-lit park. They found a bench, tree-shadowed and secluded, and sat there.

For the first time his arm stole gently around her. Her golden-bronze head slid restfully against his shoulder.

"Gee!" sighed Masie, thankfully. "Why didn't you ever think of that before?"

"Masie," said Carter, earnestly, "you surely know that I love you. I ask you sincerely to marry me. You know me well enough by this time to have no doubts of me. I want you, and I must have you. I care nothing for the difference in our stations."

"What is the difference?" asked Masie, curiously.

"Well, there isn't any," said Carter, quickly, "except in the minds of foolish people. It is in my power to give you a life of luxury. My social position is beyond dispute, and my means are ample."

"They all say that," remarked Masie. "It's the kid they all give you. I suppose you really work in a delicatessen or follow the races. I ain't as green as I look."

"I can furnish you all the proofs you want," said Carter, gently. "And I want you, Masie. I loved you the first day I saw you."

"They all do," said Masie, with an amused laugh, "to hear 'em talk. If I could meet a man that got stuck on me the third time he'd seen me I think I'd get mashed on him."

"Please don't say such things," pleaded Carter. "Listen to me, dear. Ever since I first looked into your eyes you have been the only woman in the world for me."

"Oh, ain't you the kidder!" smiled Masie. "How many other girls did you ever tell that?"

But Carter persisted. And at length he reached the flimsy, fluttering little soul of the shopgirl that existed somewhere deep down in her lovely bosom. His words penetrated the heart whose very lightness was its safest armor. She looked up at him with eyes that saw. And a warm glow visited her cool cheeks. Tremblingly, awfully, her moth wings closed, and she seemed about to settle upon the flower of love. Some faint glimmer of life and its possibilities on the other side of her glove counter dawned upon her. Carter felt the change and crowded the opportunity.

"Marry me, Masie," he whispered, softly, "and we will go away from this ugly city to beautiful ones. We will forget work and business, and life will be one long holiday. I know where I should take you—I have been there often. Just think of a shore where summer is eternal, where the waves are always rippling on the lovely beach and the people are happy and free as children. We will sail to those shores and remain there as long as you please. In one of those far-away cities there are grand and lovely palaces and towers full of beautiful pictures and statues. The streets of the city are water, and one travels about in ———"

"I know," said Masie, sitting up suddenly. "Gondolas."

"Yes," smiled Carter.

"I thought so," said Masie.

"And then," continued Carter, "we will travel on and see whatever we wish in the world. After the European cities we will visit India and the ancient cities there, and ride on elephants and see the wonderful temples of the Hindoos and the Brahmins and the Japanese gardens and the camel trains and chariot races in Persia, and all the queer sights of foreign countries. Don't you think you would like it, Masie?"

Masie rose to her feet.

"I think we had better be going home," she said, coolly. "It's getting late."

Carter humored her. He had come to know her varying, thistledown moods, and that it was useless to combat them. But he felt a certain happy triumph. He had held for a moment, though but by a silken thread, the soul of his wild Psyche, and hope was stronger within him. Once she had folded her wings and her cool hand had closed about his own.

At the Biggest Store the next day Masie's chum, Lulu, waylaid her in an angle of the counter.

"How are you and your swell friend making it?" she asked.

"Oh, him?" said Masie, patting her side curls. "He ain't in it any more. Say, Lu, what do you think that fellow wanted me to do?"

"Go on the stage?" guessed Lulu, breathlessly.

"Nit; he's too cheap a guy for that. He wanted me to marry him and go down to Coney Island for a wedding tour!"

Chicago May was a reformed criminal whose memoirs were supposed to help finance her reformation. Her guide to criminal jargon ought to have many uses. (Selection from May C. Sharpe, *Chicago May—Her Story*, n.d.)

CHICAGO MAY

. . . Here are a few definitions; some of these expressions have been explained in the text, and some are self-explanatory. This list, which is in the nature of a code, is very far from being complete. It was used by educated thieves for correspondence between members of their gangs. You will notice that the last words in many of these expressions rhyme with their definitions. The object of all this was to throw dicks off the track if they stumbled on any professional correspondence of members of the gang.

Moll Buzzers—people who rob women.

Hooks, Whizzers, or *Dips*—pickpockets.

Slims, Rats, Squealers, Squawkers, Stool-Pigeons, Stools, Pigeons or *Narks* (English)—police informers.

Bulls, Dicks, Harness-Bulls, John Elbows, or *John Laws*—police officers, depending on the kind.

Laying Down the Querre (usually called "The Queer"), comes from the French argot, and means false or counterfeit money.

Laying the Note—crooked advertising.

Taking a sleigh ride—getting morphine.

Snow-Birds—morphine addicts.

Mrs. White—the name used to and for dope-peddlers.

Pay-Off Men, or *Cons*—confidence men (or women).

Peter Men, Yeggs, Blowers—safe crackers.

Heavy Guys—stick-up men, or safe-breakers.

Gun Molls, or *Trips*—women who steal from men in the street, or carry guns.

Boosters, or *Hoisters*—shoplifters.

Stir, Can, Bird-Lime Can, Iron Horse, or *Big House*—jail.

Bouncer—the plug-ugly who throws out the victims who want to make trouble, especially in a house of prostitution.

The Madam—the proprietor of a house of prostitution.

White Slaves—inmates of a house of prostitution who cannot get away, for various reasons, principally because they are always in debt to the Madam.

Bracelets—handcuffs.

Johns, Suckers—men who are lured by crooks, mostly women.

Sods, Fairies, Sads, Masocks—degenerates or sexual perverts according to the type.

Trailer—helper or assistant.

Pinch—arrest.

Grand—$1000.00.

Century—$100.00.

Prowlers, Hotel Prowlers, etc.—sneak thieves, as the adjective describes.

Sparklers, sparks, shiners, stones, ice (English), etc.—diamonds.

Touch—either borrowing or stealing.

Spring—to set free, or "beat" the case.

Call Out—to use a stolen check to get baggage, etc.
Gopher—one who tunnels to steal.
Honky-tonk—gaudy saloon with back-room hangout.
Jolt—prison sentence.
Dud—substitute or fake.
Tail—follow or shadow.
Irish lasses—glasses.
I suppose—nose.
Dot and dash—moustache.
Locating—getting prospects.
Weigh-in—to meet.
Jug—jail, prison or safe.
Stem—drill.
Screw—key.
Panhandler—professional beggar.
Punk—apprentice thief.
Hoops—rings.
Target—outside man.
Dan—dynamite.
Stickers—postage-stamps.
Steerer—shyster-lawyer.
Bindle—blanket or bundle.
White line, Dr. Hall, Mickey—alcohol.
Chuck—food.
D. D.—deaf and dumb.
Playhouse—easy prison.
Clam-up—to keep quiet.
Shive—knife.
Mulligan—stew.
Connector—beggar.
Pennies—money.
Gump—chicken.
Box—safe.
Cons—convicts or confidence men.
Flop—cheap place to sleep.
Rap—to put wise, a pinch.
Yen-Yen—hop habit.
Ditch—hide.
Soft Stuff—paper money.
Smoke—to shoot.
Smoke irons—guns.
Whittler—constable.
Yaffle—to arrest.
Rooting—working, stealing.
Office—signal.
Batter—beg.
Doss—camp.
Tumble and trips—lips.
North and south—mouth.
Under beneaths—teeth.
Heart and lung—tongue.

Out and in—chin.
Thick and thin—grin.
Train wreck—neck.
Chalk boulders—shoulders.
Chalk farm—arm.
Woolly west—breast or chest.
Brace and bits—beasts.
Darby kelly—belly.
Songs and sighs—thighs.
Mumbly pegs—legs.
High seas—knees.
Plates of meat—feet.
Oscar Joes—toes.
German bands—hands.
Long and lingers—fingers.
Simple Simon—diamond.
Brothers and sisters—whiskers.
Ocean waves—shave.
Sidney harbour—barber.
Leaning fat—hat.
Tit for tat—cap.
Charlie Rawler—collar.
Lamb fry—tie.
Seldom see—B.V.D.'s.
Do and dare—underwear.
Dig and dirt—shirt.
Fiddle and flute—suit.
Ivory float—coat.
Uncles and aunts—pants.
Johnny Rowsers—trousers.
Sunday best—vest or dress.
Oscar Hocks—socks.
Ones and twos—shoes.
Daisy Roots—boots.
Joe Roke—smoke.
Cherry ripe—pipe.
Rattle and jar—car.
Jungle—crooks' territory.
Script—money, paper money.
Aunt Jane—Tia Juana, Mex.
Jungle buzzard—hobo sneak-thief, preys on his own kind.
Bos—hoboes.
Lusher—lone drinker.
Frisk—search, steal from person.
Lump of lead—head.
Bonny fair—hair.
Tears and cheers—ears.
Centre lead—forehead.
Chips and chase—face.
Mince pies—eyes.
Gay and frisky—whisky.

Near and far—bar.
Rise and shine—wine.
Oh, my dear—beer.
Elephant trunk—drunk.
Bottles and stoppers—coppers.
Shovel and broom—room.
Weeping willow—pillow.
Loop the loop—hoop, or ring.
Bees and honey—money.
Block and tackle—watch and chain.
Heap of coke—bloke.
Fields of wheat—street.
Piperheidsieck—look or see.

A picture of New York City as a convention center and tourist mecca in the 1940s was prepared for American Legionnaires coming to their national convention. ("This is New York," 1947. Reprinted by permission of Hawthorn Books, Inc. from *The American Legion Reader*, edited by Victor Lasky. Copyright © 1953 by The American Legion. All rights reserved.)

THIS IS NEW YORK

Walter Winchell

What you want to see in New York depends on what's inside of you. There's nothing you can't see—from masterpieces to Madison Square Garden, because the shiny waters of New York Bay are a mirror held up to the rest of the world.

We like this town so well that we want you to like it too.

She's like our best girl. In general, these are her best features:

She's a wonderful cook. There's no type or kind of good food that you can't get and, authorities assure us, better cooked than anywhere else in the world. Finding it is merely a matter of casual inquiry, not thorough investigation.

Of course, New Yorkers think the best show in New York is New York itself. The pulsating lights of Times Square are part of every New Yorker's heartbeat. Love of life and its excitement make it the only spot in the world where a newspaper extra is only normal. Every night on Broadway is like Saturday night back home.

Fifth Avenue is a smart and beautiful woman. All the more so because she looks at you out of the corner of her eye.

There are dozens of other personality neighborhoods. Like the

Village, Central Park, University Heights, all outlined in the guide books. The theaters reflect the art of the times—and there are parts of these times which reflect no art whatsoever.

See what you want to see. There's a broad enough choice to give you a pretty good idea of yourself. What you want to see is the kind of guy you are.

The book shops, the museums, the Planetarium and the ballet give you some idea of the variety.

The show windows of the big stores are the flowers on New York's bonnet. And by all means, before you leave, go to the top of the Empire State or RCA building and gaze down upon the wonderful face that every New Yorker carries in his heart.

James A. Farley

There's too much to see in four days, but take your choice of the following: Times Square at night, a legitimate show, the wonderful Radio City Music Hall and the Rockettes, a big league baseball game, Rockefeller Center, the tower of the Empire State Building, the Planetarium and some of our museums, among the greatest in the world, the downtown skyline of Manhattan, the Brooklyn Bridge, in the shadows of which our great Al Smith was born, the shopping centers along Fifth and Madison Avenues, the grand view of Park Avenue at night, the Grand Army Plaza in front of the Plaza Hotel and Central Park, the Zoological Gardens, among the most beautiful in the world. I will also remind you that the Hudson River is more beautiful than the Rhine, and that our Palisades, Bear Mountain and Stony Point, where Mad Anthony Wayne made history, are famous in poem and story. Not far from these is West Point, and certainly a visit to the famous United States Military Academy would give you a great thrill.

John Kieran

If I were visiting New York for the first time I think I would like to do the following things:

Take the ferry from the Battery to Staten Island and back. It's just a ten-cent outlay and gives a million-dollar view of the Bay, the Statue of Liberty and the famous skyline of the financial center of the world.

Take a bus ride up Riverside Drive. The Hudson is one of the most scenic rivers in the world. London has the Thames, Paris the Seine, Rome the Tiber, but New York doesn't have to take a back seat with the best big-city river that I know.

Visit the Metropolitan Museum of Art, the American Museum of Natural History, the main Public Library at 42nd Street and Fifth Avenue and the Bronx Zoo. (And take in one of the Planetarium shows.)

Spend half a day wandering around Radio City and seeing what a magnificent city in itself it is.

Walk through the Waldorf-Astoria and have dinner in some little Italian, French or Swedish restaurant in the Fifties.

See some Broadway show if I could get in.

Go back home and tell the folks that New York was wonderful—I saw it all—but I'll stick to my home town after all.

Sherman Billingsley

So you're here to see the big city? Instead of the usual sightseeing trips to the Empire State Building and the Statue of Liberty, let's do things a little differently. Let's start off with Park Avenue from midtown with its expensive shops and hotels all the way up to the section where the railroad emerges from the ground and the merchants hawk their wares.

Now you're up about 110th Street turn west to Fifth Avenue where Central Park begins. Summer will be nearly ended, so you won't see the kids ice-skating but you can witness the New Yorker's way of communing with nature. It's virtually a rural countryside in the heart of the largest city in the U. S.

As you come down Fifth Avenue don't forget to shop in Saks' or Bonwit's or any of the better-known shops and buy a gift, anything in one of the famous boxes will do, for your wife, child or sweetheart.

Along Fifth Avenue you'll see Rockefeller Center. Take a minute to pause at St. Patrick's Cathedral. Regardless of your faith, it will be worth it.

Downtown around midday the Stock Exchange center is a must and on the way back Chinatown and the Bowery will open up the eyes of many visitors.

A visit to Night Court is a thrill any innocent visitor will experience instead of reading about it. If one is fortunate enough to have a friend with an automobile LaGuardia Airport is a sight with landings and take-offs to all parts of the world.

Now take a ride to the Fulton Fish Market and the produce market along West Street, ending with a ride up the West Side Highway to take a glimpse of the largest ships in the world at anchor, and a peek at the George Washington Bridge with the Palisades in the background while the cool slow ripples of the Hudson River seem to say "I'd Never Believe It" but now I see it with my own eyes.

That is a full day for any Legionnaire, and if that is not sufficient New York has the most famous night clubs in the world in case you're bored with it all.

Billy Rose

If I were a Legionnaire on a brief visit to New York, here are some of the sights I would want to see:

"Old Lady Cutting Her Fingernails," by Rembrandt, at the Metropolitan Museum of art.

The bronze plaque on the house next to the corner, Fifth Avenue and 86th Street. On this plaque a Roman God thumbs his nose at his next door neighbor. Many years ago, a next door neighbor objected to a man living in this house, for racial reasons. The thumb-nosing plaque was the answer.

The Washington Vegetable Market at 3 o'clock in the morning. This one is for the book.

A bus ride up Fifth Avenue on Sunday morning.

The George Washington Bridge. A breath-taking job in steel and wire.

The dinosaur and the other prehistoric what-nots at the Museum of Natural History. They cut a fellow down to size.

A long look at the Statue of Liberty.

Oh, yes—Broadway, 'specially if you're interested in neon.

Americans found their cross-country railroads romantic, but not their urban trains. There are few subway buffs. Rather the folklore of these dreaded necessities stresses their discomfort and the invasion of privacy they seem to represent. (From Ben Hecht, *1001 Afternoons in New York,* 1941.)

THE SUBWAY

The Ogling Corpse

Newspapermen know these stillborn fantasies better than most. They are forever running down the tales of mystery and wonder that periodically flood the talk of the town.

There is the one of the dead man in the subway who sits with eyes fixed on a lady passenger. Offended by his crude ogling, this lady finally slaps the dead man's face, whereupon the cadaver pitches out of its seat and much hysteria ensues.

The name of this finicky and mistaken lady has never been found, nor that of the defunct ogler, nor of the subway guard who witnessed it all. There is available always to the good reporter, however, a ring of hundreds on hundreds of citizens who heard the story from a neighbor whose aunt or uncle was on the train where it all happened.

subcultures

In the conflicts between capital and labor, labor has always had the best music. There are dozens of labor songs and no serious collection of songs for management. Apparently for all the union men who dreamt they "saw Joe Hill last night," no beleaguered manager has ever dreamt he saw John D. [Rockefeller].

LABOR SONG

The Preacher and the Slave

1 Long-haired preachers come out ev'ry night,
   Try to tell you what's wrong and what's right,
   But when asked about something to eat,
   They will answer with voices so sweet:

   Chorus
   You will eat (you will eat), bye and bye (bye and bye),
   In that glorious land in the sky (way up high).
   Work and pray (work and pray), live on hay (live on hay),
   You'll get pie in the sky when you die (that's a lie!).

2 And the starvation army they play,
   And they sing and they clap and they pray,
   Till they get all your coin on the drum—
   Then they tell you when you're on the bum:

3 If you fight hard for children and wife—
   Try to get something good in this life—
   You're a sinner and bad man, they tell;
   When you die you will sure go to Hell.

4 Working men of all countries, unite!
   Side by side we for freedom will fight.
   When the world and its wealth we have gained,
   To the grafters we'll sing this refrain:

   Last Chorus
   You will eat (you will eat), bye and bye, (bye and bye),
   When you've learned how to cook and to fry (way up high).
   Chop some wood (chop some wood)—'twill do you good (do you good)
   And you'll eat in the sweet bye and bye (that's no lie!).

Harlem in New York City emerged as the capital of black America in the 1920s, and going "uptown" became a vogue among white intellectuals and daring members of the middle class. (Selections from Langston Hughes, *The Big Sea*, 1940; Claude McKay, *Harlem: Negro Metropolis*, 1940.)

HARLEM HOUSE-RENT PARTIES

[In the 1920's] house-rent parties began to flourish—and not always to raise the rent either. But, as often as not, to have a get-together of one's own, where you could do the black-bottom with no stranger behind you trying to do it, too. Non-theatrical, non-intellectual Harlem was an unwilling victim of its own vogue. It didn't like to be stared at by white folks. But perhaps the down-towners never knew this—for the cabaret owners, the entertainers, and the speakeasy proprietors treated them fine—as long as they paid.

The Saturday night rent parties that I attended were often more amusing than any night club, in small apartments where God knows who lived—because the guests seldom did—but where the piano would often be augmented by a guitar, or an old cornet, or somebody with a pair of drums walking in off the street. And where awful bootleg whisky and good fried fish or streaming chitterling were sold at very low prices. And the dancing and singing and impromptu entertaining went on until dawn came in at the windows.

These parties, often termed whist parties or dances, were usually announced by brightly colored cards stuck in the grille of apartment house elevators. Some of the cards were highly entertaining in themselves:

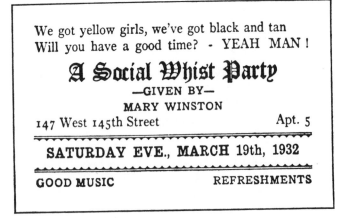

We got yellow girls, we've got black and tan
Will you have a good time? - YEAH MAN !

𝔄 𝔖𝔬𝔠𝔦𝔞𝔩 𝔚𝔥𝔦𝔰𝔱 𝔓𝔞𝔯𝔱𝔶
—GIVEN BY—
MARY WINSTON
147 West 145th Street   Apt. 5

SATURDAY EVE., MARCH 19th, 1932

GOOD MUSIC   REFRESHMENTS

NUMBERS IN HARLEM

Playing numbers is the most flourishing clandestine industry in Harlem. It is the first and foremost of the rackets and the oldest. Exciting the masses' imagination to easy "hits" by the placement of tiny stakes with glittering quick returns, it squeezes Harlem in its powerful grip. To the Negro operators it is not so enormously profitable today as in its halcyon period, when its foundations were laid and it spread with impunity, not fearing white competitors and the action of the law. At that time the operators ("kings" and "queens" as they were called) each had a turnover of a quarter of a million dollars yearly. But after a span of unbelievably fabulous gold-years, the law of the land at last became aware of them and Federal and Municipal investigations compelled well-known operators to retire to private, comfortable and even luxurious lives. Through fear or careless management the business of some slipped from their hands and they were reduced to penury. And others were driven from the field by white overlords.

Through all the changes Harlemites have played the game increasingly and apparently will as long as Harlem exists. Numbers is a people's game, a community pastime in which old and young, literate and illiterate, the neediest folk and the well-to-do all participate. Harlemites seem altogether lacking in comprehension of the moral attitude of the white world towards its beloved racket.

In its early years these whites in and around Harlem who were aware of the game were tolerantly amused, and contemptuously called it 'the nigger pool," or "nigger pennies"! "Numbers" was the only game on which a penny could be put up as a wager. But a lucky penny makes six dollars for the player, minus the small percentage for the collector who places the bet. The white world never imagined that the pennies of Harlem's humble folk were creating fortunes of thousands of dollars and "kings" and "queens" in Harlem.

. . . The avid playing of numbers enormously multiplied the appetites of the credulous in the science of numerology. Harlem was set upon a perpetual hunt for lucky numbers. House numbers, car numbers, letters, telegrams, laundry, suits, shoes, hats, every conceivable object could carry a lucky number. Any casual thing might become unusual with the possibility of being endowed with a lucky number: a horse in the street, the first person you meet, an automobile accident, a fire, a fight, a butterfly fluttering on the air, a funeral, even a dog posing against a wall! And dreams! Harlem is haunted by numbers.

Dreaming of numbers is an inevitable condition of the blissful state of sleeping. And so the obsession of signs and portents in dreams as interpreted by numbers created a business for local numerologists. They compiled books of dreams interpreted by playing numbers. Dream books of numbers were published by Prince Ali, Madame Fu Futtam, Professor Konje, Red Witch, Moses Magical and many others. Such are the best sellers of Harlem.

"Hot" lucky numbers are peddled on the streets. Some are offered with a phial of oil or a box of incense to elude the curiosity of the police. But many are brazenly sold in a little piece of folded paper. And the occult chapels have multiplied and increased their following by interpreting dreams by numbers and evoking messages from the dead with numbers attached to the messages and by figuring out signs and portents by numbers.

The religious playing of numbers naturally increases the development of mysticism in Harlem. The numbers must be guessed and played at hazard. When such numbers do not win, the addicts of the game will readily resort to those psychic types of persons who profess to be mediums of numbers. It may be crudely manifested in Harlem, but this mystical abnegation is not a Negroid monopoly. It exists among the international gamblers of Monte Carlo as well as the *aficionados* of the Spanish lottery. In fact I have been amused in foreign parts by some gamblers taking me as a kind of fetish and touching my skin before placing a bet.

Thomas Wolfe's great strophe to the placenames and the immensity of America combines many of the techniques of literary modernism with the old grandiloquence that Americans loved in their preachers, politicians, and entertainers. (Excerpt from Thomas Wolfe, *Of Time and the River*, is reprinted with the permission of Charles Scribner's Sons. Copyright 1935 by Charles Scribner's Sons.)

THOMAS WOLFE, AMERICAN NAMES

Oh, brother, there are voices you will never hear—ancestral voices prophesying war, my brother, and rare and radiant voices that you know not of, as they have read us into doom. The genteel voices of Oxenford broke once like chimes of weary, unenthusiastic bells across my brain, speaking to me compassionately its judgment on our corrupted lives, gently dealing with the universe, my brother, gently and without labor—gently, brother, gently, it dealt with all of us, with easy condescension and amused disdain:

"I'm afraid, old boy," the genteel voice of Oxenford remarked, "you're up against it over thöh. . . . I really am. . . . Thöh's no place thö faw the individual any longah,"—the genteel voice went on, un-indi-vidual brother. "Obviously," that tolerant voice instructed me, "obviously, thöh can be no cultuah in a country so completely lackin' in tradition as is yoähs. . . . It's all so objective—if you see what I main—thöh's no place left faw the innah life," it said, oh, outward brother! ". . . We Europeans have often obsöhved (it's *very* curious, you know) that the American is incapable of any real feelin'—it seems quite impawsible faw him to distinguish between true emotion an' sentimentality—an' he in-vayably chooses the lattah! . . . *Curious, isn't it?*—or do you think so, brother? Of co'se, thöh is yoäh beastly dreadful sex-prawblem. . . . Yoäh women! . . . Oh, deah, deah! . . . Perhaps we'd bettah say no moah . . . but, thöh you *ah!*—right in the eye, my brother. "Yoäh country is a matriahky, my deah fellah . . . it really is, you know." . . . if you can follow us, dear brother. "The women have the men in a state of complete subjection . . . the male is rapidly becomin' moah sexless an' emasculated"—that genteel voice of doom went on—"No!—Decidedly you have quite a prawblem befoah you. . . . Obviously thöh can be no cultuah while such a condition puhsists. . . . *That* is why when my friends say to me, 'You ought to see *America*, . . . you really ought, you know.' . . . I say, 'No thanks. . . . If you don't mind, I'd rathah not. . . . I think I'll stay at home . . . I'm sorry,' " the compassionate tones of Oxenford went on, "but that's the way I feel—it really is, you know. . . . Of co'se, I know you couldn't undahstand my feelin'—faw aftah all, you ah a Yank—but thöh you ah! Sorry!" it said regretfully, as it spoke its courteous but inexorable judgments of eternal exile, brother, and removed forever the possibility of your ever hearing it. "But that's the way I feel! I hope you don't mind," the voice said gently, with compassion.

No, sir, don't mind. We don't mind, he, she, it or they don't mind. Nobody minds, sir, nobody minds. Because, just as you say, sir, oceans are between us, seas have sundered us, there is a magic in you that we can-not fathom—a light, a flame, a glory—an impalpable, indefinable, incom-prehensible, undeniable something-or-other, something which I can never understand or measure because—just as you say, sir—with such compas-sionate regret, I am—I am—a Yank.

'Tis true, my brother, we are Yanks. Oh, 'tis true, 'tis true! I am a Yank! Yet, wherefore Yank, good brother? Hath not a Yank ears? Hath not a Yank lies, truths, bowels of mercy, fears, joys, and lusts? Is he not warmed by the same sun, washed by the same ocean, rotted by the same decay, and eaten by the same worms as a German is? If you kill him, does he not die? If you sweat him, does he not stink? If you lie with his wife or his mistress, does she not whore, lie, fornicate and betray, even as a Frenchman's does? If you strip him, is he not naked as a Swede? Is his hide less white than Baudelaire's? Is his breath more foul than the King of Spain's? Is his belly bigger, his neck fatter, his face more hoggish, and his eye more shiny than a Munich brewer's? Will he not cheat, rape, thieve, whore, curse, hate, and murder like any European? Aye—Yank! But wherefore, wherefore Yank—good brother?

Brother, have we come then from a fated stock? Augured from birth, announced by two dark angels, named in our mother's womb? And for what? For what? Father-less, to grope our feelers on the sea's dark bed, among the polyped squirms, the blind sucks and crawls and sea-valves of the brain, loaded with memory that will not die? To cry our love out in the wilderness, to wake always in the night, smiting the pillow in some foreign land, thinking forever of the myriad sights and sounds of home?

"While Paris Sleeps!"—By God, while Paris sleeps, to wake and walk and not to sleep; to wake and walk and sleep and wake, and sleep again, seeing dawn come at the window-square that cast its wedge before our glazed, half-sleeping eyes, seeing soft, hated foreign light, and breathing soft, dull languid air that could not bite and tingle up the blood, seeing legend and lie and fable wither in our sight as we saw what we saw, knew what we knew.

Sons of the lost and lonely fathers, sons of the wanderers, children of hardy loins, the savage earth, the pioneers, what had we to do with all their bells and churches? Could we feed our hunger on portraits of the Spanish king? Brother, for what? For what? To kill the giant of loneliness and fear, to slay the hunger that would not rest, that would not give us rest.

Of wandering forever, and the earth again. Brother, for what? For what? For what? For the wilderness, the immense and lonely land. For the unendurable hunger, the unbearable ache, the incurable loneliness. For the exultancy whose only answer is the wild goat-cry. For a million memories, ten thousand sights and sounds and shapes and smells and names of things that only we can know.

For what? For what? Not for a nation. Not for a people, not for an empire, not for a thing we love or hate.

For what? For a cry, a space, an ecstasy. For a savage and nameless hunger. For a living and intolerable memory that may not for a second be forgotten, since it includes all the moments of our lives, includes all we do and are. For a living memory; for ten thousand memories; for a million sights and sounds and moments; for something like nothing else on earth; for something which possesses us.

For something under our feet, and around us and over us; something that is in us and part of us, and proceeds from us, that beats in all the pulses of our blood.

Brother, for what?

First for the thunder of imperial names, the names of men and battles, the names of places and great rivers, the mighty names of the States. The name of The Wilderness; and the names of Antietam, Chancellorsville, Shiloh, Bull Run, Fredericksburg, Cold Harbor, the Wheat Fields, Ball's Bluff, and the Devil's Den; the names of Cowpens, Brandywine, and Saratoga; of Death Valley, Chickamauga, and the Cumberland Gap. The names of the Nantahalahs, the Bad Lands, the Painted Desert, the Yosemite, and the Little Big Horn; the names of Yancey and Cabarrus counties; and the terrible name of Hatteras.

Then, for the continental thunder of the States: the names of Montana, Texas, Arizona, Colorado, Michigan, Maryland, Virginia, and the two Dakotas; the names of Oregon and Indiana, of Kansas and the rich Ohio; the powerful name of Pennsylvania, and the name of Old Kentucky; the undulance of Alabama; the names of Florida and North Carolina.

In the red-oak thickets, at the break of day, long hunters lay for bear—the rattle of arrows in laurel leaves, the war-cries round the painted buttes, and the majestical names of the Indian Nations: the Pawnees, the Algonquins, the Iroquois, the Comanches, the Blackfeet, the Seminoles, the Cherokees, the Sioux, the Hurons, the Mohawks, the Navajos, the Utes, the Omahas, the Onondagas, the Chippewas, the Crees, the Chickasaws, the Arapahoes, the Catawbas, the Dakotas, the Apaches, the Croatans, and the Tuscaroras; the names of Powhatan and Sitting Bull; and the name of the Great Chief, Rain-In-The-Face.

Of wandering forever, and the earth again: in red-oak thickets, at the break of day, long hunters lay for bear. The arrows rattle in the laurel leaves, and the elmroots thread the bones of buried lovers. There have been war-cries on the Western trails, and on the plains the gunstock rusts upon a handful of bleached bones. The barren earth? Was no love living in the wilderness?

The rails go westward in the dark. Brother, have you seen starlight on the rails? Have you heard the thunder of the fast express?

Of wandering forever, and the earth again—the names of the mighty rails that bind the nation, the wheeled thunder of the names that net the continent: the Pennsylvania, the Union Pacific, the Santa Fé, the Baltimore and Ohio, the Chicago and Northwestern, the Southern, the Louisiana and Northern, the Seaboard Air Line, the Chicago, Milwaukee and Saint Paul, the Lackawanna, the New York, New Haven and Hartford, the Florida East Coast, the Rock Island, and the Denver and Rio Grande.

Brother, the names of the engines, the engineers, and the sleeping-cars: the great engines of the Pacific type, the articulated Mallets with three sets of eight-yoked driving-wheels, the 400-ton thunderbolts with J. T. Cline, T. J. McRae, and the demon hawk-eyes of H. D. Campbell on the rails.

The names of the great tramps who range the nation on the fastest trains: the names of the great tramps Oklahoma Red, Fargo Pete, Dixie Joe, Iron Mike, The Frisco Kid, Nigger Dick, Red Chi, Ike the Kike, and The Jersey Dutchman.

By the waters of life, by time, by time, Lord Tennyson stood among the rocks, and stared. He had long hair, his eyes were deep and sombre, and he wore a cape; he was a poet, and there was magic and mystery in his touch, for he had heard the horns of Elfland faintly blowing. And by the waters of life, by time, by time, Lord Tennyson stood among the cold, gray rocks, and commanded the sea to break—break—break! And the sea broke, by the waters of life, by time, by time, as Lord Tennyson commanded it to do, and his heart was sad and lonely as he watched the stately ships (of the Hamburg-American Packet Company, fares forty-five dollars and up, first-class) go on to their haven under the hill, and Lord Tennyson would that his heart could utter the thoughts that arose in him.

By the waters of life, by time, by time: the names of the mighty rivers, the alluvial gluts, the drains of the continent, the throats that drink America (Sweet Thames, flow gently till I end my song). The names of the men who pass, and the myriad names of the earth that abides forever: the names of the men who are doomed to wander, and the name of that immense and lonely land on which they wander, to which they return, in which they will be buried—America! The immortal earth which waits forever, the trains that thunder on the continent, the men who wander, and the women who cry out, "Return!"

Finally, the names of the great rivers that are flowing in the darkness (Sweet Thames, flow gently till I end my song).

By the waters of life, by time, by time: the names of great mouths, the mighty maws, the vast, wet, coiling, never-glutted and unending snakes that drink the continent. Where, sons of men, and in what other land will you find others like them, and where can you match the mighty music of their names?—The Monongahela, the Colorado, the Rio Grande, the Columbia, the Tennessee, the Hudson (Sweet Thames!); the Kennebec, the Rappahannock, the Delaware, the Penobscot, the Wabash, the Chesapeake, the Swannanoa, the Indian River, the Niagara (Sweet Afton!); the Saint Lawrence, the Susquehanna, the Tombigbee, the Nantahala, the French Broad, the Chattahoochee, the Arizona, and the Potomac (Father Tiber!)—these are a few of their princely names, these are a few of their great, proud, glittering names, fit for the immense and lonely land that they inhabit.

Oh, Tiber! Father Tiber! You'd only be a suckling in that mighty land! And as for you, sweet Thames, flow gently till I end my song; flow gently, gentle Thames, be well-behaved, sweet Thames, speak softly and politely, little Thames, flow gently till I end my song.

The anthem of the Civil Rights movement in the 1960s, "We Shall Overcome," is a modern adaptation of an old black hymn. Black strikers gave it the present lyrics in 1945. (From *Songs of the Freedom Movement*, compiled by Guy and Candie Carawan for The Student Non-Violent Coordinating Committee, 1963.)

WE SHALL OVERCOME

We shall overcome,
We shall overcome,
We shall overcome some day
Oh, deep in my heart (I know that)
I do believe (oh) we shall overcome someday.

We are not afraid,
We are not afraid,
We are not afraid today.
Oh, deep in my heart, I do believe,
We shall overcome someday.

We are not alone,
We are not alone,
We are not alone today.
Oh, deep in my heart, I do believe,
We shall overcome someday.

The truth will make us free,
The truth will make us free,
The trust will make us free today.
Oh, deep in my heart, I do believe,
We shall overcome someday.

We'll walk hand in hand,
We'll walk hand in hand,
We'll walk hand in hand today.

Oh, deep in my heart, I do believe,
We shall overcome someday.

The Lord will see us through,
The Lord will see us through,
The Lord will see us through today.
Oh, deep in my heart, I do believe,
We shall overcome someday.

Black and white together,
Black and white together,
Black and white together now.
Oh, deep in my heart, I do believe,
We shall overcome someday.

We shall all be free,
We shall all be free,
We shall all be free today.
Oh, deep in my heart, I do believe,
We shall overcome someday.

Ethnic humor is as American a staple as corn. Throughout the nation's history it has been a steady response to immigration and the problems of a polyglot society. In general, ethnic humor falls into two categories—a good-natured variety shared by the group satirized as well as the rest of society and a nastier variant aimed as a weapon at the strangers in the land. In addition, there has been a continuous tradition of regional humor, such as the "Vermont Stories" reprinted here, which share many of the same characteristics. Frequently groups absorbed the humor aimed at them and turned it into their own popular art— witness the stage Irishman of the late nineteenth century, or the Jewish comedians of the first half of the twentieth century, or the black humorist of the present. That may also occur with the contemporary "Polish" jokes:

ETHNIC AND REGIONAL HUMOR

Did you hear about the two flamingoes who got married and put pink stucco Italians on their lawn?

Who wears dirty white flowing robes and rides into town on a pig? Lawrence of Poland.

An interior decorator was telling a doctor and his wife how to decorate their new house. In the livingroom he suggested a Persian rug; then he went to the window and said: "Green side up." Upstairs in the bathroom he recommended onyx tile in the shower; again he went to the window and shouted "Green side up." In the bedroom he asked the doctor and his wife if they wanted a canopied bed and screamed out the window "Green side up." Finally, the doctor's wife asked "What is this 'green side up?'" The decorator replied: "I've got a Pole outside laying sod."

The icthyologists crossed a Coho salmon, a wall-eye, and a muskie, and got a Cowalski. It was a marvelous fish but they had a terrible time teaching it how to swim.

A guy in a bar saw a friend come in and said, "Hey, I've got a great Polish joke." "But I'm Polish," complained the friend. "That's all right. I'll tell it slowly."

What is the difference between a Hungarian and a Rumanian? Both will sell their mother but the Rumanian will deliver.

How do you sink an Italian ship? Launch it.

Vermont Stories

A leading citizen of Royalton was sitting on his porch in the cool of the evening when a tourist from New Jersey paused to chat. "Have you lived here all your life?" the stranger asked. "Not yet," was the low-pitched reply.

A farmer and his hired hand were by the road when a motorist inquired if he was on the right road for Jericho Center, and the farmer gave affirmative reply. After he had driven on the hired man remarked, "You didn't tell him the bridge was out." "Nope," said the farmer. "He didn't ask."

Sometimes I rib my fellow legislators by reporting the discussion between two old boys at a political rally where a candidate for office was going on at great length. One of them, a bit hard of hearing, asked his friend, "What's he talking about?" And received the precis: "He don't say."

Yankees from the hill-country are noted for responding to questions by asking one of their own, as epitomized in the exchange: "How's your wife?" a neighbor inquired. "Compared to what?" was the canny counterquery.

A nurse at the Waterbury State Hospital was in the yard walking a couple of patients who were recovering from mental problems. A passing bird dropped a calling card on the bald head of one, and the nurse, solicitous for his emotional balance, told him not to worry—"just stay right here and I'll go in the building and bring a piece of toilet paper."

When she had disappeared the old man said to his companion, "Ain't she a damn fool. That bird'll be a quarter a mile away 'fore she gets back."

I have heard tell of the New Yorker who had a Great Dane on a leash and tried to board a bus in Vermont. The driver opened the bus door and, looking at the pair, said: "You can't get on this bus."

"Why can't I get on the bus?" snapped the New Yorker.

"No dogs allowed on this bus," countered the driver.

To which the New Yorker retorted, not with the greatest display of understanding and courtesy, "OK, you know what you can do with your damned bus."

Equal to the occasion, the driver replied, "You do the same with your dog and you can get on."

I heard up in the Northeast Kingdom of an old-timer in Lyndonville, I think it was, who sat down one evening by the lamp to fill out a government form which was almost overdue. Like many of us under similar circumstances the old man was not in a pleasant or co-operative frame of mind to start with, and staring him in the face at the head of a box at the top righthand corner of the printed form were the words in bold type: DO NOT WRITE HERE.

Before going any further the old gentleman took a firm grip on his pen and wrote in the box, in equally bold letters, I WRITE WHERE I GODDAM PLEASE.

public enemies

The Bonus Army of 1932 consisted mostly of unemployed veterans, and often their families, who converged on Washington, D.C., from all over the nation, demanding early payment of their World War I soldiers' bonus due in 1945. They were chiefly peaceful transients who took over private property in the capital. Hoover simply ordered them dispersed from the condemned buildings, but General Douglas MacArthur went far beyond his instructions and, using bayonets instead of nightsticks, burned their shacks and drove them off Anacostia Flats on the Maryland side of the Potomac. Mrs. Evalyn McLean, a resident of the capital, recalls the marchers. (From Evalyn Walsh McLean, *Father Struck It Rich*, 1936.)

THE BONUS MARCHERS

On a day in June, 1932, I saw a dusty automobile truck roll slowly past my house. I saw the unshaven, tired faces of the men who were riding in it standing up. A few were seated at the rear with their legs dangling over the lowered tailboard. On the side of the truck was an expanse of white cloth on which, crudely lettered in black, was a legend, BONUS ARMY.

Other trucks followed in a straggling succession, and on the sidewalks of Massachusetts Avenue where stroll most of the diplomats and the other fashionables of Washington were some ragged hikers, wearing scraps of old uniforms. The sticks with which they strode along seemed less canes than cudgels. They were not a friendly-looking lot, and I learned they were hiking and riding into the capital along each of its radial avenues; that they had come from every part of the continent. It was not lost on me that those men, passing any one of my big houses, would see in such rich shelters a kind of challenge.

I was burning, because I felt that crowd of men, women, and children never should have been permitted to swarm across the continent. But I could remember when those same men, with others, had been cheered as they marched down Pennsylvania Avenue. While I recalled those wartime parades, I was reading in the newspapers that the bonus army men were going hungry in Washington.

That night I woke up before I had been asleep an hour. I got to thinking about those poor devils marching around the capital. Then I decided that it should be a part of my son Jock's education to see and try to comprehend that marching. It was one o'clock, and the Capitol was beautifully lighted. I wished then for the power to turn off the lights and use the money thereby saved to feed the hungry.

When Jock and I rode among the bivouacked men I was horrified to see plain evidence of hunger in their faces; I heard them trying to cadge cigarettes from one another. Some were lying on the sidewalks, unkempt heads pillowed on their arms. A few clusters were shuffling around. I went up to one of them, a fellow with eyes deeply sunken in his head.

"Have you eaten?"

He shook his head.

Just then I saw General Glassford, superintendent of the Washington police. He said, "I'm going to get some coffee for them."

"All right," I said, "I am going to Childs'."

It was two o'clock when I walked into that white restaurant. A man came up to take my order. "Do you serve sandwiches? I want a thousand," I said. "And a thousand packages of cigarettes."

"But, lady—"

"I want them right away. I haven't got a nickel with me, but you can trust me. I am Mrs. McLean."

Well, he called the manager into the conference, and before long they were slicing bread with a machine; and what with Glassford's coffee also (he was spending his own money) we two fed all the hungry ones who were in sight.

Next day I went to see Judge John Barton Payne, head of the Red Cross, but I could not persuade him that the bonus army men were part of a national crisis that the Red Cross was bound to deal with. He did promise a little flour, and I was glad to accept it.

Then I tried the Salvation Army and found that their girls were doing all they could. I asked the officer in charge, a worried little man, if he would undertake to find out how I could help the men. With enthusiasm he said he would, and the next day he came to my house to tell me that what the bonus army leaders said they most needed was a big tent to serve as a headquarters in which fresh arrivals could be registered. At once I ordered a tent sent over from Baltimore. After that I succeeded in getting Walter Waters to come to my house. He was trying to keep command of that big crowd of men. I talked to him, and before long we were friends. I sent books and radios to the men. I went to the house in Pennsylvania Avenue that Glassford had provided for the women and children. There was not a thing in it. Scores of women and children were sleeping on its floors. So I went out and bought them army cots. Another day I took over some of my sons' clothing, likewise some of my own, and dresses of my daughter. One of the women held up one of little Evalyn's dresses and examined it on both sides. Then she said, "I guess my child can starve in a fifty-dollar dress as well as in her rags."

One day Waters, the so-called commander, came to my house and said: "I'm desperate. Unless these men are fed, I can't say what won't happen to this town." With him was his wife, a little ninety-three-pounder, dressed as a man, her legs and feet in shiny boots. Her yellow hair was freshly marceled.

"She's been on the road for days," said Waters, "and has just arrived by bus."

I thought a bath would be a welcome change; so I took her upstairs to that guest bedroom my father had designed for King Leopold. I sent for my maid to draw a bath, and told the young woman to lie down.

"You get undressed," I said, "and while you sleep I'll have all your things cleaned and pressed."

"Oh, no," she said, "not me. I'm not giving these clothes up. I might never see them again."

Her lip was out, and so I did not argue. She threw herself down on the bed, boots and all, and I tiptoed out.

That night I telephoned to Vice-President Charlie Curtis. I told him I was speaking for Waters, who was standing by my chair. I said: "These men are in a desperate situation, and unless something is done for them, unless they are fed, there is bound to be a lot of trouble. They have no money, nor any food."

Charlie Curtis told me that he was calling a secret meeting of senators and would send a delegation of them to the House to urge immediate action on the Howell bill, providing money to send the bonus army members back to their homes.

Those were times when I often wished for the days of Warren Harding. Harding would have gone among those men and talked in such a manner as to make them cheer him and cheer their flag. If Hoover had done that, I think, not even troublemakers in the swarm could have caused any harm.

Nothing I had seen before in my whole life touched me as deeply as what I had seen in the faces of those men of the bonus army. Their way of righting things was wrong—oh, yes; but it is not the only wrong. I had talked with them and their women. Even when the million-dollar home my father built was serving as a sort of headquarters for their leader, I could feel and almost understand their discontent and their hatred of some of the things I have represented.

I was out in California when the United States army was used to drive them out of Washington. In a moving-picture show I saw in a news reel the tanks, the cavalry, and the gas-bomb throwers running those wretched Americans out of our capital. I was so raging mad I could have torn the theater down. They could not be allowed to stay, of course; but even so I felt myself one of them.

SLICK TRICKS OF THE COMMIES

Got commie trouble in your organization? Here's how they operate, their tricks and schemes to seize power and frustrate Americans from running their own groups.

Few organizations warn members against even the most common Communist tricks and swindlers. Such a head-in-sand attitude is dangerous. It has wrecked more than one labor union. For Communism attacks like cancer. Allowed to grow, it affects the vitals of the organization so that its removal is a critical, sometimes fatal operation.

Legionnaires are in a unique position to clean up these cancerous growths, and do it effectively. No individual by himself can cope with the highly disciplined commies, but a powerful organization can.

Many Legionnaires are union members. By working together they can outmaneuver any Red attempts to take over unions. However, this calls for a united front against the commies. No Legionnaire by himself is going to get very far in the rough-and-tumble battle to eliminate fanatical Reds. Legionnaires will find the job no cinch. You'll be up against tough opposition.

To give an example, I once attended a meeting of a union in which I had been active. Most members were newcomers to me. The routine meeting, with nothing important to consider, dragged on for hours because of an endless barrage of questioning to which the president was subjected by a small group apparently motivated only by concern for their union's welfare. These highly skilled interrogators, who seemed to follow each other in regular batting order, apparently wanted to make sure that their unsalaried officers were sufficiently vigilant, aggressive and constantly "on the job." The general trend of their endless, fine-point questions was not offensive or overly critical.

It was instantly plain to me that the badly harried official did not suspect that something was being put over on him, meeting after meeting, by a well-organized "Fraction" of trained Reds. His courteous, detailed explanations betrayed the pathetic fact that he assumed that his tormentors were simply asking legitimate questions. Neither he nor the non-Communist members realized that this typical Red tactic of interminable questioning was used in all Red-infested organizations to break down human patience. Exasperated officials finally "blow up" and resign or refuse to run again for office. This clears the road for Red office-seekers.

The secret purpose of this "Chinese water torture" tactic is twofold. First, it gradually undermines confidence in all non-Communist officials. Uncritical members draw the false conclusion that *perhaps* their officers are not as aggressive as they might be. They certainly sound apologetic, always making alibis. Secondly, these "progressives," whom some people suspect of being Reds, certainly have the union's best interests at heart as their vigilant attendance demonstrates. Needless to add, Communists tolerate no such criticism in unions they control.

I remarked to a former president of the local, "Well, I see you have a nice commy 'Fraction' here and they are really working the 'Diamond' in fine fashion right under your president's nose."

He looked at me in astonishment:

"What do you mean by 'commy Fraction' and the 'Diamond'?"

I was amazed to learn that this well-informed, old AFL man knew absolutely nothing about Red trickery. He had never been taught how to spot slick-working commies "boring from within." In fact, he was not even sure that these interrogators were Communists but felt they might be "just a bunch of radical troublemakers and soreheads."

The "Fraction" is a rigidly organized caucus which meets before a meeting to plot every action in minutest detail. A Communst "trade union expert" hands down the "Line." Speakers interrogators, hecklers, introducers of resolutions, and the hissing and booing squad are all carefully rehearsed. Nothing foreseeable is left to chance. The "Fraction," led by the "Fraction Secretary" moves into meeting as a smooth-working machine. A well-led "Fraction" in action suggests a pack of snarling sheep dogs harrying, splitting, and driving where they will a great flock of milling, helpless sheep.

As the Reds in any meeting seldom exceed 7 or 8 per cent of those present, the problem of exerting maximum parliamentary pressure with such slender forces is solved through use of the "Diamond" seating scheme, a most effective Communist device.

An anti-Communist union member arises to denounce the Reds. Or he criticizes Russia. Instantly the "Fraction" members surrounding him jump up, angrily denouncing him as a "Red-baiter," "fascist," "labor splitter," "imperialist war-monger." If the chairman is a Red stooge or a weak character, the wolfpack will collectively torpedo the "Red-baiter."

However, if the chairman is a non-Communist enforcing Robert's Rules of Order, they will attack in relays until the anti-Communist is silenced. Most people unfamiliar with this tactic make the erroneous deduction that with so many obvious Communists seated right around him, the same percentage carried out in the hall means that 30 to 50 per cent of those present are C.P. supporters. Outrageous heckling and whispered threats of a beating at the hands of goons generally leads anti-Communists into deciding that "discretion is the better part of valor."

Assume, however, there are other militant anti-Reds in the hall. As they take the floor an entirely new set of "Fraction" goons spring to their feet and effectively seal them off in the same vituperative, threatening manner. These men make the same erroneous conclusion as to Red strength present when they find themselves apparently surrounded by angry comrades and they, too, are probably happy to drop the thankless argument. If each person present were as fanatical and disciplined as the "Fraction" and knew that he had a strong, well-oiled machine behind him, such Communist tactics would obviously be useless. It is, however, a well-known fact that 90 per cent of any attendance at general meetings never takes an active part in the proceedings. The Communists therefore only have to worry about the troublesome 10 per cent or less who have the intelligence and courage to spot and fight Communists.

The "Diamond" is equally effective in disrupting meetings which the Communists consider damaging. Jot down the names of speakers who always support each other on "Party Line" issues. You will soon have a list of most of the "Fraction." But do not hope to trap the "Fraction" secretary—he is too important to show his hand.

Delaying adjournment for hours is another tell-tale Red trick. Long-winded harangues about "fascism," the "rising danger of imperialist war," "labor spies," etc., etc., or endless points of order are used to exhaust most non-Communists to a point where they drift out. "Hot" Communist resolutions are then steamrollered through with a minimum of parliamentary palaver. Note that Reds seldom introduce their own tell-tale resolutions, since this would reveal their identities—stooges and dupes are invariably used as cover-ups.

Many organizations have been surprised to learn that the meeting of the night before, which had apparently dwindled to a handful of wrangling radicals at a late hour, had passed some dangerous resolutions in the name of the entire group. Unwary officials might find themselves facing formal trials or investigations on phony plausible "charges." Or the union's funds, welfare, security, or good name may have been dangerously compromised by an inopportune stride. The obvious answer to this tactic is for the majority to force an adjournment vote before a single member is allowed to leave.

Anti-Communists are sometimes heartened by an apparent split in heretofore solid Red ranks. Or unionists seeking means of ridding their union of Reds are surprised to find their secret plans are known to the enemy. The answer is the little known technique of the Phony Opposition. This is composed of undetected Reds and camp followers not compromised by consistently supporting the Party "line."

In Red unions where a rising opposition becomes threatening, outstanding leaders of the Phony Opposition will run for office *against* the Red incumbents, thus neatly splitting the anti-Communist vote and assuring the re-election of the Red slate.

In critical situations where the "Fraction" faces defeat, the Phony Opposition enables the Reds to salvage something from the debacle. The Phony Opposition comes out openly in support of the majority but its role is strictly one of sabotage. Its speakers indulge in silly tactics to embarrass the position of the true opposition. They will even attack the Communists—not as a menace to the union. Oh no!—but merely on the grounds that they are "ill-advised." Unwary anti-Reds naturally welcome allies with open arms little realizing they have opened defenses to a Trojan Horse full of armed Red spies.

The Phony Opposition protects the Reds from ever being driven out of any organization. A secret battalion has been left behind in the very heart of the enemy's camp. The bitterly acquired knowledge that it is almost impossible to form any broad anti-Communist front without attracting phony "anti-Communists" has discouraged more than one unionist into abandoning the struggle against such experts in low cunning, deceit and treachery.

Watch for the shopworn, old "It is no accident" gag used to "amalgamate" opponents with some utterly unpopular cause or person. Joe Zilch who questions some raw Communist swindling in his union is most effectively squelched by: "It is no accident that Brother Zilch starts Red-baiting some of this union's most hard-working members just at this time when Wall Street warmongers are pounding their tom-toms of hate against our ally, Russia."

Keeping the pot of discontent bubbling by endless phony beefs is another common tactic known as "Raising the Issue." As Reds solemnly mouth the same gibberish, they in time unwittingly betray themselves by their peculiar terminology.

"Manufacturing martyrs" by framing some poor dupe in a labor skirmish and then collecting thousands of dollars for "legal defense" is another commy trick which serves to embarrass the police, besides bringing in money needed for other purposes. Scaring off oppositionists by phoned threats of physical violence at 2 A.M. is also very effective.

Don't fall for the Red hokum that they are invincible. Hitler peddled the same line for years. This is merely Communist self-hypnosis, serving a double purpose of frightening their enemies and bolstering their own morale. One has to swallow a great deal to be a Communist, to say nothing of public and social liabilities. Deprived of the comfort of religion, public esteem and good conscience which a socially useful life confers, Communists find most soothing the delusion that they are the elite of the future, the sure inheritors of absolute power over man and property. Red arrogance and colossal self-righteousness are nothing but opiates intended to deaden all doubts and to still any twinges of conscience and self-respect.

Thomas Alva Edison was a fit hero for the new age of technology. All those sinister things going on in science could be humanized by a man in a rumpled suit who enjoyed fishing and earned $50,000 a year from his inventions. The description below accompanied a drawing of Edison. (From *Harper's Weekly*, XXIII [August 2, 1879], 607.)

THOMAS EDISON IN HIS WORKSHOP

It is utter, black midnight, and the stillness and awe of that lonely hour have settled upon the pleasant hills and pretty homes of the remote New Jersey village. Only one or two windows gleam faintly, as though through dusty panes, and the traveller directing his stumbling steps by their light, enters a door, passes to a stairway guarded by the shadows of strange objects, and gropes his way upward.

A single flaring gas flame flickers at one end of a long room, disclosing an infinite number of bottles of various sizes, carved and turned pieces of wood, curious shapes of brass, and a wilderness of wires, some straight, others coiled and spiral and kinked, the ends pinched under thumbscrews, or hidden in dirty jars, or hanging free from invisible supports—an indiscriminate, shadowy, uncanny foreground. Picking his way circumspectly around a bluish, half-translucent bulwark of jars filled with azure liquid, and chained together by wires, a new picture meets his bewildered eyes. At an open red brick chimney, fitfully outlined from the darkness by the light of fiercely smoking lamps, stands a roughly clothed gray-haired man, his tall form stooping under the wooden hood which seems to confine noxious gases and compel them to the flue. He is intent upon a complex arrangement of brass and iron and copper wire, assisted by magnets and vitriol jars, vials labelled in chemical formulæ, and retorts in which to form new liquid combinations. His eager countenance is lighted up by the yellow glare of the unsteady lamps, as he glances into a heavy old book lying there, while his broad shoulders keep out the gloom that lurks in all the corners and hides among the masses of machinery. He is a fit occupant for this weird scene; a midnight workman with supernal forces whose mysterious phenomena have taught men their largest idea of elemental power; a modern alchemist, who finds the philosopher's stone to be made of carbon, and with his magnetic wand changes every-day knowledge into the pure gold of new applications and original uses. He is THOMAS A. EDISON, at work in his laboratory, deep in his conjuring of Nature while the world sleeps.

The author of the quadruplex telegraph, the telephone, and the phonograph was born at Milan, Ohio, in February, 1847, of parents whose ancestors came from Holland. Going to the public schools until the age of fourteen, he then began to sell newspapers upon the trains of the Grand Trunk Railway, and perceiving the advantage to be derived, conceived the idea of establishing bulletin-boards at the principal stations on his route, and telegraphing ahead the features of the morning's news, which in those war days were likely to be startling enough. Interest was excited, and his sales correspondingly increased. These bulletin-boards are a common institution on Western railways now, but his was the first. Next he wanted to do his own telegraphing, and so got an operator to teach him how. Then, to perfect his knowledge, he and a companion erected a line between their houses at their own expense, which was small, since young EDISON made every thing himself. To get the wire charged was the great difficulty; and not knowing that the sparks thus evolved were not the kind they needed, the two youthful electricians captured a wretched cat, tied the two poles of their circuit to opposite ends of the animal, and diligently rubbed the fur, right way and wrong. This, of course, was a failure, but the amateur line proved a success after all. Then young EDISON got some type and a press, set it up in the baggage-car, and printed the *Grand Trunk Herald* every day on the express train. When this came to an end, he put up a chemical laboratory in the bagage-car, and experimented until an explosion occurred which set the car afire, when he and his laboratory were ignominiously bundled out. After that he was employed as a railway telegraph operator, and then went to Cincinnati in the employment of the Western Union Company. It was here that his *penchant* for experimenting began to be so strongly manifested. Sleeping almost where night overtook him, and living upon the cheapest possible fare, he spent every penny of his salary in buying apparatus and material for his investigations. The results were that he patented the duplex machine, by which two dispatches could be transmitted on the same wire at the same time, and that he was discharged from his place for continually taking the company's instruments to pieces to try to improve them. From Cincinnati EDISON went to Louisville to receive the press reports at midnight. These come at the rate of forty words a minute, and must be taken off as they go by. EDISON was not proficient enough to do this, and therefore contrived an arrangement by which the paper on which the message was printed in MORSE's characters should pass through a second machine, where an embossing point travelling over the indented paper should make and break the circuit so as to report in sound what the original machine had printed, but only at half the speed, so that he could easily record it. This went on a few weeks, until the printers complained of the lateness of their copy, and the ingenious operator was again discharged; but his invention was far more important than he suspected, for it was the parent of the phonograph.

In 1872 the quadruplex system of telegraphy was got into shape by him, by which four messages can be sent simultaneously on one wire, two one way and two the other, and which is in daily use now. This was quickly followed by other very important inventions, but the two which carried EDISON's fame the farthest, and aroused such widespread popular interest in his work, are the telephone and the phonograph, both of which have been fully described in the journals of the day.

These with other patents now bring him a large revenue, and the Western Union Telegraph Company pay him a good yearly bonus for the simple refusal of the first right to buy any and all of his discoveries which relate to telegraphy, so that his present annual income is perhaps $50,000. Though only thirty-one, Mr. EDISON's tall form is somewhat bent with much stooping over his work, and his brown hair is streaked with gray. He wears no beard or mustache, and in rest would hardly be called a handsome man; but when he speaks, the face instantly speaks too, and the keen blue eyes, far apart, light up with quick and happy intelligence. Careless in matters of personal appearance, riding rough-shod over the factitious requirements of society, happy only in his laboratory and his home nearby, reckless of money when applied to his scientific needs, regarding time as the one precious thing, EDISON is a man of such strong characteristics as make an indelible impress upon the world wherever he goes. He works, and always has worked, incessantly, and with all sorts of irregularity. Never fond of any athletic games, he had his amusement in experimenting, took his exercise in occasional fishing excursions, and finds recuperation in long deep sleep.

His laboratory is a wonderful place. Down stairs are his office and unpacking room, where are hosts of books, and his steam-engines and machinery, where the best workmen turn for him the delicate parts of iron and brass which are to be put together in his cunning constructions. Up stairs is the work-room. Plenty of windows give light and air and a pleasant view. Gearing from the engine can be attached any where needed. Telegraph wires run to New York and Washington, and a circuit of 3000 miles can be secured if necessary to ascertain whether some designed improvement which works well enough in the laboratory will cope with conditions of long out-door lines. Everywhere are the implements and evidences of his craft: a battery of 250 cells; a wilderness of insulated wires, so that anywhere and everywhere electrical attachments can be made; gas jets innumerable, the gas being made on the premises;

telegraphic machines, simple, duplex, triplex, and quadruplex; a coil which will throw a spark nine inches; telescopes, microscopes, spectroscopes. The tables are crowded with parts of new models and fragments of old machines. In one corner is a fine organ; in another a photographic kit; in a third a glass case of delicate material; all around the walls shelves full of chemical mixtures in little bottles, more than 2000 of which have been made and retained, labelled, by EDISON. In the middle of the room are several machines whose names end in *phone*, the biggest of which, naturally, is the megaphone, consisting of a tripod supporting two narrow hollow cones of paper, ending at the apex in rubber tubes. You put the tubes in your ear, go off a mile, some one speaks in an ordinary tone, and you hear it plainly. To conclude, there is an instrument so delicate as to detect the heat derived from the rays of a single star!

This sad sad song of World War I was a favorite about the hangars of Long Island from which Charles Lindbergh flew in 1927. (From John J. Niles, *Songs My Mother Never Taught Me*, 1920.)

A POOR AVIATOR LAY DYING

A poor aviator lay dying.
At the end of a bright summer's day.
His comrades had gathered about him.
To carry his fragments away.

The airplane was piled on his wishbone,
His Hotchkiss was wrapped round his head;
He wore a spark-plug on each elbow,
'Twas plain he would shortly be dead.

He spit out a valve and a gasket,
And stirred in the sump where he lay,
And then to his wondering comrades,
These brave parting words he did say:

"Take the magneto out of my stomach,
And the butterfly valve off my neck,
Extract from my liver the crankshaft,
There are lots of good parts in this wreck.

"Take the manifold out of my larynx,
And the cylinders out of my brain,
Take the piston rods out of my kidneys,
And assemble the engine again."

In the 1920s, radio, movies, and mass-produced consumer goods created more than ever a national culture, a massive audience that could all together enjoy one or another sensation. Heavyweight prize fights, murders, or seamy divorce trials could be "ballyhooed" to the entire nation. The greatest spectacular of the 1920s, however, was not an event manufactured by press agents or reporters, but the spontaneous reaction to Charles Lindbergh's solo flight across the Atlantic in 1927. His modestly written and winning account of the flight, We, graced bookshelves in homes all over the country. (Excerpt from Charles A. Lindbergh, We. Reprinted by permission of G. P. Putnam's Sons. Copyright 1927, © 1955 by Charles A. Lindbergh.

CHARLES LINDBERGH: WE

On the morning of May nineteenth, a light rain was falling and the sky was overcast. Weather reports from land stations and ships along the great circle course were unfavorable and there was apparently no prospect of taking off for Paris for several days at least. But at about six o'clock I received a special report from the New York Weather Bureau. A high pressure area was over the entire North Atlantic and the low pressure area over Nova Scotia and Newfoundland was receding. It was apparent that the prospects of the fog clearing up were as good as I might expect for some time to come. The North Atlantic should be clear with only local storms on the coast of Europe. The moon had just passed full and the percentage of days with fog over Newfoundland and the Grand Banks was increasing so that there seemed to be no advantage in waiting longer.

We went to Curtiss Field as quickly as possible and made arrangements for the barograph to be sealed and installed, and for the plane to be serviced and checked.

We decided partially to fill the fuel tanks in the hangar before towing the ship on a truck to Roosevelt Field which adjoins Curtiss on the east, where the servicing would be completed.

I left the responsibility for conditioning the plane in the hands of the men on the field while I went into the hotel for about two and one-half hours of rest; but at the hotel there were several more details which had to be completed and I was unable to get any sleep that night.

I returned to the field before daybreak on the morning of the twentieth. A light rain was falling which continued until almost dawn; consequently we did not move the ship to Roosevelt Field until much later than we had planned, and the take off was delayed from daybreak until nearly eight o'clock.

At dawn the shower had passed, although the sky was overcast, and occasionally there would be some slight precipitation. The tail of the plane was lashed to a truck and escorted by a number of motorcycle police. The slow trip from Curtiss to Roosevelt was begun.

The ship was placed at the extreme west end of the field heading along the east and west runway and the final fueling commenced.

About 7:40 A.M. the motor was started and at 7:52 I took off on the flight for Paris.

The field was a little soft due to the rain during the night and the heavily loaded plane gathered speed very slowly. After passing the half-way mark, however, it was apparent that I would be able to clear the obstructions at the end. I passed over a tractor by about fifteen feet and a telephone line by about twenty, with a fair reserve of flying speed. I believe that the ship would have taken off from a hard field with at least five hundred pounds more weight.

I turned slightly to the right to avoid some high trees on a hill directly ahead, but by the time I had gone a few hundred yards I had sufficient altitude to clear all obstructions and throttled the engine down to 1750 R.P.M. I took up a compass course at once and soon reached Long Island Sound where the Curtiss Oriole with its photographer, which had been escorting me, turned back.

The haze soon cleared and from Cape Cod through the southern half of Nova Scotia the weather and visibility were excellent. I was flying very low, sometimes as close as ten feet from the trees and water.

On the three-hundred-mile stretch of water between Cape Cod and Nova Scotia I passed within view of numerous fishing vessels.

The northern part of Nova Scotia contained a number of storm areas and several times I flew through cloudbursts.

As I neared the northern coast, snow appeared in patches on the ground and far to the eastward the coastline was covered with fog.

For many miles between Nova Scotia and Newfoundland the ocean was covered with caked ice, but as I approached the coast the ice disappeared entirely and I saw several ships in this area.

I had taken up a course for St. John's, which is south of the great circle from New York to Paris, so that there would be no question of the fact that I had passed Newfoundland in case I was forced down in the North Atlantic.

I passed over numerous icebergs after leaving St. John's, but saw no ships except near the coast.

Darkness set in about 8:15 and a thin, low fog formed over the sea through which the white bergs showed up with surprising clearness. This fog became thicker and increased in height until within two hours I was just skimming the top of storm clouds at about ten thousand feet. Even at this altitude there was a thick haze through which only the stars directly overhead could be seen.

There was no moon and it was very dark. The tops of some of the storm clouds were several thousand feet above me and at one time, when I attempted to fly through one of the larger clouds, sleet started to collect on the plane and I was forced to turn around and get back into clear air immediately and then fly around any clouds which I could not get over.

The moon appeared on the horizon after about two hours of darkness; then the flying was much less complicated.

Dawn came at about 1 A.M., New York time, and the temperature had risen until there was practically no remaining danger of sleet.

Shortly after sunrise the clouds became more broken, although some of them were far above me and it was often necessary to fly through them, navigating by instruments only.

As the sun became higher, holes appeared in the fog. Through one the open water was visible, and I dropped down until less than a hundred feet above the waves. There was a strong wind blowing from the northwest and the ocean was covered with white caps.

After a few miles of fairly clear weather the ceiling lowered to zero and for nearly two hours I flew entirely blind through the fog at an altitude of about 1500 feet. Then the fog raised and the water was visible again.

On several more occasions it was necessary to fly by instrument for short periods; then the fog broke up into patches. These patches took on forms of every description. Numerous shorelines appeared, with trees perfectly outlined against the horizon. In fact, the mirages were so natural that, had I not been in mid-Atlantic and known that no land existed along my route, I would have taken them to be actual islands.

As the fog cleared I dropped down closer to the water, sometimes flying within ten feet of the waves and seldom higher than two hundred.

There is a cushion of air close to the ground or water through which a plane flies with less effort than when at a higher altitude, and for hours at a time I took advantage of this factor.

Also it was less difficult to determine the wind drift near the water. During the entire flight the wind was strong enough to produce white caps on the waves. When one of these formed, the foam would be blown off, showing the wind's direction and approximate velocity. This foam remained on the water long enough for me to obtain a general idea of my drift.

During the day I saw a number of porpoises and a few birds but no ships, although I understand that two different boats reported me passing over.

The first indication of my approach to the European Coast was a small fishing boat which I first noticed a few miles ahead and slightly to the south of my course. There were several of these fishing boats grouped within a few miles of each other.

I flew over the first boat without seeing any signs of life. As I circled over the second, however, a man's face appeared, looking out of the cabin window.

I have carried on short conversations with people on the ground by flying low with throttled engine, and shouting a question, and receiving the answer by some signal. When I saw this fisherman I decided to try to get him to point towards land. I had no sooner made the decision than the futility of the effort became apparent. In all likelihood he could not speak English, and even if he could he would undoubtedly be far too astounded to answer. However, I circled again and closing the throttle as the plane passed within a few feet of the boat I shouted, "Which way is Ireland?" Of course the attempt was useless, and I continued on my course.

Less than an hour later a rugged and semi-mountainous coastline appeared to the northeast. I was flying less than two hundred feet from the water when I sighted it. The shore was fairly distinct and not over ten or fifteen miles away. A light haze coupled with numerous storm areas had prevented my seeing it from a long distance.

The coastline came down from the north and curved towards the east. I had very little doubt that it was the southwestern end of Ireland, but in order to make sure I changed my course towards the nearest point of land.

I located Cape Valencia and Dingle Bay, then resumed my compass course towards Paris.

After leaving Ireland I passed a number of steamers and was seldom out of sight of a ship.

In a little over two hours the coast of England appeared. My course passed over southern England and a little south of Plymouth; then across the English Channel, striking France over Cherbourg.

I was flying at about a fifteen-hundred-foot altitude over England

and as I crossed the Channel and passed over Cherbourg, France, I had probably seen more of that part of Europe than many native Europeans. The visibility was good and the country could be seen for miles around.

The sun went down shortly after passing Cherbourg and soon the beacons along the Paris-London airway became visible.

I first saw the lights of Paris a little before 10 P.M., or 5 P.M., New York time, and a few minutes later I was circling the Eiffel Tower at an altitude of about four thousand feet.

The lights of Le Bourget were plainly visible, but appeared to be very close to Paris. I had understood that the field was farther from the city, so continued out to the northeast into the country for four or five miles to make sure that there was not another field farther out which might be Le Bourget. Then I returned and spiralled down closer to the lights. Presently I could make out long lines of hangars, and the roads appeared to be jammed with cars.

I flew low over the field once, then circled around into the wind and landed.

Albert Einstein, the long-haired, violin-playing scientific genius who fled Nazi Germany and settled in Princeton, New Jersey, in 1933, seems an odd folk hero. Yet without question, he was a household word, a national treasury, an image of accomplishment held up to millions of young people. Anyone growing up in the 1930s and 1940s heard countless times that there were only six (or ten or some such small integer) men in the world who understood the theory of relativity. (One never heard of women who understood these mysteries!) Americans were beginning to understand that pure science was a serious business: the dawning of the atomic age would simply drive the lesson home more forcibly. (Edwin Muller, "Einstein, a Study in Simplicity." Copyright © 1940 by The Reader's Digest Association Inc. Reprinted with permission.)

ALBERT EINSTEIN: A NEW FOLK HERO

Princeton people no longer stare at Einstein; they have become subconsciously aware of him as a massive reality in the background, like Nassau Hall or the football stadium. Einstein may be the "greatest thinker of the age" but he has none of the grand manner.

They found that out upon the Herr Doktor's arrival five years ago.

At that time public curiosity boiled. Even the senior faculty members turned to gaze, as he took his first walk. Others shamelessly followed the great man, wondering what profound thoughts seethed behind that vast forehead. Where was he going and what would he do?

If Einstein was aware of all this he gave no sign of it. Finally he turned meditatively into a drugstore. Some of the bolder spirits pressed right up to the window where they could see the great man—eating an ice cream cone.

Einstein lives in a frame house in a quiet back street. The room in which he works is a small chamber, one end of which is almost filled by a big window that looks out upon a garden. He greets you wearing a loose coat, a zipper shirt open at the neck. The mane of fine white hair trembles a little in the breeze. The great eyes under the bushy brows are deeper and softer than any of his pictures can indicate. With a gentle smile of apology he asks for a moment at his table, as he pens a few final sentences of tiny, neat script and mathematical symbols.

His life has been spent in covering thousands of these blank sheets, most of which have gone into the wastebasket. He gropes intuitively, his pen driving on hour after hour. Coming to a blank wall, he plays the piano or violin or goes for a walk. But, consciously or unconsciously, his mind is still on the problem. Essential parts of his theory of relativity occurred to him while wheeling his son in a baby carriage, and during a solitary ramble in Prague.

As you study Einstein's face, you are struck with the look of a man at peace with himself, who has found the way to supreme happiness—a discovery at least comparable to that of relativity.

Is he happy because he has won a renown that seems secure for the ages? His theory of relativity has completely changed the conception of the universe. It has been called the greatest single stride that science has ever made. The 12-page leaflet in which it was presented is, perhaps, the most important document of the century. Within 15 years of its publication 3775 books and pamphlets have been written about it.

More surprising is his reputation with the general public. His face is as widely known as any movie star's. Something about him commands instant response and deference. On a battlefield tour after the war he was lunching at Rheims. A few tables away sat two French officers of high rank and a distinguished lady. They had quickly recognized Einstein. When he got up to leave, all three rose without a word and bowed low and respectfully to the great physicist.

Fame, however, has not made him happy. On the contrary, he literally runs from reporters, photographers and all the hangers-on of glory. When he travels, every day is a struggle between his violent desire to keep curiosity seekers at arm's length and his inability to hurt anybody's feelings.

Part of Einstein's serenity, no doubt, comes from his having had immense potentialities for work. But, equally or more, it is because he has remained a simple, human being with a love for his fellow man.

In all his habits his bent is for simplification. He uses the same soap to wash and to shave with because he doesn't see the need of complicating life by keeping two kinds. In warm weather socks seem superfluous, so at home he doesn't wear them. He throws away letters that don't interest him, no matter how important the people from whom they come. He is sublimely indifferent to money. Once for several weeks he used for a bookmark a $1500 check from the Rockefeller Foundation. Then he lost the book.

His pleasures too are of the simpler sort: walking, sailing a boat. When he sails he sometimes wears a towel draped around his head, making him look like a benevolent pirate. He doesn't believe in wasting mental energy on such games as bridge and chess. He likes to write doggerel, to play parlor games—though only the easier kinds. No alcohol. Smoking is a permitted luxury—three pipes a day. He's not much of a reader. "Reading," he says, "after a certain age diverts the mind too much from its creative pursuits. Any man who reads too much and uses his own brain too little falls into lazy habits of thinking."

He has never had an intellectual's disdain for service to others. When he won the Nobel Prize, he gave the entire $25,000 to charity, though he could ill afford to do it. He is an active champion of causes he believes in.

Once a liner on which he was a passenger stopped over in New York for five days. Greatly in need of rest, he laid down the law: no interviews, no photographs, no public appearances.

But therein he reckoned without himself. The first reporter found the vulnerable spot. "You ought to give us the interview, Dr. Einstein, because it would help the cause of Zionism." Before the ship left Quarantine he had promised to address a public luncheon, a dinner, to broadcast. The whole five days became a turmoil of activity—for Zionism.

That Einstein has a wholesome disregard for the tyranny of custom was shown when, as the guest of honor at a dinner given by the president of Swarthmore, he was called on for a speech. "Ladies and gentlemen," he said, "I am sorry but I have nothing to say—" and sat down. Then he arose and added, "In case I do have something to say, I'll come back." Six months later he wired the president, "Now I have something to say." Another dinner was held, and Einstein made his speech.

Einstein's earliest years were spent in Munich, where his father conducted an unsuccessful electrical business. It never occurred to young

Einstein that he was a Jew until one day his teacher showed the class a nail from the True Cross, one that the Jews had driven into the feet of Christ. Pupils turned to stare at Einstein. After that he knew what it was to be a Jew.

In those days too he got his bias toward pacifism. In the 1880's the streets of Munich were full of steel helmets. The little boy conceived a horror of drums and marching soldiers that has lasted all his life.

The course of his early life impelled him to internationalism. While he was still in his teens his family moved to Italy, where he spent some of his happiest days. Then he went to Switzerland to school. He was not a brilliant pupil. He failed completely on his first entrance examination to the school at Zurich. His mind was not responsive to the organized teaching and discipline of schools. The greater part of what he has learned he taught himself. At 14, Kant was his favorite philosopher.

In later years he was a professor in Austria-Hungary, then in Germany. He has been a citizen of many lands and an ardent patriot of none. He yearns for the good of the human race, not to push forward any section of it at the expense of others.

"Nationalism," he says, "is an infantile disease. It is the measles of mankind."

When he was 26 he published his first work on relativity. Then for 10 years he built it patiently, stone by stone. At last, in 1915, the structure was complete.

He had started with the daring assumption that there could be no such thing as absolute time, that two events that are simultaneous to one observer may not be simultaneous to another. That led to the conception of time as a fourth dimension. Every body in the universe, moving relatively to every other body, has its own length, breadth and thickness— and its own time specification.

When Hitler came into power, Einstein shook the dust of Germany from his feet. The Nazis made characteristic gestures of farewell to their greatest scientist—turned him out of the Academy of Sciences, seized his sailboat and other personal property, confiscated his bank account. As a crowning irony they solemnly searched his house for arms.

A woman once asked Einstein if he was convinced that his theory was true.

"I believe it to be true," he answered. "But it will only be proved for certain in the year 1981, when I am dead."

"What will happen then?"

"Well, if I am right the Germans will say I was a German and the French will say I was a Jew; if I am wrong the Germans will say I was a Jew and the French will say I was a German."

In Princeton Einstein has made himself at home again. He works harder than ever. But he remains a simple, emotional, very human being. Before you meet Einstein, you look forward to the experience of talking with a great man. But afterward you realize that you have had a more moving experience—you have seen and talked with a good man.